POSITIVISM AND SOCIOLOGY

Positivism and Sociology

edited with an introduction by

Anthony Giddens

HEINEMANN
LONDON

Heinemann Educational Books Ltd

LONDON EDINBURGH MELBOURNE AUCKLAND TORONTO
HONG KONG SINGAPORE KUALA LUMPUR
IBADAN NAIROBI JOHANNESBURG
LUSAKA NEW DELHI

ISBN 0 435 82340 X
Paperback ISBN 0 435 82341 8

Published by Heinemann Educational Books Ltd
48 Charles Street, London W1X 8AH

Printed in Great Britain by Fletcher & Son Ltd
Norwich, Norfolk

CONTENTS

ACKNOWLEDGEMENTS

The editor and publishers are grateful for permission to quote from the following:

Max Weber: 'Roscher und Knies und das Irrationalitätsproblem', *Wissenschaftslehre*, pp. 127–37. Publisher: J. C. B. Möhr, Tübingen, Germany.

Alfred Schutz: 'Weber's Methodological Concepts', *Phenomenology of the Social World*, pp. 24–42. Publisher: Heinemann Educational Books, London, 1972.

Harold Garfinkel: 'The Rational Properties of Scientific and Common-sense Activities', *Behavioural Science*, 1960. Publisher: Mental Health Research Institute, University of Michigan, at Mount Royal and Guilford Avenues, Baltimore 2, Maryland 21202, U.S.A.

Alain Touraine: 'Pour une sociologie actionnaliste', *Archives européennes de Sociologie*, Vol. 5, 1964, pp. 1–24.

Jean-Daniel Reynaud and Pierre Bourdieu: 'Une sociologie de l'action, est-elle possible?' and Alain Touraine: 'La raison d'être d'une sociologie de l'action', *Revue française de sociologie*, Vol. 7, 1966, pp. 508–27. Publisher: Editions du CNRS, 15 quai Anatole-France, Paris 7e, France.

Ernest Gellner: 'The New Idealism—Cause and Meaning in the Social Sciences', in I. Lakatos and Musgrave: *Problems in the Philosophy of Science*. Publisher: North-Holland Publishing Co., Amsterdam.

Hans Albert: 'Der Mythos der totalen Vernunft', and Jürgen Habermas: 'Gegen einen positivistisch halbierten Rationalismus', in T. Adorno: *Der Positivismusstreit in der deutschen Soziologie*, pp. 193–266. Publisher: Hermann Luchterhand Verlag Grubtl, Neuwied and Berlin, Germany, 1969.

Herbert Marcuse: 'On Science and Phenomenology', *Boston Studies in the Philosophy of Science*, 1965. Publisher: Humanities Press, New York.

PREFACE

A few remarks are necessary about the contents of this book. The word 'positivist', like the word 'bourgeois' has become more of a derogatory epithet than a useful descriptive concept, and consequently has been largely stripped of whatever agreed meaning it may once have had. I make no claim, therefore, that the sources which make up this collection bear upon more than a fraction of the problems frequently linked to the notion of positivism—even as I have defined the latter term in the Introduction to the book. But there are close connections between the issues discussed by the authors represented here, even if the divergencies between their theoretical points of view make certain of them rather strange bedfellows.

Much of the best—and, it must be admitted, the worst—writing in social philosophy, or in any other subject for that matter, is born out of polemic. The majority of the selections in this book have a distinctly polemical ring to them, and virtually all of them take the form of a discussion by a prominent author of the work of another; the only exception to this is the article by Touraine, which is more synoptic in character, but which is followed by a critical attack upon Touraine's work, together with a reply by that author. Six of the selections reproduced here have not appeared in English before. They have all posed difficulties of translation, and several of them, even after much polishing, remain stylistically somewhat alien when presented in English, as the reader will readily see. I should perhaps point out, if it is not obvious, that in my Introduction I have maintained a proper editorial modesty in the face of some considerable provocation from the ideas stated by certain of the authors. Many of these ideas I think to be mistaken; but a direct confrontation with them is not very useful unless undertaken in some detail, and this I shall do in a work of my own concerned with problems of social theory and social philosophy. Thus I have contented myself with merely describing some of their main arguments. I have also refrained from referring to the larger works of the authors in question, save when strictly necessary, since they are mostly very well known.

A.G.
King's College, Cambridge
Cambridge, January 1974

INTRODUCTION

The writer, Auguste Comte, who invented the word 'sociology' (a 'barbarous neologism', as Durkheim later remarked) also coined the term 'positive philosophy'. As Comte envisaged it, sociology was to be the very culmination of positivism: the science of man completed the historical evolution of the hierarchy of the scientific disciplines, and for the first time made possible an adequate understanding of that evolution. Comte's writings, of course, are informed by a definite view of the logic of scientific method and the character of scientific knowledge. The hierarchy of the sciences expresses both an historical and a logical order of relationships between the various fields of scientific endeavour. In the historical aspect, human knowledge in general, and the specific sciences in particular, pass through the successive phases of 'theological', 'metaphysical' and 'positive' thought. These processes of development, according to Comte, are primarily governed by a simple principle: those disciplines relating to phenomena furthest from man's own involvement and control develop first, and the history of science as a whole is one of a progressive movement inwards towards the study of man himself. The mechanism of scientific development provides the key to the logical relations between the sciences. The earliest sciences to come into being are those which deal with facts of the greatest generality; thus each field of study in the hierarchy of the sciences is predicated upon those which lie below it, although its own concepts and generalizations are irreducible. Sociology, which concerns itself with human social conduct, presupposes the laws of biology, which apply to all organisms, while the latter in turn presume the laws of chemistry, etc.

The neatness of Comte's theoretical scheme belies the complexity of the problems which it conceals. Comte's work both shares in and best exemplifies the views of the nature of science that dominated nineteenth-century thought—which not only took scientific knowledge to be the paradigm of all (valid) knowledge, but also saw in science the solution to the major practical problems facing mankind. It was fashionable at one time to suppose that there were two Comtes: the author of the 'Positive Philosophy', the sober analyst of scientific history and method, and the creator of the bizarre utopia of the 'Positive Polity'. But such an interpretation was the child of an age which had forsaken the nineteenth-century vision of the transformative powers of scientific knowledge, and had tempered an acknowledgement of the achievements of natural science with a scepticism about whether these bore any immediate consequences for social progress.

After Comte, very few philosophers or social thinkers willingly called themselves 'positivists', and there are evident differences between his views and those of others to whom the label has since been applied. The term has become one of opprobrium, and has been used so broadly and vaguely as a weapon of critical attack, both in philosophy and in sociology, that it has lost any claim to an accepted and standard meaning. Moreover, philosophers and sociologists today have rather different points of reference in mind when they use the term. For many of the former it has become identified, not primarily with Comte at all, but with the 'logical positivism' of the 1930s—although it is certainly not consistently used in the fairly restricted sense which it had when applied to certain of the conceptions originally developed by the Vienna circle.

Since there is no longer much consistency in the general employment of the word, it would seem appropriate to attempt to impose some order upon the flux of differing usages. Positivism *as a philosophy* I take to imply simply two main elements. First, what Kolakowski has called the 'rule of phenomenalism', which asserts the uniqueness of experience as the basis of knowledge. Only that qualifies as 'knowledge' which can in some sense, more or less directly, be related to a 'reality' immediately apprehended by the perceiver. This is often regarded as separable from the postulate of 'nominalism'—that is to say, the notion that an abstract concept or generalization, such as may be involved in science, in Kolakowski's words, 'gives us no extra, independent knowledge in the sense that, via its abstractions, it opens access to empirically inaccessible domains of reality'.[1] But actually these are merely different aspects of the fundamental supposition of the

[1] Kolakowski, Leszek, *Positivist Philosophy*, London, 1972, pp. 15–16.

experiential foundation of all (viable) knowledge in sensorily apprehended 'reality'. Secondly, as necessarily following from the first proposition, the idea that judgements of value have no empirical content of a sort which renders them accessible to any tests of their 'validity' in the light of experience. There is no kind of observation of the sensory environment which can have a direct bearing upon the content of value judgements or normative assertions.

Defined in this way, positivism certainly does not begin with Comte (any more than sociology itself does!), but has a long history in Western philosophy. The implications which have been placed upon the views indicated above, the mode in which they have been expressed and the inferences which have been drawn from them, have been many and varied. Some of the problems raised by the various competing and overlapping strands of positivistic thought in philosophy, however, are not as such relevant to the issues posed in sociological analysis. If 'positivism' has meant somewhat different things to philosophers and sociologists, this is partly because the introduction of positivistic assumptions into sociology creates a series of quite specific difficulties which cannot be resolved on the level of generalized philosophical inquiry. Positivism in philosophy in some sense revolves around the contention, or the implicit assumption, that the notions and statements of science constitute a framework by reference to which the nature of any form of knowledge may be determined. Positivism in sociology may be broadly represented as depending upon the assertion that the concepts and methods employed in natural sciences can be applied to form a 'science of man', or a 'natural science of society'. Since this of course relies upon some sort of stated or unstated view of the character of natural science, it is obviously to some degree tied to the sorts of problems involved in the epistemological assumptions of philosophical positivism. But we may distinguish three principal sets of issues specific to the importation of positivism into sociology, aspects of which most of the articles in this book are concerned. The 'positivistic attitude' in sociology may be said to comprise the following connected suppositions:

1. That the *methodological* procedures of natural science may be directly adapted to sociology. According to this standpoint,

the phenomena of human subjectivity, of volition and will, do not offer any particular barriers to the treatment of social conduct as an 'object' on a par with objects in the natural world. Positivism here implies a particular stance concerning the sociologist as *observer* of social 'reality'.

2. That the *outcome* or end-result of sociological investigations can be formulated in terms parallel to those of natural science: that is to say, that the goal of sociological analysis can and must be to formulate 'laws' or 'law-like' generalizations of the same kind as those which have been established in relation to natural reality. Positivism here involves a definite view of the sociologist as *analyst* or 'interpreter' of his subject-matter.

3. That sociology has a *technical* character, providing knowledge which is purely 'instrumental' in form; in other words, that the findings of sociological research do not carry any logically given implications for practical policy or for the pursuit of values. Sociology, like natural science, is 'neutral' in respect of values. From this aspect, positivism presumes a specific standpoint upon the sociologist as *practically involved* in the social order.

Obviously, acceptance of any one of these three suppositions does not necessarily entail adoption of the other two.

1. *Subjectivity and meaning.* Broadly speaking, there can be said to be two discrete traditions in social theory relating to problems of method and to the identification of the 'subject-matter' with which sociology is held to be concerned. One is quite evidently 'positivistic' in both the general and the more specific senses of the term which I have described previously. This is precisely the tradition of social theory of which Comte stands as a prominent representative, but which stretches back well before him to Montesquieu and Condorcet, and which finds its most sophisticated defence later on in the nineteenth century, in Durkheim's works. In certain important respects, the French positivists were highly critical of British social theory, founded upon the model of orthodox political economy. But although the former insisted upon a 'holistic' conception of social reality, while the latter asserted the primacy of the 'individual', they shared common assumptions of a methodological sort, and the

dominant strain in nineteenth-century British social thought may also be correctly designated as positivistic. The second tradition in social theory, a complex tissue of interweaving strands, but quite definitely in opposition to both French and British positivism, is that which arose in Germany in the latter period of the nineteenth century.

The complexity of this second tradition is well illustrated by the intellectual struggles which Max Weber was forced to undergo in order to achieve even the semblance of a reconciliation between the differing fragments which were his theoretical inheritance. The conception of sociological and historical method which Weber worked out drew heavily from the writings of prior authors who rejected one or more of the three elements of positivism noted above; but he also attempted to synthesize these received views with others which were quite definitely positivistic. In Weber's thought, perhaps the main axis of this confrontation is represented in his attempt, via neo-Kantian philosophy, to reconcile the 'subjectivism' and 'irrationalism' of the German historical school with the naturalistic views of Menger. Weber's essays on Roscher and Knies, one of the most important places in which he tackles these problems, are among the few of his more theoretical writings which have not yet appeared in English translation. The essays are heavily polemical in character, but contain a number of lengthy passages—one of which is translated here—that elucidate and develop themes not treated in as much depth in his other, more well-known, methodological writings.

Weber's methodological essays deal with two overlapping themes: that of 'subjectivism' versus 'objectivism', and that of 'irrationality' versus 'rationality' in the explication of human conduct. In the essays on Roscher and Knies, Weber attempts to show that these authors confuse the two dimensions in such a manner as to obscure the logical distinctions presupposed by any form of sociological or historical study. From the premise that human action necessarily is 'subjective' in character, they draw the conclusion that it possesses an 'irrational', or perhaps more accurately, an 'a-rational' quality, in the sense that it is not specifically 'calculable' or 'predictable' in the way in which occurrences in the natural world are. This sort of viewpoint is linked with a rejection of 'causality' as relevant to the explanation of any form of conduct which is 'motivated conduct'. Weber questions this line of reasoning, by trying to recast the relationship between subjectivism and objectivism on the one hand, and irrationality and rationality on the other. The essential basis of his argument may be simply stated as follows. We may, and must, accept that human action has a 'subjective' component which differentiates it qualitatively from the sphere of natural reality. But it is mistaken to suppose that recognition of the subjective character of action necessarily involves either the relinquishment of the possibility of confronting it 'objectively', as the natural scientist confronts natural reality, or the abandonment of causal explanation. The interpretation of human action in terms of motives can be 'causal' interpretation precisely in so far as we are able to analyse it in terms of chains of rationality—that is to say, by linking 'motives' or 'purposes' to the 'means' whereby the actor seeks to attain particular goals. In so far as conduct is rational, it is also highly predictable: it is therefore erroneous to suppose that subjectivity may be equated with 'incalculability'.

It has been assumed by the writers of the historical school, Weber points out, that 'freedom of will' is ultimately the most fundamental factor separating the human universe from that of nature. In fact, Weber claims, the 'freer' an individual's action, the less his act is conditioned either by the internal impress of affect or by external compulsion of some sort, the more clearly it may be analysed in terms of a means–ends scheme of rationality, and the more accurately its course and outcome may be predicted by the observer: 'The more this is the case, the less room there is for any sort of romantic naturalistic conception of "personality", that conception which paradoxically seeks the sacred quality of personality in an "irrationality" based upon the dull, undifferentiated, vegetative "foundation" of personal life . . .'[1] It is precisely the rational character of 'freely willed' behaviour which distinguishes man from the animals; not, as is proposed by these writers, some mystical quality of the irrational. 'Irrationality' of action is actually the trait by which we recognize the insane—individuals whose behaviour is refractory to our interpretative 'understanding' and thereby is specifically 'incalculable'. The interpretation of rational action, Weber emphasizes, depends upon the use of generalizations about typical processes of action—

[1] Below, p. 27.

what he usually calls *Erfahrungsregeln*, or empirical rules. While these often remain unstated, and may not even be known to the actual individual whose behaviour is being analysed, no form of interpretative understanding can proceed without using them. The operation of 'free will', which may be conceived to be realized to the degree to which an individual acts rationally in a given situation, in terms of the relating of means to ends, thus *presupposes* that human behaviour conforms to 'laws', or ascertained regularities.

We thus reach the conclusion that, while the social sciences (including under this term sociology and also history and economics) must of necessity be founded upon a method—interpretative analysis of subjective 'meanings', or means–ends chains—which is distinct from that employed in natural science, where 'understanding' in this sense is obviously impossible, this is not only compatible with causal generalization about human behaviour, but presumes it. Since Weber places this standpoint within a context of neo-Kantian philosophy, following Windelband, Rickert and Simmel, his notion of the significance of theoretical generalizations in the social sciences takes a very particular form. According to this conception, reality, whether natural or social, is extensively and intensively infinite; therefore any approach to the analysis of a given event or phenomenon in reality must be selective, and guided by values, as stated in the principle of value-relevance (*Wertbeziehung*). It follows that the discovery of scientific 'laws' in no sense exhausts the analysis of that area of reality to which such laws apply. On the contrary, the more general the generalization—the more successful it is in incorporating a range of occurrences which may be subsumed under it—the more abstract it is, and the *less* it tells us about the specific event or phenomenon in question. The more, because of particular values we hold which direct our interests along such a line, we are interested in a datum 'for its own sake', the more we are forced to complement analysis in terms of generalization with the analysis (which again cannot be 'exhaustive') of historical individuals. In the social sciences, Weber holds, this sort of interest tends to be pre-eminent: sociology is in a sense subordinate to history.

Schutz's *Der sinnhafte Aufbau der sozialen Welt*, originally published in 1932, but only translated into English quite recently,

takes up and attempts to expand upon certain of the basic suppositions detailed in Weber's methodological writings. Given
that his primary concern is to elaborate a conception of sociological method employing ideas adapted from Husserl's phenomenology, Schutz directs his attention mainly to effecting a
critique of Weber's treatment of subjectivity and rationality—
a theme also taken up, via a discussion of Schutz's own works, in
Garfinkel's article reproduced below. According to Weber's
exposition of interpretative sociology, the aim of sociology is to
analyse and explain social action through the study of the subjective meanings whereby individuals orient their conduct. But
Schutz tries to show that Weber fails to pursue his arguments far
enough. What he takes as the basic 'material' of analysis, the
subjective meanings of action, 'by no means defines a primitive,
as he thinks it does. It is, on the contrary, a mere label for a highly
complex and ramified area that calls for much further study.'[1]
The constitution of 'meaning' in social action is problematic in
a double sense: on the one side from the perspective of the
analyst, who shares in the meaning-structure of the social world
at the same time as he seeks to detach himself from it, in order to
observe it from the outside; and from the perspective of the social
actors themselves, for whom meanings are not fixed and irreducible, but are continually in flux and in the process of being
constructed and dissolved in an active fashion.

When Weber speaks of 'meaningful action', Schutz points out,
he has in mind—as I have described above—action which can be
interpreted by the observer in terms of a means–ends scheme of
rationality. This is shown by the fact that he places both affective
responses and traditional conduct, behaviour governed by un-
thinking habit or custom, at the margins of action which is
meaningful and thus amenable to the method of interpretative
sociology. Rational action serves Weber as the model for all
meaningful action, and the criterion of instrumental rationality
is the basis of the array of ideal types which he establishes for the
study of social conduct. The upshot of this, according to Schutz,
is that Weber confuses 'meaningful' with 'motivated' action. It is
mistaken, Schutz asserts, to suppose that either emotional behaviour or habitual reactions are *ipso facto* devoid of meaning.
In his discussion of interpretative sociology, Weber distinguishes

[1] Schutz, Alfred, *The Phenomenology of the Social World*, London, 1972, p. 8.

between the 'direct understanding' and the 'explanatory understanding' of the subjective meaning of an observed action.
The first refers to a situation in which the observer grasps the
significance of the act directly, either because its rational content
is immediately perceived by him, or because he has an emphatic
understanding of it; the latter involves comprehending the motive
which leads the individual to engage in the conduct in question,
and is achieved by placing that conduct in the context of a broader
complex of meanings. But this, Schutz argues, is a distinction
which confuses more than it clarifies. When Weber speaks of
'direct understanding', he is certainly referring to the subjective
experience of the actor; 'explanatory understanding' necessarily
involves the analyst in considering far more than the subjective
meaning with which the individual himself invests his action.
If, however, we examine 'direct understanding' more closely, we
find that this also implies looking beyond what is designated by
Weber. We see a man wielding an axe: but in order to know that
he is 'chopping wood', we have to locate what we observe in a
wider context of meaning, which may *not* in fact be exactly the
same as that attributed to his behaviour by the actor himself.
We must distinguish the subjective from the objective context
of meaning, a differentiation which cross-cuts that drawn by
Weber. There is a certain logic in the distinction proposed by the
latter author, but its import is quite different from that which he
indicates: when we 'directly' understand the meaning of the
action of an individual, we do so within the framework of everyday life, participating in the action itself. Rather than referring
to a procedure which is to be employed by the social scientist,
Weber's 'direct understanding' merely concerns the sort of understanding which everyone makes use of in his day-to-day life;
while this may adequately serve the practical demands of everyday
social existence it conceals a potentially complicated set of influences which themselves have to be examined.

The main source of difficulty posed for sociology in the interpretation of meanings, according to Schutz, is that meaning is
not simply constituted subjectively, but *intersubjectively*. It is not
hard to see, examining the course of Husserl's philosophical
development over the course of his career, that his most fundamental problem, within the confines of the premises which he
began from—a problem which he did not resolve even to his own

satisfaction—was that of bridging the apparently unfathomable gulf between subjectivity and intersubjectivity as parameters of existential knowledge. For intersubjectivity is already *presupposed* in the analysis of the *Lebenswelt* of the subject. In Schutz's sociological phenomenology, the matter does not, of course, present itself in the same form; but a parallel dilemma arises in the latter author's separation of subjective and objective meaning. Schutz, however, bypasses the problem rather than solves it—although a substantial part of his work is concerned with discussing its manifications. Objective meaning inheres in signs and expressions which 'are meaningful and intelligible in their own right—in their, so to speak, anonymous nature—regardless of whether anyone is thinking of them, regardless of whether anyone is using them'.[1] Thus a term or phrase in a language has an objective meaning regardless of whether or not anyone happens to be uttering it at any particular time. Objective meaning, Schutz holds, can be studied from two points of view—as constituted and 'given' (as in the case of the above-mentioned example), and as in the process of becoming, in the process of being constituted.

These considerations, Schutz says, allow us to identify more clearly the defects in Weber's account of interpretative sociology. In speaking of the subjective meanings of action, Weber fails to treat 'action' within a time perspective. In this respect, W. F. Whyte's comment on Talcott Parsons' 'action theory'—there is a stage, there is a set, but the actors do not move—could, following Schutz's critique, be equally well applied to Max Weber. Weber's analysis, Schutz points out, conflates action as a completed act, in the latter's terms an 'objectified act', and action as a flow of events (again, as constituting rather than constituted). The theorem that the actor 'attaches meaning to his action' is a metaphorical expression; meaning is a reflexive mode of attending to experience, whether as a matter of forming, means—ends projects (subjective meaning), or as a matter of interpreting completed acts (objective meaning).

In Weber's writings, the question of rationality in social activity is one which continually appears, in several guises. The affirmation of the intrinsic rationality of conduct that is 'freely' directed by the individual is a major thesis in his analysis of his eminent precursors in the historical school; although he also sought to

[1] Below, pp. 42–3.

place defined limits upon the scope of reason in denying the possibility of rationally evaluating the ends of activity themselves. In constructing typological concepts for the study of society, he insisted that 'rational ideal types', setting out purely rational modes of action, must be the basis of interpretative sociology; the actual behaviour of individuals is to be explained in terms of its deviation from rational conduct. The polarity of rationality and irrationality appears yet again in Weber's empirical sociology itself, in his many discussions of the increasing penetration of rationality into the various institutional spheres of modern society, and once more is offset by a contrast with 'unreason' (charisma). Even a cursory comparison of Weber's different writings reveals that he uses the term 'rational' in a shifting and inconsistent way. Schutz's attempt to reformulate the Weberian treatment of subjectivity, as he recognizes, obviously has immediate implications for the notion of rationality of conduct; these are summarized and developed by Garfinkel.

The course of sociological research, Garfinkel believes, has followed an opposite line to that advocated by Weber. Rather than finding it most useful to analyse social conduct by treating the 'nonrational' as a factor of deviation from the 'rational', 'in most of the available theories of social action and social structure rational actions are assigned residual status'.[1] Neither of these positions is satisfactory, and we have instead to discriminate different modes or aspects of rationality in conduct, no single one of which can be said to be more basic than the others. In fact the numerous modes of rationality—fourteen in all!—which Garfinkel distinguishes really divide into two main types: what Garfinkel calls the 'scientific rationalities', and the 'rationalities of everyday life'. The mistake underlying most treatments of rationality in the social sciences is to suppose that the first can serve as a model for the study of the second. The essential core of Garfinkel's argument is that the (ideal) conduct of scientific inquiry, far from embodying norms of rationality which can be applied usefully to the interpretative analysis of social conduct, has to be regarded as a separate and very special type of activity.

2. *Problems of generalization.* Few works dealing with problems of the philosophy of the social sciences in recent years have stimu-

---

[1] Below, p. 54.

lated as much controversy (at least, in the English-speaking world) as Winch's concise but forceful work *The Idea of a Social Science*, first published in 1958. While the author owes a debt above all to Wittgenstein, the book takes up similar questions of subjectivity and meaning to those dealt with against a different intellectual background by Weber and Schutz, but reaches conclusions which are substantially divergent from theirs. Neither Weber nor Schutz doubt that a 'science of society' is possible. In their varying ways, they each emphasize the significance of the interpretative method as a necessary instrument of analysis in the social sciences, and in doing so certainly recognize a major methodological division between social and natural science. But this does not compromise the possibility of establishing generalizations about social conduct which do not differ *logically* from those characteristic of natural science. Winch, however, specifically rejects this view.

Philosophy, Winch believes, stands in a different relationship to sociology than to natural science: 'it is often supposed that newly developing disciplines, with no settled basis of theory on which to build further research, are particularly prone to throw up philosophical puzzles; but that this is a temporary stage which should be lived through and then shaken off as soon as possible. But, in my view, it would be wrong to say this of sociology; for the philosophical problems which arise there are not tiresome foreign bodies which must be removed before sociology can advance on its own independent scientific lines. On the contrary, the central problem of sociology, that of giving an account of the nature of social phenomena in general, itself belongs to philosophy.'[1]

We can demonstrate the validity of this position, according to Winch, by considering Wittgenstein's notion of 'following a rule', and elucidating certain consequences which this has for sociological analysis. Following a rule in linguistic usage must necessarily be a 'public' phenomenon, having reference to the responses of others; the notion of a rule is inseparable from a social setting in which that rule is applied. The concept of following a rule, Winch holds, gives us important insights into the nature of what Weber calls subjectively meaningful action. We can say, in fact, that meaningful action is that which is rule-governed; and this in

[1] Winch, Peter, *The Idea of a Social Science and its Relation to Philosophy*, London, 1971, p. 43.

turn shows us why we cannot generalize about human conduct in the same form as we can when dealing with phenomena in the natural world. In Winch's words, 'the notion of a human society involves a scheme of concepts which is logically incompatible with the kinds of explanation offered in the natural sciences'.[1] Motives cannot be regarded (as Weber thought) as causal factors in human behaviour. To discover the motives of a given act is to 'understand' it: understanding, when applied to human action, means nothing more or less than this. To say that a person was motivated to act in such and such a way is to say that his behaviour is 'intelligible' or 'meaningful' in terms of the rules of conduct which pertain in the society of which he is a member. To interpret observed regularities in social conduct is not to offer the sort of law-like causal generalization familiar in natural science, but to inquire into the character of the rule to which it is oriented. These rules, not the procedures of investigation of the sociologist, supply the criteria of identity whereby we judge two acts, of the same individual or of different individuals, to be 'the same'.

What Gellner refers to as this 'new idealism' has not been very favourably received by sociologists, and his article indicates some of the chief objections which have been raised. As Gellner points out, in seeking to apply Wittgenstein's doctrine to the social sciences, Winch reverses the formula involved in the former's philosophy of meaning. 'If "meaning = use", then "use = meaning." ... Where Wittgenstein taught philosophers not to ask for the meaning but for the use, Winch advises social scientists not to look for the cause, but for the meaning'.[2] Winch does not see that this undermines Wittgenstein's philosophy itself; for if we accept that language, and the social meanings it expresses, delimits the boundaries of 'our' world, but also assert that there exists a (potentially infinite ?) plurality of social contexts in which different rules of meaning have become elaborated, we are caught in a hopeless paradox. There are two ways out of this paradox; and it is not stretching Gellner's case too far to say that each of these is itself paradoxical. One is to suppose that there are criteria for judging the 'validity' of propositions which stand outside variations in forms of language or conceptual structure. But this by its very nature means abandoning Wittgenstein's original premise. The

[1] Ibid., p. 72.
[2] Below, pp. 134-5.

other path which can be followed, the one taken by Winch, is towards a conceptual relativism. But this view cannot be reconciled with some essential aspects of sociological method and with certain basic features of social life itself. The latter, Gellner suggests, concern the oppositions or 'contradictions' which exist both within and between different societies or cultural *milieux*. Consider, say, a zealous reforming movement which drives its proselytizing appeal from the conviction that existing rules of religious practice or 'meaning' do not genuinely express revealed truth. A view which holds that meaning is wholly given in social usage cannot cope with such a circumstance; moreover, the type of situation illustrated by the case of the reforming zealot is not merely marginal in character—it exemplifies something which is generic to social life. This in an important sense again brings us back to questions of the nature of rationality, since the reformer may be declaring that existing beliefs/practices are irrational, in the light of the 'proper' exegisis of doctrine.

for Winch, this is a new rule, Allso, 'situation' is emergent

'For most modern thinkers,' Gellner indicates, 'relativism is a *problem*: for Winch and Wittgenstein, it is a *solution*. Other thinkers start from the fact of the diversification of belief and morals, and try to find the touchstone of <u>correct</u> belief, etc. This, I think, is the general form of the mainstream of modern Western thought ... But Wittgenstein and Winch *arrive* at relativism, they don't start from it, and they arrive at it as a solution to quite another problem, the problem of meaning. Meaning, they say, is not an echo, a reduplication, a structural mirroring of the thing meant, aided perhaps by the struts of a formal framework (*this* was the rejected theory of Wittgenstein's youthful *Tractatus*): it is the possession of a place, a role, in a "language", a "form of life", a culture.'[1] These relativities have to be treated as problematic, not only in relation to internal 'contradictions' within any given society, but also in terms of what Gellner refers to as the '<u>unequal cognitive power</u>' of different cultures. We must reject the view, Gellner concludes, which presumes that any form of belief or 'rule of meaning', when interpreted within its social context, is as valid as any other.

not culturally aware here.

Arguing that the 'effectiveness of scientific industrial civilization and its diffusion are the central facts of our time', which any adequate approach to the basic issues of sociological method

[1] Below, pp. 149–50.

must be able to encompass theoretically, Gellner states a conclusion which in fact forms something of a starting-point for
Touraine. In the article reproduced below, Touraine sets out an
initial formulation of ideas subsequently expounded at length in
his *Sociologie de l'action* (Paris, 1965). Although Touraine's conception of 'action theory' (*actionalisme*) borrows nothing from the
sort of intellectual sources discussed by Gellner, questions of
what significance must be given to the nature of 'meaning' in
social action, and of the implications of this for causal generalization again appear as basic here. But Touraine is less concerned
with philosophical problems underlying these phenomena
than with deficiencies in existing forms of theoretical generalization in sociology.

As Reynaud and Bourdieu point out, in their critique of the
above book, Touraine's sociology of action begins from the idea
that human conduct is intrinsically 'meaningful'. Rather than
discussing the nature of terms such as 'meaning', 'motive',
'purpose', etc., as applied to human behaviour in general, he
seeks to accomplish precisely what Gellner says is taken for
granted in Winch's analysis—the sources of the creation of new
forms of meaning in society. Touraine's *actionalisme* has to be
distinguished, as he stresses, from Parsons' 'action theory',
which belongs to a leading contemporary school of social theory
that Touraine wishes to criticize—or at least, to show the limitations of. Functionalism, Touraine proposes, can be seen to have
come into being at a particular stage in the development of
modern society when, for definite reasons, men became preoccupied with the character of 'social cohesion' and the (given)
existence of social norms. Action theory, as Touraine sets it out,
involves a different perspective; and in a specific sense, it implies
a criticism of Weber's *verstehende Soziologie* as well as of functionalism. For, according to Touraine, we must abandon the
conception that, as Weber put it, 'the individual is the "atom"
of sociological analysis', and recognize that 'subjectivity' and
'meaning' are not merely to be conceptualized as properties of
the individual subject. Touraine's 'historical subject' is not the
individual actor. The values or symbolic systems (which includes
language) embodied in social conduct at any point in time are not
creations of any single individual, nor can they be said to represent some sort of aggregate of individual actions; nor are these

values normally present in, or even necessarily accessible to, the consciousness of the individual actor. The study of the historical subject involves analysing 'the emergent structure of a totalizing activity, the unity of the dialectical movements of historical action'.[1] The highly opaque style of expression which Touraine adopts makes for a very real difficulty in elucidating the nature of the key concept of the 'historical subject'. Touraine emphasizes that the notion does not represent a return to outmoded conceptions of group mind or collective consciousness. The historical subject does not have a fixed empirical referent, and is most aptly regarded as a methodological principle for understanding the *unité totalisante* of social action as the creator of meaning. But neither does it imply a reversion to a philosophy of history: 'When we speak of the historical subject, of systems of action and projects, we do not construct a philosophy of history, but an historical sociology (*une sociologie de l'historicité*) and, more than that, we build an understanding of the formation of social systems—which others study from the functional point of view. The historical subject is not a concrete totality, such as feudal society or industrial society; it is not therefore an interpretation of an observable entity, but the basic principle of a type of analysis, a mode of analysing the normative orientation of conduct.'[2]

The process of labour, Touraine suggests, such as conceived in Marxian theory, can be regarded as the exemplar of the creation of values by the activity of the historical subject. This should not be considered merely in terms of the material process of creation, whereby men modify their physical environment in such a way as to produce goods or commodities; rather, the 'products' of labour are the symbols or meanings which men bring into being in differentiating themselves from the senseless world of nature. There are, according to Touraine, always two aspects to this: 'the double exigency of creation and control'. The point of reference here is the same as is involved in Schutz's distinction between subjective and objective meanings—what is created becomes externalized (objectified) as a reality outside the consciousness of the actor, and hence confronts him as a phenomenon which may escape his control. The dialectic of subject and object,

---

[1] Quoted below, p. 105.
[2] Below, p. 126.

conceived of in these terms, represents a type of analysis that can be applied universally; but there are definite reasons, Touraine suggests, why the modes of creation and control vary between different forms of society, and why action analysis should have a particular significance to industrial societies. For the advent of industrialism, and the secularized interpretation of the world which both precedes it and is furthered by it, allows men to free themselves from the constraints of previous ages, and to seek actively to control their destiny in ways foreign to the bounded and stable universe of traditional society.

philosophy of
history,
nonetheless

3. *Values, interests and scientific knowledge.* If Weber's methodological writings form the *fons et origo* of most subsequent discussions of 'subjectivity' and 'meaning' by social scientists, they also constitute the classic point of reference for problems of value-interpretation. The famous *Methodenstreit* of the turn of the century is by now familiar to everyone; its much more recent successor, the so-called '*Positivismusstreit*' is less well known outside Germany. But some of the issues raised in the latter controversy are the same as those which were so vigorously debated over half a century earlier, albeit within a rather different theoretical framework.

The articles by Albert and Habermas which appear below represent part of the latter debate which, like the earlier controversy, had its immediate origins within a specific institutional setting—in this case, the meetings of the German Sociological Association held in Tübingen some twelve years ago. The occasion gave rise to some acrimony, and has an odd sequel. Karl Popper was invited to open a discussion about 'The logic of the social sciences', which he did in the form of twenty-seven theses that summarized views which he has stated at length in his various works. This was followed by a 'reply' by Theodor Adorno which, however, instead of attacking Popper's stated position directly, set out an alternative one. Thus the anticipated confrontation between the two never got off the ground, and the 'positivism debate' really followed a subsequent intervention by Jürgen Habermas, criticizing Popper's position. The aftermath was a similarly polemical paper by Hans Albert, stimulating a rejoinder from Habermas (both reprinted below), followed by a series of further interchanges between the two. The whole collection of papers, with new contributions from Adorno were published as *Der Positivismusstreit in der deutschen Soziologie*. The curious thing is that the debate is like Hamlet without the Prince; for Popper insists that, not only are his 'twenty-seven theses' not discussed anywhere in the book, but that to call his views 'positivist' betrays a complete misunderstanding of them.[1]

This brings us back to the point at which I started in writing this Introduction. For Popper uses the term 'positivism' in a quite specific and precisely defined sense, whereas his opponents do not. Popper stresses: 'I have fought against the aping of the natural sciences by the social sciences, and I have fought for the doctrine that the positivistic epistemology is inadequate even in its analysis of the natural sciences which, in fact, are not carefully generalizing from observation as is normally believed, but are essentially speculative and daring; moreover, I have taught, for more than 38 years, that all observations are theory-impregnated, and that their main function is to check and refute, rather than to prove, our theories. Finally, I have not only stressed the meaningfulness of metaphysical assertions and the fact that I am myself a metaphysical realist, but I have also analysed the important historical role played by metaphysics in the formation of scientific theories.'[2] The main theme, however, which Adorno and Habermas wish to say separates their standpoint from that of Popper does not so much concern the matters referred to in the quotation, as the problem of the *critical* role of theory—or perhaps more accurately, in their terms, the problem of the role of critical theory. Now once more there are terminological difficulties here, since 'criticism' plays a fundamental part in Popper's ideas as well. In opposition to those who have seen objectivity in science as resting upon some state of mind of the individual scientist confronting his subject-matter, Popper treats this as possible only because of the 'public' criticism to which hypotheses are submitted, whereby they can be falsified. The process of conjecture and refutation is thus the central feature of Popper's

[1] See Theodor W. Adorno: *Der Positivismusstreit in der deutschen Soziologie*, Neuwied, 1960; (English translation, *The Positivist Dispute in German Sociology*, London, 1974). For a short account, David Frisby: 'The Popper–Adorno Controversy: the methodological dispute in German sociology', *Philosophy of Social Science*, Vol. 2, 1972. Popper comments on the debate in 'Reason or Revolution', *Archives européennes de sociologie*, Vol. 11, 1970.

[2] Ibid., p. 262.

epistemology of science. But this presupposes a relationship between 'theory' and 'criticism' which Adorno and Habermas reject in attempting to set out their own notion of 'critical theory', particularly in relation to the social sciences.

Habermas makes this clear in the article reprinted in this book. His discussion, he says, is not directed towards analysing the procedures of research in natural science, nor even in what he calls 'behavioural-scientific sociology', but 'exclusively towards the positivistic interpretation of such research processes'.[1] Such an interpretation, according to him, has the effect of closing off a whole range of problems from rational assessment, including the evaluation of the norms of scientific method itself. Habermas recognizes that Popper rejects 'empiricism'—which is actually close to what the former means when he uses the term 'positivism' —since he holds that, as it is expressed in the above quotation, 'all observations are theory-impregnated'. What Habermas disputes are the further inferences which he believes Popper draws from this, and the unexamined nature of 'falsifiability': 'He rightly discredits every form of primary knowledge, but even mistakes can only be found to be such on the basis of criteria of validation. For their justification we must adduce arguments; but where then are we to look for these if not in precisely that dimension—not of the origin but namely of the formation of knowledge—which has been ruled out? Otherwise the standards of falsification remain arbitrary . . . He assumes the epistemological independence of facts from the theories which should descriptively grasp these facts and the relations between them. Accordingly, tests examine theories against "independent" facts. This thesis is the pivot of the positivistic problematic which Popper still retains.'[2] What Popper fails to do, according to Habermas at least, is to reconcile the supposedly inherent 'uncertainty' of scientific information (i.e., that its status never goes beyond that of 'not falsified') with the technical confidence with which it is everywhere applied in modern civilization. The 'technical-cognitive interests' which supply this confidence, and which therefore in a very significant sense determine the validation of scientific knowledge—validation in practice—remain unanalysed in Popper's approach.

[1] Below, p. 195.
[2] Below, p. 200.

Can rationalism be rationally justified? It is really over the significance of this question that the views of Habermas (and Adorno) diverge from those of Albert (and Popper). Albert seeks to attack the position adopted by Habermas in two primary respects. First that Habermas himself relapses into a naïve positivism at a key stage of his argument because, in stressing the role of 'technical-cognitive interests' in relation to the validation of scientific information, he confuses logical with the sociological questions in an illegitimate fashion. Secondly that, as a result of this confusion, Habermas avoids rather than solves the 'substantiation problem'. For Habermas, however, each of these points rests upon a misunderstanding. The main issue, as he sees it, escapes each of these observations. He does not wish to question the logical distinction between the genesis of ideas or theories and the mode of their resolution, nor to attempt to formulate a logical solution to the substantiation problem. Rather, he wants to open up to rational criticism that area of analysis which he claims, since it defines the scope of reason in Popper's scheme, is left purely residual—or alternatively, assumed *a priori*, which comes to the same thing. This is directly tied in to the fact/value problem, since Habermas wishes to disavow the traditional separation between the 'is' and the 'ought'. Here lies the crux of Habermas's argument. Critical theory, as he conceives of it, means abandoning the idea that the parameters which define the character of scientific discourse may be identified with rational knowledge as such, and this in turn entails the recognition that 'validation' is not limited to the technical procedures of scientific method. At this vital point in his discussion, however, Habermas's exposition, never overly transparent, slips into the sort of quasi-Hegelian murkiness which Albert rather understandably finds it difficult to penetrate.

The substance of Habermas's position appears to be as follows. Factual propositions and value-standards are not independent of one-another, but are dialectically connected. Any form of evaluation of statements, regardless of whether or not they are 'factual' in character, involves three elements—the 'descriptive', the 'postulatory' and the 'critical'. Each of these presupposes the other two: 'The descriptive usage is in no way limited to a certain class of "facts". The postulatory usage covers the establishment of norms, of standards, of criteria and definitions of all types, no matter whether practical, logical or methodological rules are involved. The critical usage employs arguments for considering, evaluating, judging and justifying the choice of standards . . .'[1] Every description makes reference to standards of evaluation, and involves attitudes which are in need of justification and thus are open to criticism. When it goes beyond the sort of procedures applied in scientific method, criticism becomes the critique of ideology, and seeks to evaluate historically created conditions in the context of historically generated values. It is in this latter, dialectical fashion, that we can discern that science itself helped to create an outlook (positivism) which robs those who practice it of the capability of examining their own activity as ideological, i.e., in relation to the 'technical-cognitive interests' which shape it.

The discussion of Husserl's work by a third Frankfurt philosopher, Herbert Marcuse, is particularly interesting because it unites this theme of the limitations of scientific rationality with the phenomenological philosophy which was the proximate source of Schutz's attempt to reframe the basis of interpretative sociology. Husserl identifies a process of the 'decomposition of reason' from the Classical era up to the present age. The Greek concept of reason was founded upon a notion of the intellect as self-determining, as controlling human destiny, within a universe that has an inherent rational structure; in other words, subjective and objective reason are integrated. The consequence of this, as Marcuse presents Husserl's argument, is an identification of the real and the rational which transcends the given fact, and indeed is thus set off against it; 'theoretical' and 'practical' reason are harmonized. The triumph of scientific rationality, however, has destroyed this all-embracing concept of reason, and has dislocated science from the broader framework of ends which define the ultimate meanings of human existence. But this transformation, as Marcuse puts it, *'remains hidden to science itself*, hidden and unquestioned . . . Reason looses its philosophical power and its scientific right to define and project ideas and modes of Being beyond and against those established by the prevailing reality.'[2] The result is, in Habermas's terminology, the autonomy of 'technical-cognitive interests'—an apparent autonomy only, which

---

[1] Below, p. 216.
[2] Below, p. 229.

actually legitimizes an impoverishment of human reason. Thus here we have almost come full circle: what seemed to Comte, and to most other nineteenth-century thinkers, to be the highest and most complete attainment of man, in this perspective appears as a fundamental source of limitation upon the cognitive power of the human intellect!

Anthony Giddens

1 MAX WEBER

Subjectivity and Determinism[1]

Wherever we 'understand' human action as conditioned by clearly conscious and willed 'purposes', and wherever we clearly recognize the 'means' used by the actor, this understanding undoubtedly attains a particularly high level of 'certainty'.[2] If, however, we now inquire into the basis for this, it readily becomes apparent that it lies in the fact that the relationship between 'means' and 'ends' is a rational one, and as such is particularly suitable for establishing specific causal observations of a general nature which assume a 'law-like' character. There is no rational action without the causal rationalization of that part of reality which is implicated both as object and as means of manipulation, i.e., without its being integrated into a complex of empirical rules (*Erfahrungsregeln*), which state what we may expect to be the result of a given course of conduct.

Certainly it is completely, and in every respect, mistaken to claim that the 'teleological' 'understanding' of a process should intrinsically be seen as a 'reversal' of a causal one. But it is correct to say that without the belief in the verifiability of empirical rules no action based upon the evaluation of the means to an intended result could take place. Furthermore, it is correct to say, associated with this, that given one clearly-defined objective, the choice of the means is not necessarily equally clear. Rather this choice, not in every case completely indefinite or ambiguous, is 'determined' in terms of a disjunctive variety of

[1] First published as 'Roscher und Knies und das Irrationalitätsproblem' in *Wissenschaftslehre*. Translated by Peter Markl.

[2] *Translator's note*: This expression, 'evidence', is used here instead of 'inner view and visibility of the processes of consciousness'. This is in order to avoid the ambiguities of the expression 'experience' or 'obviousness'. Weber affirms that this is not the sense logicians attribute to 'evidence'. His 'evidence' is to be 'carefully distinguished' from 'validity'. Logically the notion contains only the possibility of the interpretation of comprehensible connections.

elements the number of which varies according to circumstances. The rational interpretation can thus take the form of a conditional judgement of necessity. (Schema: with a given purpose X and according to known rules of the event in question, for its attainment the actor 'had' to choose the means Y, from the respective means y, y', y''.)

Therefore, this coincides with a teleological 'evaluation' (*Wertung*) of the action which is empirically stated. (Schema: the choice of the means y, according to the known rules governing the event, guarantees a higher chance of realizing purpose x than means y' or y'', or this choice realizes this purpose with least sacrifice, etc. One choice is therefore 'more purposive' than the other; or one might even say: it alone is 'efficacious' (*zweckmässig*).) Once what really happens is recognized this 'evaluation' appears simply as an hypothesis or an ideal-typical construct: actual conduct is compared with rational action. This is what rational action is, according to general causal rule of experience (empirical rules), if one looks at it 'teleologically'. Thus, we can observe either a rational motive which could have ruled the actor, and which we intend to discover by demonstrating that his actual conduct was an adequate means for the end he 'might' have aimed at—or a comparison of the two in order to explain why a motive of the actor which, given the choice of means, we know leads to a result different from that intended by the actor subjectively. In neither case, however, do we proceed to a 'psychological' analysis of the 'personality' by means of some odd mode of inquiry, but, aided by our nomological knowledge, to an 'objective' analysis of a given situation.[1]

Here, then, 'interpretation' is reduced to the general knowledge

---

[1] (Most of Weber's original footnotes have been excluded—Ed.) It is thus the height of misunderstanding if in the construction of the abstract theory— e.g., the 'law of marginal utility'—one sees products of 'psychological' and even 'individual-psychological' interpretation, or an attempt at a 'psychological explanation' of 'economic value'. The specific character of these constructions, their heuristic value and the limits of their empirical applicability are based on the fact that they do not contain the least bit of 'psychology' in any sense of that term. Some representatives of the school who operate with these schemata have, of course, helped to create this error. For they have sometimes insisted upon analogies with 'thresholds of appeal', which these purely rational constructions—possible only against the background of thinking in terms of money—had nothing in common except certain superficial characteristics.

that we can act 'purposively', but this means to act on the basis of the consideration of different 'possibilities' of a future event, such that different conceivable modes of action (or abstentions from action) could be envisaged. Because of the eminently factual significance of 'purposive' action in empirical reality in this sense, 'teleological' rationalization can be used as a constructive means towards the creation of cognitive models (*Gedankengebilden*). These have an unusual heuristic value for the causal analysis of historical relationships. As constructive cognitive structures they can, first of all, be of a purely individual kind: interpretative hypotheses relating to concrete unique relationships; for instance in the example (already mentioned)[1] of the construction of the politics of Frederick William IV based on the one hand upon certain presumed purposes, and upon the constellation of the 'great powers' on the other. This serves, then, as a cognitive means for the purpose of measuring his real policy in terms of its degree of rational content and thereby of recognizing both the rational elements (in relation to the purpose) on the one hand, and the non-rational elements of his actual political action on the other.

In this way, an historically valid interpretation of this action can be achieved; that is, an estimation of the causal importance of both elements, and thus a valid classification of the 'personality' of Frederick William IV as a causal factor in the historical context. Or—and this is what interests us here—these can be ideal–typical constructs of a general character, like the 'laws' of abstract political economy which, under the assumption of strictly rational behaviour, speculatively construct certain imagined sets of economic conditions. In each case, however, the relation of such rational teleological constructs to the reality which is dealt with by the empirical sciences is not, of course, like that of a 'law of nature' and 'constellation' but only that of an ideal-typical notion, which serves to facilitate an empirically valid interpretation by comparing given facts with a possibility for interpretation. This is, in this respect, similar to the role played by teleological interpretation in biology. We do not 'disclose' through rational interpretation—as Gottle thinks—'actual conduct', but 'objectively possible' relationships.

Teleological evidence, even in these constructions, does not

---

[1] (This appears in a previous part of the article—Ed.)

signify a specific measure of empirical validity; but the 'evident' rational construction, 'correctly' formed, may allow us to distinguish directly the teleologically irrational elements in a concrete piece of economic action, and thereby make the actual course of that action understandable. Such schemes of interpretation, therefore, are not merely, as has been said, 'hypotheses' analogous to scientific hypothetical 'laws'. They can function as hypotheses in a heuristic sense for the interpretation of concrete events. But, contrary to scientific hypotheses, the statement that they do not in any concrete case contain a valid interpretation, does not impugn their interpretative value. It does so as little as, for instance, the empirical invalidation of pseudo-spherical space comprises the 'correctness' of its construction. Even if interpretation with the help of a rational scheme was then not possible in a given case—because the 'purposes' assumed in the schema did not exist as motives in the concrete instance—this in no way excludes the possibility of its usefulness.

If a hypothetical 'law of nature' definitely fails in only one instance, it collapses once and for all as a hypothesis. The ideal-typical constructions of political economy, however, do not —correctly understood—claim general validity, whereas a 'law of nature' must make this claim if it is not to lose its significance. A so-called 'empirical' law in the end is an empirically validated rule, having a problematic causal interpretation. A teleological schema of rational action, on the other hand, is an interpretation with a problematic empirical validation: the two are thus logically polar opposites. But both schemata are 'ideal-typical conceptual constructions'. The categories 'purpose' and 'means', in their application to empirical reality, bring about the rationalization of the latter—only because of this is the construction of such schemata possible. Here again, and in a conclusive way, we are able to cast light upon the postulate of the specifically empirical irrationality of 'personality' and of 'freedom' of action.

The 'freer', i.e., the more based on the actor's 'own' considerations—undisturbed by 'foreign' ('external') coercion or irresistible 'affect'—the actor enters into a decision, the more completely—*ceteris paribus*—may the motivation be analysed in terms of the categories of 'purpose' and 'means', and the more completely therefore can it be rationally analysed and categorized in terms of a schema of rational action. The greater the role played by nomological knowledge, however—for the actor on the one hand and for the analysing investigator on the other— the more 'determined' is the former in relation to the 'means'. And this is not all. In fact, the 'freer' the action, in the sense used here, i.e., the *less* it takes the form of a 'natural occurrence', the more that notion of 'personality' becomes validated which finds its 'essence' in the constancy of its inner relation to definite ultimate 'values' and life 'meanings'. In being pursued, these become translated into purposes, and thereby transformed into teleological-rational action. The more this is the case, the less room there is for any sort of romantic naturalistic conception of 'personality', that conception which paradoxically seeks the sacred quality of personality in an 'irrationality' based upon the dull, undifferentiated, vegetative 'foundation' of personal life: i.e., upon the interminglings of a mass of psycho-physical conditions of temperament and sentiment, but which in no way distinguishes the human 'person' from the animal.

For it is this Romanticism which stands behind the 'enigma of personality' in the sense in which Treitschke occasionally, and many others very frequently, talk about it and which wherever possible manages to introduce 'freedom of will' into these regions of natural life. The contradiction in this latter endeavour can be directly grasped in immediate experience: it is through just these 'irrational' elements of our actions that we 'feel' (often) directly 'determined', or at least 'constrained' in a way which is not the 'result' of our 'volition'.

In the historian's interpretation, 'personality' is not an 'enigma', but rather the totality of that which is 'understandable'. Even where rational interpretation ceases to be applicable, human action is not irrational in the sense of being 'incalculable', or resistant to causal classification—not any more than any individual event as such. However it is highly elevated above the irrationality of the purely 'natural' wherever rational 'interpretation' is possible. The impression of the uniquely irrational character of the 'personal' occurs because the historian measures the action of his hero, and the ensuing outcomes, against the ideal of teleological-rational action rather than, as he ought to do—in order to compare what is actually comparable—to contrast it with the occurrence of individual events in 'dead nature'. Least of all, however, should any concept of 'freedom of will' be related to that irrationality. It is the actor who is empirically 'free', i.e., acting according to his own considerations, who is bound by the recognizable and unequal means which, in terms of the objective situation, govern the achievement of his purposes.

The manufacturer in the competitive struggle, or the stock-broker in the stock exchange, are hardly helped by the belief in their 'freedom of will'. They can choose between economic extinction or following very definite maxims of economic behaviour. If, to their obvious disadvantage, they do not follow them, we might—among other possible hypotheses—consider that they were lacking 'freedom of will'. The laws of theoretical economics—in just the same manner as any purely rational interpretation of a unique historical event—precisely presuppose the existence of 'freedom of will', in any sense which is possible on empirical grounds. In any other sense than that of purposive-rational action, the 'problem' of 'freedom of will', in any form in which it could possibly occur, is placed completely outside the scope of history, and is meaningless to it.

The historians' 'interpretative' research in terms of motives is causal assessment in absolutely the same logical sense as causal interpretation of any particular individual event in nature.[1] For their aim is to postulate 'sufficient' grounds (at least as a hypothesis), in just the same way as is necessarily the case with research into natural phenomena, if it is concerned with individual components. Such research cannot be oriented towards determining the necessity of a given action (in the sense of laws of nature), if it is to avoid falling victim to Hegelian Emanationism or some version of modern anthropological occultism. For the human as well as for the extra-human *concretum* ('living' or 'dead'), as a necessarily limited part of the cosmic cluster of events, cannot be

---

[1] We may certainly agree that no causal observation whatever is equivalent to 'enactment' or 'lived experience' (*Erleben*). We cannot investigate here what significance can be attributed to this state of affairs in relation, for instance, to metaphysical constructions. But such a lack of equivalence also applies to every articulated 'understanding of chains of motivations'. There is no plausible reason for the principle of empirical causal explanation not to apply beyond the limit of 'understandable' motivation. The attribution of 'understandable' occurrences follows the same basic laws as the classification of natural events. On the ground of the empirical there is only one break in the principle of causality where the causal equation ends as a possible, or at least ideal, aim of scientific work.

integrated in its totality within purely 'nomological' knowledge
—since there is always (not only in the field of the 'personal') an
intensive infinity of aspects from which, seen logically, any
conceivable particular event, which for the science can only be
postulated as given, can be considered causally significant for a
(causal) historical interrelation. The way in which the categories
of causality are used—in a certain sense, which may be fully
acknowledged, the content of the categories itself changes in
such a way, that of its elements the one or the other looses its
meaning just when the principle of causality is seriously applied
in the last consequence. Its full, so to say, 'original', sense contains two aspects: the concept of 'effect' as, so to speak, a dynamic
connection between qualitatively different occurrences, on the one
hand, and the idea of the dependence upon 'rules' on the other.
'Effect', as the material content of the category of causality and with
it the concept of causal 'origin', looses its sense and disappears
wherever it gains expression as a purely spatial causal relationship
of the sort found in the quantifying abstractions of mathematics.

If one still wants to maintain a sense of causal categories
here, it would only be through a rule of successive movements
through time, and even this only in the sense that it amounts to
an expression of a metamorphosis of something which—in its
essence—remains for ever the same. Inversely the concept of
'rule' disappears from the category of causality as soon as the
qualitative singularity of the world process running through time
and also the qualitative uniqueness of any segment of space-time
from this process is reflected. Then the notion of causal law—
just like the causal equation for the notion of causal 'functioning'
—looses its sense in the case of any singular development of the
whole or of part of the cosmos. And if one wants to maintain a
sense of the causal category for the infinity of those concrete
happenings, which cannot ever be fully grasped by cognition,
then only the concept of 'being-caused' remains. That is in the
sense that in every time differential, that which is plainly 'new'
had to occur out of that which is 'past' in precisely the way it
actually did occur.

Basically, however, this serves only to point out the fact that
it came to be 'as it is now' just this way and no other, in absolute
uniqueness but nevertheless in a continuum of occurrences.

Those empirical disciplines which work with the category of

causality and which deal with aspects of reality—to which belong history and all the 'cultural' sciences, of whatever kind—use this category in its full implication throughout. They look at conditions and changes of reality as 'causes' and 'effects', and try in part to work out 'rules' of 'causation' through abstraction from concrete circumstances, and in part to 'explain' concrete 'causal' circumstances by relating them to those 'rules'.

However, the role played by the formulation of the 'rules', and the logical form this takes, is a question of the specific aim of a given investigation, if a formulation of 'rules' takes place at all. Formulation in terms of judgements of causal necessity is not the sole aim, and the impossibility of the apodictic form is by no means limited to the 'sciences of man' (*Geisteswissenschaften*). For history especially, moreover, the form of the causal explanation follows from its postulate of understandable 'interpretation'. To be sure, even this will and should work with concepts of satisfactory certainty and achieve the maximum possible clarity in the causal link, on the grounds of the sources available.

However, the historians' interpretation is not orientated according to our capacity to sort 'facts' as examples into general categories and formulae, but to our familiarity with the task which we are daily confronted with, namely to 'understand' the motives of individual human action. Hypothetical interpretations which our intuitive 'understanding' offers us, are verified by us in the light of 'experience'. But we saw in the case of the falling rock[1] that the formulation of judgements of necessity as the sole aim of any causal assessment of a specific constellation of given phenomena is only possible in terms of abstract and partial conditions. The same applies in history. History can only (*a*) postulate that a 'causal' relationship of a particular kind has existed, and (*b*) make this 'understandable' by relating it to the laws of that which happened.

On the one hand, the strict 'necessity' of the concrete historical occurrence remains for history not only an ideal postulate but also one that lies in infinity; on the other hand one cannot deduce a concept of non-deterministic 'freedom', which would be relevant or in any way specific to historical research from the irrationality of each particular occurrence, which is part of a

[1] (In a previous section of the article, Weber refers to the example of predicting where the fragments of a splintered rock will fall to illustrate that exact prediction is usually only possible under artificial conditions—Ed.)

totality. For historical research, 'freedom of will' must be regarded as completely outside of its considerations, and it is wholly senseless to see it as the basis of such research. Put negatively the situation is this: *both* the ideas of 'freedom' and 'freedom of will' are beyond the bounds of any 'experience' which they could be used to verify, and in fact neither actually influence practical work in history. Thus if one often finds in methodological discussions the sentence that 'even' man in his objective action is subjected to an 'always similar' (therefore: lawlike) 'causal nexus', then this is an unproven *protestatio fidei* in favour of metaphysical determinism, which does not relate to actual scientific practice. From it the historian can draw no sort of consequence for his practical work.

For much the same reason the rejection of the metaphysical belief in 'determinism'—in whatever sense this may be meant—on behalf of a historian, say on religious or other grounds, beyond experience, remains totally irrelevant in principle and as an experience so long as the historian holds to the principle of the interpretation of human action in terms of comprehensible motives—given that these motives can always in principle be subjected to verification in terms of experience.[1]

The belief that, for any area of knowledge, deterministic postulates include the methodological postulate of establishing categories and 'laws' as the only aim, is as great an error as the assumption which matches it in the reverse: that a metaphysical belief in the 'freedom of will' should exclude the application of categories and 'rules' to human behaviour. There is no basis for the belief that human' freedom of will' must be connected with a specific 'incalculability' or in any way with any specific kind of 'objective' irrationality of human action. We have seen that the opposite is the case.

[1] For the principle of historical conceptualization would still remain the same even if the 'material' of a concrete historical interrelation consisted solely of events caused by hysteria, hypnotism or paranoia, which would appear to us 'natural' in so far as they could not be interpreted. Even then the 'significance' produced through an interrelation of values—a significance which would be attributed to an individual constellation of such events in connection with an equally individual 'environment'—would be the starting-point, the recognition of individual connections would be the aim, and individual causal classification would be the means of scientific work. Thus Taine, who occasionally allows for such notions, does not cease to be an 'historian'.

2 ALFRED SCHUTZ

Subjective and Objective Meaning[1]

Weber distinguishes between two types of understanding:
'The first is the direct observational understanding (*aktuelles Verstehen*) of the subjective meaning (*gemeinter Sinn*) of the given act as such, including verbal utterances. We thus understand by direct observation, in this sense, the meaning of the proposition $2 \times 2 = 4$ when we hear or read it. This is a case of the direct rational understanding of ideas. We also understand an outbreak of anger as manifested by facial expression, exclamations or irrational movements. This is direct observational understanding of irrational emotional reactions. We can understand in a similar observational way the action of a woodcutter or of somebody who reaches for the knob to shut a door or who aims a gun at an animal. This is rational observational understanding of actions. Understanding may, however, be of another sort, namely, explanatory understanding (*erklärendes Verstehen*). Thus we understand in terms of motive (*motivationsmässig*) the meaning an actor attaches to the proposition twice two equals four, when he states it or writes it down, in that we understand what makes him do this at precisely this moment and in these circumstances. Understanding in this sense is attained if we know that he is engaged in balancing a ledger or in making a scientific demonstration, or is engaged in some other task of which this particular act would be an appropriate part. This is rational understanding of motivation, which consists in placing the act in an intelligible and more inclusive context of meaning (*Sinnzusammenhang*). Thus we understand the chopping of wood or aiming of a gun in terms of motive in addition to direct observation if we know that the woodchopper is working for a wage or is chopping a supply of firewood for his own use or possibly is doing it for

[1] First published in *The Phenomenology of the Social World*. Translated by George Walsh and Frederick Lehnert.

recreation. But he might also be 'working off' a fit of rage, an irrational case. . . . In all the above cases the particular act has been placed in an understandable *sequence of motivation* (*Sinnzusammenhang*), the understanding of which can be treated as an *explanation* of the actual course of behavior. Thus for a science which is concerned with the subjective meaning of action, explanation requires a grasp of the complex of meaning (*Sinnzusammenhang*) in which an actual course of understandable action thus interpreted belongs. In all such cases, even where the processes are largely affectual, the subjective meaning (*subiektiver Sinn*) of the action, including that also of the relevant meaning complexes, will be called the 'intended' meaning (*gemeinter Sinn*). This involves a departure from ordinary usage, which speaks of intention in this sense only in the case of rationally purposive action.'[1]

This very illuminating thesis deserves closer examination.

From the preceding passage it ought to be clear that Weber is using the term 'intended meaning' in two different senses. First, he is referring to the subjective meaning which the action has for the actor. According to him, this subjective meaning can be understood 'observationally', that is, it can be grasped by direct observation. But second, he is referring to the broader framework of meaning in which an action 'thus interpreted' (i.e., interpreted according to its subjective meaning) belongs. It is this broader context of meaning which is uncovered by motivational or clarifying understanding.

Let us look first at *observational understanding*, and, under that heading, first at the observational understanding of 'affects' and 'thoughts'. How can we arrive at an understanding of the subjective meaning of these experiences through direct observation? Whether a given affectual action is meaningful behaviour and thus genuine action is very difficult to determine, as Weber himself justly emphasizes.[2] Suppose that I 'internally perceive' *A*'s outburst of anger, as Scheler would say. Or, to use Weber's

---

[1] Weber, *Wirtschaft und Gesellschaft*, p. 3; cf. also point 3, ibid., as well as Weber's essay 'Über einige Kategorien der verstehenden Soziologie', *Gesammelte Aufsätze zur Wissenschaftslehre*, especially pp. 408 ff.

[2] Weber, *Wirtschaft und Gesellschaft*, p. 12.

terminology, suppose that in an act of observational understanding I grasp the look on *A*'s face and his gestures as an outburst of anger. But have I thereby determined whether *A* is
merely reacting, whether his behaviour is 'over the line of what
can be considered meaningfully oriented', whether it 'consists in
an uncontrolled reaction to an exceptional stimulus', or whether *A*
is merely having a tantrum and that the only meaning the outburst has for him is the release of his pent-up feelings? Direct
observation gives me no answer to this question. While I know he
is angry, I remain in the dark as to what that anger means to him
subjectively.

Now this is also true of the 'observational understanding' of
thoughts, such as the judgement $2 \times 2 = 4$. Husserl has recently
distinguished two different senses of the meaning of a judgement.[1]
First, there is the content of the judgement (*Urteilsinhalt*): 'that
$2 \times 2 = 4$'. Second, there is the epistemic attitude (*subjektiv
doxisch Setzungsmodus*) which the person using or uttering the
judgement has towards the judgement content. He may, for
instance, hold it to be certainly true or only probably true; he
may merely suspect that it is true; or he may be simply supposing
it true for the sake of argument. Or, finally, he may be denying
it. The *judgement content*, it should be noted, remains the same
throughout these changes of epistemic attitude. Now, it is this
very epistemic attitude which, according to Weber, determines
what the utterer of the judgement 'means'. In other words, what
he means when he utters it consists in whether he really believes
it, only suspects it may be true or what not. And yet this epistemic attitude is precisely what *cannot* be determined by direct observation.

We encounter a parallel difficulty when we come to the observational understanding of an *act*. Weber would say that I understand by direct observation the meaning of a man's behaviour
when I see him performing such acts as chopping wood, grasping
a doorknob in order (N.B.!) to shut the door or aiming a rifle
at an animal. These observed movements of the other person's
body Weber cites as the substratum of observational understanding. However, it is obvious that they have *already* been
understood and interpreted as soon as they are called 'woodchopping', 'knob-grasping' or 'taking aim'. What if the man

[1] *Formale und transzendentale Logik*, pp. 192 f. [The remainder of this paragraph is a paraphrase.]

wielding the axe is not really chopping wood but merely appears to be doing so? What if the man holding the doorknob is not grasping it in order to shut the door but is merely holding it steady in order to repair it? What if the hunter is not taking aim at all but is merely watching the animal through the telescopic sight on his rifle? Observational understanding of the other person's outward behaviour is clearly not enough to settle these points. These are questions of subjective meaning and cannot be answered by merely watching someone's behaviour, as Weber seems to think. On the contrary, we first observe the bodily behaviour and then place it within a larger context of meaning. One way we may do this is by giving the behaviour in question a name. But this context of meaning need not, in fact cannot, be identical with the context of meaning in the mind of the actor himself. Let us call it the *objective* context of meaning as opposed to the actor's *subjective* context of meaning.

Now let us turn to motivational understanding. Weber says that this consists in understanding the meaning-context within which an action belongs, once the action's subjective meaning is itself understood. But in the same place he speaks of this meaning-context as one of which this action would be, *from our point of view*, an appropriate part. This is confusing if not downright contradictory, for we have no means of knowing that the meaning-context which we think appropriate is at all the same as what the actor has in mind. This is a question to which we shall return later. It suffices at the moment that we have proved the impossibility of motivational understanding on the basis of observation alone. Data derived from some other source are essential. To understand a person's motives it will not do to 'size up' his actions on the basis of a 'taking-stock' drawn from the context. Motivational understanding requires instead a certain amount of knowledge of the actor's past and future. I look at the two men in Weber's example. One of them is working on a mathematical equation, the other is cutting wood. Information about the *past* of the two men that would be essential might be that the first has embarked on the demonstration of a point in science and that the second has been employed as a woodchopper. Information about the *future* of the two men that would be essential might be that the scientist regards this particular equation as relevant to his demonstration and that the employer is going to pay for this particular bit of woodchopping. Knowledge of the two men's past is necessary if *I* am to find an intelligible meaning-context into which I can fit their acts. Knowledge of the two men's future is essential if I am to determine whether their acts *in the subjective meaning which those acts have for them* fit into the meaning-context I have already recognized.

In both of these cases I am looking for the 'motive'. By *motive* Weber understands 'a complex of . . . meaning which seems *to the actor himself or to the observer* an adequate (or meaningful) ground for the conduct in question'.[1] Weber is here quite logically applying to the meaning-context, which without further elaboration he calls the 'motive', the distinction he has already made between the subjective and objective meaning of an action. Now, what is meant by calling the motive 'a complex which seems *to the actor* a meaningful ground for his conduct'? Obviously, again two different things. First there appears to me, as the meaningful ground of my behaviour, a series of future events whose occurrence I propose to bring about. I am orienting my behaviour to this end. But there is a second sense in which I sometimes speak of the meaningful ground of my behaviour. Here I refer to those past experiences of mine which have led me to behave as I do. In the first case I regard my behaviour as the means of accomplishing some desired goal. If I am trying to find my motive in this sense, I ask myself the following question: 'Which of all the future events I expect to happen are distinguished from the rest by the fact that my expectation of their occurrence constitutes or jointly constitutes the meaning of my behaviour?' In the second case I regard my present behaviour as the result of past experiences, as the effect of preceding 'causes'. If I am searching for my motive in this sense, then I ask myself a different question: 'Which of all my past experiences are distinguished from the rest by the fact that they constitute or jointly constitute the meaning of my behaviour?' Note that in both cases the motive being sought after lies outside the time span of the actual behaviour.

Weber fails to distinguish between these two quite different questions, and the results of that failure, as we shall see, are far-reaching. Furthermore, he does not answer the question of whether the meaning which the action has for an actor is identical with what appears to the latter to be his motive, i.e., the meaning-

[1] Weber, *Wirtschaft und Gesellschaft*, p. 5.

complex which he takes to be the meaningful ground of his behaviour. In other words, when we have discovered a man's motive, have we discovered the intended meaning of his action? Ordinary usage would seem to say yes. When I have discovered what a man is trying to do and what in his past has led him to try to do it, have I not discovered the meaning of his action? Certainly, if I ask him what he means by acting in such and such a way, he will commonly answer in one of two ways. Either he will say 'I am doing it *in order to* . . .' or 'I am doing it *because* . . .'. However, we must make clear that these statements are mere abbreviations for highly complex 'meaning-experiences' of the actor and that the statement of the 'motive' by no means gives an exhaustive account of the whole structure of 'intended meaning'. On the contrary, the actor takes for granted the meaning of his action: it is self-evident to him in the proper sense of the term. If he asks himself what his motives were, he takes this self-evident meaning as his point of departure and then looks for past experiences which were relevant to his action or for future events towards which his action is conducive. It can, therefore, be said that the actor must already know the intended meaning of his action before he can inquire about its motive. Notice how this applies to Weber's examples. When a man engaged in formulating a scientific demonstration utilizes for that purpose the proposition $2 \times 2 = 4$, this proposition must already be meaningful to him before he selects it as one of the steps towards his conclusion. Likewise the man who seeks employment as a woodcutter must first know what woodcutting is before he concludes that he can make a living at it.

So much for the problem of the person seeking for the subjective context of meaning within which, *from his point of view*, his action belongs. But what about the context of meaning which appears *to the observer* as the meaningful basis of the observed person's behaviour? Weber's motivational understanding has as its object the discovery of motives. Now, we have already shown that the motive of an action cannot be understood unless the meaning of that action is first known. But it is the actor who has this knowledge, not the observer. The observer lacks the self-evident starting point which is available to the actor. All he can do is start out with the objective meaning of the act as he sees it, treating this objective meaning as if it were without question the intended meaning of the actor. Weber sees this clearly enough when he says that motivational understanding must search for the context of meaning which is from our point of view appropriate (or which makes sense to us), into which the action, interpreted according to the intended meaning of the actor, fits. However, this so-called 'intended' meaning cannot give us any more information in motivational than in observational understanding. In neither case do we advance a step beyond the interpretation of objective meaning.

Indeed, Weber's distinction between observational and motivational understanding is arbitrary and without any logical basis in his own theory. Both types of understanding start out from an objective meaning-context. The understanding of subjective meaning has no place in either. One can treat observational understanding, whenever it concerns itself with subjective meaning, as if it were an inquiry into motives. In such a case one must be willing to take the answer one gets at a convenient cutoff point, since the search for 'the' motive always leads to an infinite regress. For instance, the woodcutter is wielding the axe in order to chop the wood to bits. Conversely, one can treat motivational understanding as if it were observational. This is done by dealing with every statement about the motive as if it were a statement of the observer's experiences of the circumstances surrounding the act. These experiences must, of course, be arranged in a continuous series and cover a sufficient span. Such a series might consist of the observation of the signing of the wage contract, of the wielding of the axe, of the splitting of the wood and of the collection of the wages. All of these observations would then be lumped together as one unified act of the subject under observation: 'working for a lumber company'.

Nevertheless, there is a valid epistemological point underlying the distinction between observational and motivational understanding. In everyday life we directly experience the acts of another. We interpret those external events which we call 'another's act' as indications of a stream of consciousness lying outside our own. To the extent that we do these things, we can 'understand' the events in question, reading the indications as they occur, and thus directly witness the action as it unfolds, witness it 'in the mode of actuality'. Observational understanding is then focused on the action as it takes place, and we, as beings living alongside the actor and sharing his present, participate experientially in the very course of his action. In essence, therefore, observational or direct understanding is simply the understanding we exercise in daily life in our direct relations with other people. Precisely for that reason, however, the inference from the overt behaviour to the intended meaning lying behind it is anything but a cut-and-dried matter.[1]

Motivational understanding, on the other hand, is not tied to the world of directly experienced social reality (*Umwelt*). It can take as its object any action of the more distant worlds of contemporaries (*Mitwelt*), or predecessors (*Vorwelt*), or even to a certain extent of successors (*Folgewelt*). For this kind of understanding does not take as its starting point an *ongoing* action. Rather, as we will later demonstrate, its object is the *accomplished act*. This may be considered as something really completed in the past or as something whose future completed form is now being envisaged. It may be regarded as motive in terms of origin or motive in terms of goal, as we said above. Furthermore it should be noted that motivational understanding starts out on the basis of an established objective meaning as merely an indication of the existence of a subjective meaning. This is all the more reason why a higher degree of scientific clarity and exactitude is attainable in motivational understanding. From this we must in turn conclude that the 'interpretive understanding' which is definitive of interpretive sociology cannot be observational understanding. Rather, the scientific method of establishing subjective meaning is motivational understanding, whereas the kind of understanding proper to everyday life is observational in character.

But this is by no means the end of our problems. We have seen that the intended meaning eludes the grasp not only of the simple everyday act of 'getting the meaning' but of the two kinds of understanding as well. We have seen, further, that external behaviour is merely an 'indication' of the existence of subjective meaning and that all meaning-contexts are given to us only objectively. Inasmuch as we have drawn a sharp distinction between subjective and objective meaning, a closer analysis of these two concepts is in order before we proceed any further.

---

[1] Husserl, *Logische Untersuchungen*, II, 25.

So far we have been using the term 'objective meaning' in a merely negative sense, that is, to refer to a meaning *other* than the subjective one in the mind of the actor. It is time that we stated in detail the positive meaning that we assign to the term.

Let M^1 be the meaning which a given action A has for a given actor X. Let the action A manifest itself by some bodily movement of X. Let A be observed by his friend F and by a sociologist S. Suppose, further, that the action A makes sense to both observers. Both of them will then connect the external course of the action A, which they take as an indication of X's subjective experiences, with a meaning. However, we have already demonstrated that the intended meaning M^1 which X gives to his action cannot be discovered either by observational or motivational understanding. What will happen, then, is that F will, on the basis of his practical experience, interpret the external action A as having the meaning M^2, and S will, on the basis of the ideal-typical constructs of interpretive sociology, assign to the action yet a third meaning, M^3. Whereas in Weber's terminology M^1 would be the subjective or intended meaning which A attributed to his own act, M^2 and M^3 would constitute the objective meaning of this act. But after all, M^2 is only the objective meaning relative to F, and M^3 is only the objective meaning relative to S. Therefore, to call M^2 and M^3 objective meaning-contents is merely to say that they are different from M^1. As a matter of fact, since M^1 can only be inferred from the evidence of A's external behaviour, the intended meaning must be regarded as a limiting concept with which M^2 and M^3 would never coincide even under optimum conditions of interpretation.

Let us first try to clear up the concept of objective meaning as exemplified in M^2 and M^3. One interpretation should be ruled out at once. This is that M^2 is the subjective meaning which F gives to X's act A and that M^3 is the subjective meaning which S gives to it. Such a reading would entirely miss what Weber has in mind when he uses the term 'subjective or intended meaning'. For it is obvious that an action has only one subjective meaning: that of the actor himself. It is X who gives subjective meaning to his action, and the only subjective meanings being given by F and S in this situation are the subjective meanings they are giving to their own actions, namely, their actions of observing X. It is obvious that there are so many riddles surrounding the problem of subjective meaning that at this early stage of the discussion we can hardly expect to achieve a clear understanding of its nature.

F and *S*, of course, see *X*'s action *A* as an event of the external world. As they live in that world, they seek to understand it. They not only live *in* their subjective experiences, they reflect *on* them. They not only have direct experience of the world, but they think and speak of their experiences, using concepts and judgements. They thus explain their experiences of the world, understanding them by means of interpretive schemes. The world and their experience of the world make sense for them just as they do for you and for me and for every rational being. This usage of 'sense' or 'meaning' signifies no more than that a rational being takes up a certain attitude towards any object he may confront. Since *F* and *S* witness the course of the act as an event of their world, experience it pre-predicatively, and proceed to explain it, they 'interpret' this, their experience; and its meaning for them is merely an explanation of one item of their own experience.

But the phenomena of the external world have meaning not only for you and me, for *F* and *S*, but for everyone living in it. There is only one external world, the public world, and it is given equally to all of us. Therefore, every act of mine through which I endow the world with meaning refers back to some meaning-endowing act (*Sinngebung*) of yours with respect to the same world. Meaning is thus constituted as an intersubjective phenomenon. The problem of how the intersubjectivity of all knowledge and thought can be transcendentally deduced is something beyond the scope of the present study, even though its analysis would completely clarify the concept of objective meaning. This most difficult and basic problem of every phenomenology of knowledge was stated in Husserl's *Formal and Transcendental Logic*[1] but by no means solved.

When we speak of objective meaning, we refer not only to those broad contexts of meaning we have just discussed. We intend to attribute objective meaning also to certain ideal objectivities (*ideale Gegenständlichkeiten*), such as signs and expressions. In so doing, we mean to say that these ideal objectivities are meaningful and intelligible in their own right—in their, so to speak,

[1] Especially § 96, pp. 210 ff. Cf. also Husserl, *Méditations cartésiennes*, Meditation V.

anonymous nature—regardless of whether anyone is thinking of them, regardless of whether anyone is using them. For instance, the expression $2 \times 2 = 4$ has an objective meaning regardless of what is in the minds of any or all of its users. A linguistic expression can be understood as an objective complex of meaning without reference to the speakers of the language. A theme from the *Ninth Symphony* is meaningful in itself wholly apart from the question of what Beethoven meant to express by it. Here the term 'objective meaning' signifies a unit of meaning considered as an ideal object. But only in so far as an expression can be considered in terms of *what it means (Bedeutung)* can it be regarded as truly objective. In his *Logical Investigations* Husserl taught us to distinguish between 'meaning' (*Bedeuten*) as an act and 'that which is meant' (*Bedeutung*), the latter being an ideal unity in contrast to the multiplicity of all possible acts of meaning. Husserl's distinction between 'essentially subjective and occasional' expressions, on the one hand, and 'objective' expressions, on the other, is only a special case of this general and fundamental insight. 'An expression is *objective* if it binds its meaning merely by its appearance-content of sound and can be understood without regard to the person uttering it or the circumstances of its utterance.' On the other hand, an expression is *essentially subjective and occasional* when it is 'such that its occasional and actual meaning must be oriented with respect to the speaking person and his condition'.[1]

Now the question is whether this sense of the term 'objective meaning' is the same as what we had in mind when we identified the objective meaning of the action A with the two meaning-interpretations M^2 and M^3 given that action by F and S. This is obviously not the case, not even if X's action is the utterance of an expression with objective meaning, such as a sentence. For, in the last analysis, F and S are not interested in what X has to say, that is, the content of his statement considered as an ideal objectivity. Rather, any observer of the social world is interested in interpreting *the phenomenon* of *X's utterance* of this statement here, now, and in such and such a manner. (By utterance we mean lip movements, sound waves, word meanings, and sentence meaning.) This interpretation consists in taking the utterance as a sign that A is undergoing certain conscious experiences, of which the having of an intention would be one example. From this point

[1] *Logische Untersuchungen*, II, 80.

of view, the precise content of the utterance is of only indirect interest. What F and S want to know is whether A said it and why. In the terminology we have established thus far, it would be proper to say that the utterance of the statement here and now by A is objectively meaningful.

Now, to be sure, the ideal objectivities (*ideale Gegenständlichkeiten*) which form the meaning-content of expressions and of the great systems of language, art, science, myth, etc., of which they are inseparable parts, play their own specific role in everyone's interpretation of the behaviour of other persons. All such interpretations presuppose the use of such *interpretive schemata*. This holds also for the account of the objective meaning observable by F and S as action D takes place. The interpretation of such courses of action takes place regularly according to schemata that are on hand to begin with, even though they are selected by F and S and are therefore relative to them.

Our analysis, so far cursory and superficial, must now proceed to a deeper level. The two concepts of subjective and objective meaning[1] will in the process undergo extensive modification, and only ... [at a later point ...][2] will we be in a position to give each of them a satisfactory definition. At this point we shall be content to add a few preliminary remarks on the direction of our investigations.

From our treatment of the different senses of the term 'objective meaning', it is clear that we call the real and ideal objectifications of the world surrounding us 'meaningful' as soon as we focus our attention upon them. We have known ever since Husserl's *Ideas*[3] that meaning-endowment is the act wherein pure sense experiences ('hyletic data') are 'animated'. What in a cursory glance we see as meaningful has already been constituted as such by a previous intentional operation of our consciousness. The most profound treatment given by Husserl to this question is to be found in his *Formal and Transcendental Logic*, although there he is concerned

---

[1] Lest there be any confusion with a concept to be found in a number of contemporary authors, it should be noted that our use of the term 'objective meaning' is without axiological implications. The fact that objective meaning may occasionally presuppose objective values (*objektive Werte*) and the fact that ideal objectivities (*Gegenständlichkeiten*) are constituted out of objective values are both matters that lie beyond the scope of this study.

[2] Schutz here refers to a subsequent chapter in his book.

[3] *Ideen*, pp. 172 ff.

with the sphere of logical objectivities. He explains the process by which meaning originates and notes that intentionality is really a synthesis of different operations,

> which are included in the intentional unity existing at a given time, and in their manner of being given on each occasion, as *a sedimented series of strata* [*sedimentierte Geschichte*], a series of strata which, however, in each case *can be laid bare by a rigorous method of investigation.*[1]

> Every meaning structure can be analyzed in terms of the *meaning stratification that is essential to it.* . . . All intentional unities have an intentional origin, are 'constituted' unities, and in every case one can subject the 'completed' unities to an analysis in terms of their over-all origin and of course their essential form, which is to be grasped eidetically.[2]

> Whereas 'static analysis' is governed by the unity of the intended object [*Gegenstand*] and in that way, by the unclear mode of givenness, following its reference as intentional modification, resists clarification, on the other hand, genetic intentional analysis is directed upon the entire concrete context in which every consciousness and its intentional object as such stand.[3]

This phenomenon of constitution can be studied in genetic-intentionality analysis, and, from an understanding of this intentionality, the genesis of meaning can be traced. Conversely, every objectivity which can be regarded as an already given and constituted meaning-content can be analysed in terms of its meaning-stratification. The *solitary Ego* can assume either point of view. *On the one hand*, I can look upon the world presenting itself to me as one that is completed, constituted and to be taken for granted. When I do this, I leave out of my awareness the intentional operations of my consciousness within which their meanings have already been constituted. At such times I have before me a world of real and ideal objects, and I can assert that this world is meaningful not only for me but for you, for us and for everyone. This is precisely because I am attending not to those acts of consciousness which one gave them meaning but because I

---

[1] *Formale und Transzendentale Logik*, p. 217.
[2] Ibid., pp. 184–5.
[3] Ibid., p. 277.

already presuppose, as given without question, a series of highly complex meaning-contents. The meaning-structure thus abstracted from its genesis is something that I can regard as having an objective meaning, as being meaningful in itself, just as the proposition $2 \times 2 = 4$ is meaningful regardless of where, when, or by whom it is asserted. *On the other hand*, I can turn my glance towards the intentional operations of my consciousness which originally conferred the meanings. Then I no longer have before me a complete and constituted world but one which only now is being constituted and which is ever being constituted anew in the stream of my enduring Ego: not a world of being, but a world that is at every moment one of becoming and passing away—or better, an emerging world. As such, it is meaningful for me in virtue of those meaning-endowing intentional acts of which I become aware by a reflexive glance. And as a world that is being constituted, never completed, but always in the process of formation, it points back to the most basic fact of my conscious life, to my awareness of the actual ongoing or passage of my life, to my duration; in Bergson's words, to my *durée*,[1] or, in Husserl's terminology, to my internal time-consciousness.[2] In everyday life, occupying as I do the position of the *natural attitude* (or *standpoint*), I live *within* the meaning-endowing acts themselves and am aware only of the objectivity constituted in them, i.e., objective meaning. It is only after I, 'by a painful effort', as Bergson says, turn away from the world of objects (*Gegenstände*) and direct my gaze at my inner stream of consciousness, it is only after I 'bracket' the natural world and attend only to my conscious experiences within the phenomenological reduction, it is only after I have done these things that I become aware of this process of constitution. To the solitary Ego occupying the natural attitude, the problem of objective and subjective meaning is quite unknown. It only comes to light after the carrying-out of the phenomenological reduction; and in so far as it concerns the

---

[1] *Essai sur les données immédiates de la conscience* (Paris, 1889); *Matière et mémoirs* (Paris, 1896); *L'Evolution créatrice* (Paris, 1907); *L'Energie spirituelle* (Paris, 1920); *Introduction à la métaphysique* (Paris, 1903); and finally, *Durée et simultanéité* (Paris, 1922).

[2] *Vorlesungen zur Phänomenologie des inneren Zeitbewusstseins* (ed. Heidegger), Suppl. VIII, *Jahrbuch für Philosophie und phänomenologische Forschung*, Vol. IX (Halle, 1928).

realm of logical objects and the corresponding antithesis of 'formal' and 'transcendental' logic, it has been stated with incomparable mastery by Husserl.

The distinction between the two ways of looking at the meaningful which we have just pointed out is, however, not the same as the distinction between objective and subjective meaning. We encountered the latter problem in the course of an analysis of the meaningful interpretation of the *social* world. 'Meaning' was for us not the generic 'predicate' of my intentional consciousness but had a specific social connotation. When we make the transition to the social sphere, there accrues, in fact, to the pair of concepts 'objective and subjective meaning' a new and sociologically relevant significance. I can, on the one hand, attend to and interpret in themselves the phenomena of the external world which present themselves to me as indications of the consciousness of other people. When I do this, I say of them that they have objective meaning. But I can, on the other hand, look over and through these external indications into the constituting process within the living consciousness of another rational being. What I am then concerned with is subjective meaning. What we call the world of objective meaning is, therefore, abstracted in the social sphere from the constituting processes of a meaning-endowing consciousness, be this one's own or another's. This results in the anonymous character of the meaning-content predicated of it and also its invariance with respect to every consciousness which has given it meaning through its own intentionality. In contrast to this, when we speak of subjective meaning in the social world, we are referring to the constituting processes in the consciousness of the person who produced that which is objectively meaningful. We are therefore referring to his 'intended meaning', whether he himself is aware of these constituting processes or not. The world of subjective meaning is therefore never anonymous, for it is essentially only something dependent upon and still within the operating intentionality of an Ego-consciousness, my own or someone else's. Now in the social world the question can in principle be posed—and this by means of a special technique yet to be described—as to what the subjective meaning is of any datum of objective meaning-content which we attribute to another mind. Furthermore, it can be asserted that it is possible to comprehend the meaning-content with a maximum degree of clarity. We can fulfil this claim if, by 'subjective meaning', we mean nothing more than the referral of constituted objectivities (*Gegenständlichkeiten*) to the consciousness of others.[1] On the other hand, we shall be unsuccessful if, by 'subjective meaning', we mean the 'intended meaning' of other persons. The latter remains a limiting concept even under optimum conditions of interpretation. Here let it suffice to state emphatically that the maximum possible grasp of subjective meaning in the social world cannot be expected on the common-sense level. In ordinary life we call a halt to the process of interpreting other people's meanings when we have found out enough to answer our practical questions; in short, we stop at the point that has direct relevance to the response we shall make ourselves. The search for the other person's subjective meaning will very likely be abandoned if his action becomes evident to us as objective content in a manner that relieves us of any further trouble. This is, perhaps, most obviously true of strictly 'rational' action, so-called, on the part of the person being observed. In such cases the overt meaning is sufficient for us to respond appropriately; we do not therefore try to interpret the other person's behaviour beyond a relatively superficial level. Otherwise, if we have any doubts about the objective meaning of a person's conduct, we ask ourselves, 'What is the fellow up to?' and so on. To this extent we can say of every meaning-interpretation of the social world that it is 'pragmatically determined'.

In order to get clear as to the essence of interpretive sociology, we took as our starting point Weber's definition of social action. Our first step was to analyse the statement, 'The actor attaches a meaning to his action.' We carried out part of this analysis in section 2[2] but found it necessary to make a digression in order to clarify the concepts of objective and subjective meaning. We can now get back on to the main track of our argument.

First of all, we must point out an ambiguity in the term 'action'. This word can, first of all, mean the already constituted act (*Handlung*) considered as a completed unit, a finished product, an

---

[1] Or, in the sphere of the solitary Ego, to the 'intended meaning' constituted each time in its own consciousness.

[2] Not reprinted here.

Objectivity. But second, it can mean the action in the very course of being constituted, and, as such, a flow, an ongoing sequence of events, a process of bringing something forth, an accomplishing. Every action, whether it be my own or that of another person, can appear to me under both these aspects. My *action as it takes place* presents itself to me as a series of *existing* and *present* experiences, experiences that are coming to be and passing away. My *intended* (*intendiertes*) *action* presents itself to me as a series of *future* experiences. My *terminated, completed act* (which is my expired action) presents itself to me as a series of *terminated* experiences which I contemplate in memory. The meaning of my action consists not only in the experiences of consciousness I have while the action is in progress but also in those future experiences which are my intended action and in those past experiences which are my completed action. We can at this point utilize the distinction we made at the end of the preceding paragraph between meaning-contents that are already constituted and meaning-contents still in the process of constitution. The distinction can now be applied specifically to action in such a way as to differentiate between the action in progress (*actio*) and the already finished and constituted act (*actum*) which has been produced by the former.

Likewise we should distinguish between the action of the other person and his act. The other person's conscious experiences in which his action is constituted present themselves to me as events of the external world. These may be his bodily movements or they may be changes in the external world brought about by such bodily movements. At any rate, we interpret these movements or changes as indications of another person's conscious experiences. Now we can regard these indications either as the other person's *actio* or as his *actum*, depending on whether our attention is focused on his conduct as it transpires before our eyes or on the act-objectivity (*Handlungsgegenständlichkeit*) produced and constituted by that conduct.

An act is therefore always something enacted (*ein Gehandelt-worden-sein*) and can be considered independently of the acting subject and of his experiences. Every act presupposes an action, but this by no means implies that reference to the action must enter into discussion of the act. In contrast to the act, the action is *subject-bound*. Whereas the act is, so to speak, performed anonymously, the action is a series of experiences being formed in the concrete and individual consciousness of some actor, be it myself or someone else.

We have already seen that it is only by studying the structure of the meaning-configuration in the stream of an Ego-consciousness that we can ever come to an understanding of the deep-seated difference between objective and subjective meaning. Meaning harks back to the internal time-consciousness, to the *durée* in which it was constituted originally and in its most generic sense. We see this point borne out in our analysis of the concepts of action and act. All action takes place in time, or more precisely in the internal time-consciousness, in the *durée*. It is duration-immanent enactment. Act, on the other hand, is duration-transcendent enactedness.

Having cleared up this point, we can now return to the question of what is meant by Weber's statement that the actor attaches meaning to his action. Does the actor give meaning to his action or to his act in the sense that we have defined these terms? In other words, is it the conscious processes which are being constituted in his *durée* which he endows with meaning, or is it the completed and constituted deed?

Before we answer this question, we must point out that we are speaking metaphorically when we say that a meaning is 'attached' to an act. This is also true of Max Weber. For although Weber's concept of action, like that of Sander,[1] contains a number of ambiguities, one thing about it is certain. This is that he did not mean by 'action' the physical event or bodily movement on the part of the actor. Nor did he think of the meaning as something which the individual in question 'attached' to his bodily movement in the sense of sending it along a parallel track in a kind of pre-established harmony. Weber's definition of action, in fact, includes also a person's inner behaviour or activity to the extent that these can properly be regarded as meaningful. We have already demonstrated that this thesis must not be understood to assert that all behaviour that is not action is therefore meaningless. Obviously, what he means is that action, as opposed to behaviour in general, has a specific kind of meaning.

The first characteristic that suggests itself as a possible way of

[1] Sander, 'Der Gegenstand der reinen Gesellschaftslehre', *Archiv für Sozialwissenschaften*, Vol. LIV, pp. 367 ff.

differentiating between action and behaviour is the *voluntary* nature of action as opposed to the automatic nature of behaviour. If this were what Weber had in mind when he defined action as meaningful behaviour, then meaning would consist in choice, in decision, in the freedom to behave in a certain way while not being forced to act in that way. However, that would take care of only one of the two meanings of 'free choice'. The term 'free choice' covers highly complex conscious events, and these need systematic study. The phenomenon of 'will' should by no means be left unanalysed as a vague label used to describe a metaphysical position. Rather, the analysis of voluntary behaviour must be carried out without reference to metaphysical problems.

A second superficial difference distinguishes action as behaviour which is *conscious* from unconscious or reactive behaviour. In that case, the meaning 'attached' to behaviour would consist precisely in the consciousness of that behaviour. However, what is 'known' in this consciousness is evidently the truth about the behaviour as it is disclosed to him whose behaviour it is. How difficult is the disclosure of this truth Husserl has shown in his *Formal and Transcendental Logic*. It is, for example, a complicated problem whether a person's behaviour is known to him simply in one particular mode of givenness or, rather, whether there are different modes or tenses of givenness for one's past, present and future (i.e., intended) behaviour. This problem must be cleared up by any analysis of meaningful behaviour.

This brief survey ought to be enough to show that an analysis of the constituting process (*Konstitutionsanalyse*) is necessary if we are going to understand the concept of meaningful action. In short, we must examine the formation and structure of those lived experiences which give meaning to an action. This investigation must, however, proceed to a still deeper level. For even what we call behaviour is already meaningful in a more primitive sense of the term. Behaviour as a lived experience is different from all other lived experiences in that it presupposes an activity of the Ego. Its meaning is therefore established in Acts wherein the Ego takes up one attitude or position after another. However, I can also attribute meaning to those of my experiences which do not involve activity (*Aktivität*). Even the fact that I become aware of the meaning of an experience presupposes that I notice it and 'select it out' from all my other experiences. In each moment of its duration the Ego is conscious of its bodily state, its sensations, its perceptions, its attitude-taking Acts and its emotional state. All these components constitute the 'thus' or 'whatness' (*So*) of each Now (*Jetzt*) of the Ego's conscious life. If I call one of these experiences meaningful it is only because, in taking heed of it, I have 'selected it out' of and distinguished it from the abundance of experiences coexisting with it, preceding it and following it. Let us call an experience that has been 'selected out' in this way a 'discrete' (*wohlumgrenztes*) experience and say that we 'attach a meaning to it'. We have now defined the first and most primitive sense of the word 'meaning'.

Notice, however, that we have ourselves just used the phrase 'attach a meaning to', a metaphor to which we had previously taken exception. The later course of our investigations will fully justify our negative attitude towards this metaphor. By no means is the meaning of an experience a new, additional and secondary experience which is somehow 'attached' to the first. By no means, either, is meaning a *predicate* of an individual experience—a conclusion suggested by such usages as 'having meaning', 'meaning-bearing' and 'meaningful'. To anticipate ourselves, we will say that *meaning is a certain way of directing one's gaze at an item of one's own experience*. This item is thus 'selected out' and rendered discrete by a reflexive Act. Meaning indicates, therefore, a peculiar attitude on the part of the Ego towards the flow of its own duration. This holds true of all stages and levels of meaning. Thus that theory is completely wrong which maintains that one's behaviour is distinct from one's conscious experience of that behaviour and that meaning belongs only to the latter. The difficulty lies chiefly in language, which, for certain deep-seated reasons, hypostatizes as behaviour certain experiences of which we become aware and afterwards predicates of this behaviour as its meaning the very way of directing the gaze upon these experiences which made them into behaviour in the first place. In just the same way, action is only a linguistic hypostatization of experiences of which we have become heedful and whose meaning (supposedly attached to them) is nothing more than the particular manner or 'how' (*Wie*) of this heeding (*Zuwendung*).

3 HAROLD GARFINKEL

The Rational Properties of Scientific and Common-sense Activities[1]

INTRODUCTION

The programme of his discipline requires that the sociologist scientifically describe a world that includes as problematical phenomena not only the other person's actions but the other person's knowledge of the world. As a result, the sociologist cannot avoid *some* working decision with respect to the various phenomena intended by the term 'rationality'.

Commonly, sociological researchers decide on a definition of rationality by selecting one or more features from among the properties of scientific activity as it is ideally described and understood.[2] The definition is then used methodologically to aid the researcher in deciding the realistic, pathological, prejudiced, delusional, mythical, magical, ritual and similar features of everyday conduct, thinking and beliefs.

But because sociologists find with such overwhelming frequency that effective, persistent and stable actions and social structures occur despite obvious discrepancies between the lay person's and the ideal scientist's knowledge and procedures, they have found that the rational properties which their definitions discriminated are empirically uninteresting. They have preferred instead to study the features and conditions of non-rationality in human condut. The result is that in most of the available theories

[1] First published in *Behavioural Science*.
[2] One definition that enjoys current favour is known as the rule of empirically adequate means. A person's actions are conceived by the researcher as steps in accomplishing tasks whose possible and actual accomplishment is empirically decidable. Empirical adequacy is then defined in terms of the rules of scientific procedure and the properties of the knowledge that such procedure produces.

of social action and social structure rational actions are assigned residual status.

With the hope of correcting a trend, it is the purpose of this paper to remedy this residual status by re-introducing as a problem for empirical inquiry (*a*) the various rational properties of conduct, as well as (*b*) the conditions of a social system under which various rational behaviours occur.

RATIONAL BEHAVIOURS

'Rationality' has been used to designate many different ways of behaviour. A list of such behaviours can be made without treating any one as definitive of the term 'rationality'. Alfred Schutz's classical paper on the problem of rationality (1943) inventories these meanings and is our point of departure.

When the various meanings of the term which Schutz inventoried are phrased as descriptions of conduct the following list of behaviours results. In the remainder of the paper, these behaviours will be referred to as 'the rationalities'.

1. *Categorizing and comparing.*   It is commonplace for a person to search his experience for a situation with which to compare the one he addresses. Sometimes rationality refers to the *fact* that he searches the two situations with regard to their comparability, and sometimes to his *concern* for making matters comparable. To say that a person addresses the tasks of comparison is equivalent to saying that he treats a situation or a person or a problem as an instance of a type. Thereby the notion of a 'degree of rationality' is encountered. The extensiveness of a person's concern with classification, the frequency of this activity, the success with which he engages in it are frequently the behaviours meant by saying that one person's activities are more rational than another's.

2. *Tolerable error.*   It is possible for a person to 'require' varying degrees of 'goodness of fit' between an observation and a theory in terms of which he names, measures, describes or otherwise intends the sense of his observation as a datum. He may pay a little or a lot of attention to the degree of fit. On one occasion he will allow a literary allusion to describe what has occurred.

On another occasion and for the same occurrences he may search the mathematical journals for a model to order them. It is sometimes said, then, that one person is rational while another is not or is less so, when that person pays closer attention than does his neighbour to the degree of fit between what he has observed and what he intends as his finding.

3. *Search for 'means'.* Rationality is sometimes used to mean that a person reviews rules of procedure which in the past yielded the practical effects now desired. Sometimes it is the fact that a person seeks to transfer rules of practice which had a pay-off in situations of like character; sometimes it is the frequency of this effort; at other times the rational character of his actions refers to the person's ability or inclination to employ in a present situation techniques that worked in other situations.

4. *Analysis of alternatives and consequences.* Frequently the term rationality is used to call attention to the fact that a person, in assessing a situation, anticipates the alterations which his actions will produce. Not only the fact *that* he 'rehearses in imagination' the various courses of action which will have occurred; but the care, attention, time and elaborateness of analysis paid to alternative courses of action are frequent references. With respect to the activity of 'rehearsing in imagination' the competing lines of actions-that-will-have-been-completed, the clarity, extent of detail, the number of alternatives, the vividness and the amount of information which fills out each of the schemata of competing lines of action are often the intended features in calling a person's actions 'rational'.

5. *Strategy.* Prior to the actual occasion of choice a person may assign to a set of alternative courses of action the conditions under which any one of them is to be followed. Von Neumann and Morgenstern (1947) have called the set of such decisions a player's strategy. The set of such decisions can be called the strategy character of the actor's anticipations. A person whose anticipations are handled with the belief that his circumstances tomorrow will be like those he has known in the past is sometimes said to be acting with less rationality than the one who addresses

alternatively possible future states of his present situation by the use of a manual of 'what-to-do-in-case-of's'.

6. *Concern for timing.*   When we say that a person intends through his behaviours to realize a future state of affairs, we frequently mean that the person entertains an expectation of the scheduling of events. The concern for timing involves the extent to which he takes a position with regard to the possible ways in which events can occur temporally. A definite and restricted frame of scheduled possibilities is compared with a 'lesser rationality' that consists of the person orienting the future fall of events under the aspect of 'anything can happen'.

7. *Predictability.*   Highly specific expectations of time scheduling can be accompanied by a concern with the predictable characteristics of a situation. A person may seek preliminary information about the situation in order to establish some empirical constants, or he may attempt to make the situation predictable by examining the logical properties of the constructs he uses in 'defining' it or by reviewing the rules that govern the use of his constructs. Accordingly, making the situation predictable means taking whatever measures are possible to reduce 'surprise'. Both the desire for 'surprise in small amounts' and the use of whatever measures yield it are frequently the behaviours intended by the term rationality.

8. *Rules of procedure.*   Sometimes rationality refers to rules of procedure and inference in terms of which a person decides the correctness of his judgements, inferences, perceptions and characterizations. Such rules define the distinct ways in which a thing may be *known*—distinctions, for example, between fact, supposition, evidence, illustration and conjecture. For our purposes two important classes of such rules of correct decisions may be distinguished: 'Cartesian' rules and 'tribal' rules. Cartesian rules propose that a decision is correct because the person followed the rules without respect for persons, i.e., that the decision was made without regard for social affiliation. By contrast, 'tribal' rules provide that a decision is or is not correct according to whether certain interpersonal solidarities are respected as conditions of the decision. The person counts his decision right

or wrong in accordance with whom it is referentially important that he be in agreement.

The term rationality is frequently used to refer to the application of Cartesian rules of decision. Because conventions may impose constraints on such decision-making, the extent to which the constraints are suppressed, controlled or rendered ineffective or irrelevant is another frequent meaning of rationality.

9. *Choice.* Sometimes the fact that a person is aware of the actual possibility of exercising a choice and sometimes the fact that he chooses, are popular meanings of rationality.

10. *Grounds of choice.* The grounds upon which a person exercises a choice among alternatives as well as the grounds he uses to legitimize a choice are frequently pointed out as rational features of an action. Several different behavioural meanings of the term 'grounds' need to be discriminated.

(*a*) Rational grounds sometimes refer exclusively to the scientific *corpus*[1] of information as an inventory of propositions which is treated by the person as correct grounds of further inference and action.

(*b*) Rational grounds sometimes refer to such properties of a person's knowledge as the 'fine' or 'gross' structure of the characterizations he uses, or whether the 'inventory' consists of a set of stories as compared with universal empirical laws, or the extent to which the materials are codified, or whether the *corpus* in use accords with the *corpus* of scientific propositions.

(*c*) In so far as the grounds of choice are the strategies of action, as was noted before in point 5, another sense of rationality is involved.

(*d*) Grounds of a person's choice may be those which he quite literally *finds* through retrospectively interpreting a present outcome. For example, in the effort to determine what was 'really' decided at a prior time, a person may realize such grounds in the course of historicizing an outcome. Thus, if a present datum is treated as an-answer-to-some-question, the datum may motivate the original question. Selecting, arranging and unifying the historical context of an action after its occurrence so as to present

---

[1] The concept of the *corpus* of knowledge is taken from the work of Felix Kaufmann (1944, pp. 33–66).

a publicly acceptable or coherent account of it is a familiar meaning of 'rationalization'.

11. *Compatibility of ends–means relationships with principles of formal logic.* A person may treat a contemplated course of action as an arrangement of steps in the solution of a problem. He may arrange these steps as a set of 'ends–means' relationships but count the problem solved only if these relationships are accomplished without violating the ideal of full compatibility with the principles of formal scientific logic and the rules of scientific procedure.[1] The fact that he may do so, the frequency with which he does so, his persistence in treating problems in this way or the success that he enjoys in following such procedures, are alternative ways of specifying the rationality of his actions.

12. *Semantic clarity and distinctness.* Reference is often made to a person's attempt to treat the semantic clarity of a construction as a variable with a maximum value which must be approximated as a required step in solving the problem of constructing a credible definition of a situation. A person who withholds credence until the condition of approximate maximum value has been met is frequently said to be more rational than another who will lend credence to a mystery.

A person may assign a high priority to the tasks of clarifying the constructs which make up a definition of a situation and of deciding the compatibility of such constructs with meanings intended in terminologies employed by others. On the other hand, a person may pay little attention to such tasks. The former action is sometimes said to be more rational than the latter.

13. *Clarity and distinctness 'for its own sake'.* Schutz points out that a concern for clarity and distinctness may be a concern for distinctness that is adequate for the person's purposes. Different possible relationships, ideal or actual, between (*a*) a concern for clarity and (*b*) the purposes which the clarity of the construct serves reveal additional behavioural meanings of rationality. Two variables are involved: (1) how highly one esteems clarification for its own sake, and (2) the value assigned by the per-

---

[1] When treated as a rule for defining descriptive categories of action, this property is known as the rule of the empirical adequacy of means.

son to the accomplishment of a project. One relationship between these variables makes the task of clarification itself the project to be accomplished. This is the meaning of 'clarification for its own sake'. But the relationship between the two variables may be treated by a person as consisting in some degree of independent variability. Such a relationship would be meant when treating as an ideal 'clarification that is sufficient for present purposes'. Rationality frequently means a high degree of dependence of one upon the other. Such a dependence when treated as a rule of investigative or interpretive conduct is sometimes meant in the distinction between 'pure' and 'applied' research and theory.

14. *Compatibility of the definition of a situation with scientific knowledge.* A person can allow what he treats as 'matters of fact' to be criticized in terms of their compatibility with the body of scientific findings. The 'allowed legitimacy of such criticism' means that in the case of a demonstrated discrepancy between what the person treats as correct grounds of inference (the meaning of 'fact') and what has been demonstrated as correct, the former will be changed to accommodate to the latter. Thus a person's actions are said to be rational to the extent that he accommodates or is prepared to accommodate to what is scientifically the case.

Frequently rationality refers to the person's feelings that accompany his conduct, e.g., 'affective neutrality', 'unemotional', 'detached', 'disinterested' and 'impersonal'. For the theoretical tasks of this paper, however, the fact that a person has such feelings is uninteresting. It is of interest, however, that a person uses his feelings about his environment to recommend the sensible character of the thing he is talking about or the warrant of a finding. There is nothing that prohibits a scientific investigator from being passionately hopeful that his hypothesis will be confirmed. He is prohibited, however, from using his passionate hope *or* his detachment of feeling to recommend the sense or warrant of a proposition. A person who treats his feelings about a matter as irrelevant to its sense or warrant is sometimes said to be acting rationally, while a person who recommends sense and warrant by invoking his feelings is said to act with less rationality. This holds, however, only for ideally described scientific activities.

SCIENTIFIC RATIONALITIES

The foregoing rationalities may be used to construct an image of a person as a type of behaviour. A person can be conceived who may[1] search a present situation for its points of comparability to situations that he knew in the past and may search his past experience for formulas that have yielded the practical effects he now seeks to bring about. In this task he may pay close attention to these points of comparability. He may anticipate the consequences of his acting according to the formulas that recommend themselves to him. He may 'rehearse in imagination' various competing lines of action. He may assign to each alternative, by a decision made prior to the actual occasion of choice, the conditions under which any one of the alternatives is to be followed. Along with such structurings of experience as these, the person may intend through his behaviours to realize a projected outcome. This may involve his paying specific attention to the predictable characteristics of the situation that he seeks to manipulate. His actions may involve the exercise of choice between two or more means for the same ends or of a choice between ends. He may decide the correctness of his choice by invoking empirical laws. And so on.

In extending the features of this behavioural type to incorporate all of the preceding rationalities, a distinction arises between the interests of everyday life and the interests of scientific theorizing. Where a person's actions are governed by the 'attitude of daily life', all of the rationalities can occur *with four important exceptions*. Phrased as ideal maxims of conduct, these excepted rationalities state that the projected steps in the solution of a problem or the accomplishment of a task, i.e., the 'means–ends relationships', be constructed in such a way (1) that they remain in full compatibility with the rules that define scientifically correct decisions of grammar and procedure; (2) that all the elements be conceived in full clearness and distinctness; (3) that the clarification of both the body of knowledge as well as the rules of investigative and interpretive procedure be treated as a first priority project; and (4) that the projected steps contain only scientifically verifiable assumptions that have to be in full compatibility with

[1] By 'may' is meant available as one of a set of alternatives. It does not mean likelihood.

the whole of scientific knowledge. The behavioural correlates of these maxims were described before as rationalities 11 through 14. For ease of reference I shall refer to these four as 'the scientific rationalities'.

It is the crux of this paper and of a research programme that would follow if its arguments are correct, that *the scientific rationalities, in fact, occur as stable properties of actions and as sanctionable ideals only in the case of actions governed by the attitude of scientific theorizing. By contrast, actions governed by the attitude of daily life are marked by the specific absence of these rationalities either as stable properties or as sanctionable ideals.* Where actions and social structures governed by the presuppositions of everyday life are concerned, attempts to stabilize these features or to compel adherence through socially systematic administration of rewards and punishments are the operations required to multiply the anomic features of interaction. All of the other rationalities, 1 through 10, however, can occur in actions governed by either attitude, both as stable properties and sanctionable ideals.

The preceding assertions are meant as empirical matters not as doctrinal ones. The reconstruction of the 'problem of rationality'[1] proposed by this paper depends upon the warranted character of these assertions. Their test depends upon a viable distinction between the 'attitude of daily life' and the 'attitude of scientific theorizing'. It is necessary, therefore, that the different presuppositions that make up each attitude be briefly compared. After this is done, we shall return to the main thread of the argument.

[1] For the sociological theorist, the 'problem of rationality' can be treated as consisting of five tasks: (1) clarifying the various referrents of the term 'rationality' which includes stating the behavioural correlates of the various 'meanings' of rationality as (*a*) the individual's actions as well as (*b*) the 'system's' characteristics; (2) deciding on the ground of the examination of experience rather than by an election of theory which of the behavioural designata go together; (3) deciding an allocation of behavioural designata between definitional and empirically problematical status; (4) deciding the grounds for justifying any of the many possible allocations that he may finally choose to make; and (5) showing the consequences of alternative sets of decisions for sociological theorizing and investigation.

PRESUPPOSITIONS OF THE TWO ATTITUDES

The attitudes of daily life and scientific theorizing[1] were described by Alfred Schutz in his studies of the constitutive phenomenology of common-sense situations (1943; 1944; 1945; 1951; 1953). Because the arguments of this paper depend upon the assumption that these attitudes do not shade into each other, it is necessary that the presuppositions that comprise each be briefly compared.

1. The first assumption Schutz refers to is the 'epoché' of the natural attitude. He shows that in everyday situations the 'practical theorist' achieves an ordering of events while seeking to retain and sanction the presupposition that the objects of the world are as they appear. The person coping with everyday affairs seeks an interpretation while holding a line of 'official neutrality' towards the interpretive rule that one may doubt that the objects of the world are as they appear. Stated as a property of events, this assumption consists of the expectation that a relationship of undoubted correspondence exists between actual appearances of the object and the-intended-object-that-appears-in-this-determined-fashion. Out of the set of alternative relationships between the actual appearances of the object and the intended object, as for example, the relationship of *doubtful* correspondence between the two, the person expects that the presupposed undoubted correspondence is the sanctionable one, and that the other person employs the same expectancy in a more or less identical fashion.

In the activities of scientific theorizing quite a different role of interpretive procedure is used. It provides that interpretation be conducted while holding a position of 'official neutrality' towards the *belief* that the objects of the world are as they appear. The activities of everyday life, of course, permit the actor's doubt that the objects are as they appear; but this doubt is in principle a doubt that is limited by 'practical considerations', i.e., his doubt is limited by his respect for certain valued, more or less routine features of the social order as seen from within, that he specifically does not and will not call into question. By contrast, the activities of scientific theorizing are governed by the strange ideal of doubt that is in principle unlimited and that

[1] To avoid misunderstanding I want to stress that the concern here is with the attitude of scientific theorizing. The attitude that informs the activities of actual scientific inquiry is another matter entirely.

specifically does not recognize the normative social structures as constraining conditions.

2. Schutz speaks of a second assumption as the person's practical interest in the events of the world. An invariant feature of the presuppositions of daily life is the person's belief that events can actually and potentially affect his actions and can be affected by his actions. Under this presupposed feature of events, the accuracy of his ordering of events is assumed by the person to be tested and testable without suspending the relevance of what he knows as fact, supposition, conjecture, fantasy and the like by virtue of his bodily and social positions in the real world. For the person in daily life, events, their relationships, their causal textures are not matters of mere theoretic interest. He does not sanction the notion that in dealing with the events of his environment it is correct to address them with the interpretive rule that he knows nothing or that *all* of what he knows he knows only 'until further notice'. What he knows, in the way he knows it, he assumes to be an integral feature of himself as a social object. He *sanctions* his competence as a bona-fide member of the group as a condition for adequately appreciating the sense of his everyday affairs; he does not treat this competence as irrelevant.

By contrast, the interpretive rules of the attitude of scientific theorizing provide that the accuracy of a model is to be tested while suspending judgement on the relevance of what the theorizer knows by virtue of his social and bodily positions in the real world.

3. Schutz describes the time perspective of daily life. The person who is said to orient events in the attitude of everyday life accords to possible events a temporal accent which is drawn from what the person assumes is a scheme of temporal relationships that he and other persons employ in equivalent and standardized fashion. The conversation that he is having consists for him of not only the events of his stream of experience, but of what was, is or may be said at a time that is designated by the successive positions of the hands of the clock. The conversation is not only progressively realized through a succession of realized meanings of the course of utterances, but as of any point in its course, the conversation has a time of beginning, of duration and of termination. Its events are co-ordinate with a socially employed scheme of temporal determinations. For the person oriented to a situation in a 'prac-

tical way' his interest in standard time is not like his interest when he is theorizing scientifically.

In the attitude of daily life the interest in an interpersonally validated scheme of standard time is directed to the problems such a scheme solves for the user in scheduling and co-ordinating his inner life and bodily movements to those of others. By contrast, the interest in standard time that occurs in the attitude of scientific theorizing—assuming in the first place that the scientific theorizier is concerned with matters of fact—is confined to the use of such a scheme as a means of conceiving an empirically possible world rather than as a means of scheduling his actions. Other attitudes provide alternative and contrasting ways of temporally punctuating events. For example, in the play *Ethan Frome*, the lovers' fate comes before and as a condition for appreciating the sequence of steps that led up to it. But in situations of everyday life the person assigns to events the properties of standard time relationships. He assumes, too, that the scheme of standard time is entirely a *public* enterprise, a kind of 'one great clock identical for all'.

4. The person assumes a particular 'form of sociality'. This assumption consists of the belief that some characteristic disparity exists between the image of himself that he attributes to others and the image that he has of himself, i.e., a characteristic disparity between his public and private life. He assumes, too, that alterations of this characteristic disparity remain within his autonomous control. The assumption serves as a rule whereby the everyday theorist groups his experiences with regard to what goes properly with whom. There corresponds thereby to the common intersubjective world of communication the unpublicized knowledge, concerned with matters that one person knows that he assumes others do not know. The events of everyday situations are communicated by this integral background of 'meanings held in reserve'. This assumption too is heavily modified in the rules that govern the actions of scientific theorizing. In the sociality of scientific *theorizing*, the theorizer is outside of a role. All matters relevant to his depiction of a possible world are public and publicizable. It is difficult to see how one might shame the scientific theorizer or make him indignant.

5. The attitude of daily life contains the assumption of a common intersubjective world of communication. The events of

everyday life are informed by this integral background of sense. This assumption of a common intersubjective world of communication is startlingly modified in the actions of scientific theorizing. The 'relevant other persons' for the scientific theorizer (colleagues, for example) are at best forgivable instances of highly abstract 'investigators' who are, in the ideal, disembodied manuals of proper ways of proceeding.

These two sets of presuppositions do not shade into each other, nor are they distinguishable in degree. Rather, passing from the use of one set to the use of the other—from one 'attitude' to another—produces a radical alteration in the person's structurings of events and their relationships. In the literal mathematical sense the two attitudes produce logically incompatible sets of events. The nature of the difference between the systems of events that are constituted by the two sets of interpretive presuppositions is illustrated in the following example. The related events that a viewer witnesses on his television screen when he attends to 'the story' may be compared with the events he witnesses when he attends to the scene as a set of effects accomplished by actors behaving in accordance with instructions from a producer. It would be the grossest philosophical didacticism to say that the viewer has seen 'different aspects of the same thing', or that the events of the story are 'nothing but' uncritically appreciated events of the production.

METHODOLOGY

It is the scientific rationalities which writers on social organization and decision making commonly refer to as features of 'rational choice'. It is proposed here, however, that the scientific rationalities are neither properties of nor sanctionable ideals of choices exercised within the affairs governed by the presuppositions of everyday life. If the scientific rationalities are neither stable properties nor sanctionable ideals of everyday life, then the troubles encountered by researchers and theorists with respect to the concepts of organizational purposes, the role of knowledge and ignorance in interaction, the difficulties in handling meaningful messages in mathematical theories of communication, the anomalies found in studies of betting behaviour, the difficulties in rationalizing the concept of abnormality in light of cross-cultural materials may be troubles of their own devising. The troubles would be due not to the complexities of the subject matter, but to the insistence on conceiving actions in accordance with scientific conceits instead of looking to the actual rationalities that persons' behaviours, in fact, exhibit in the course of managing their practical affairs.

Schutz (1943, pp. 142–3) tells us what it means to say that an actor has rational choice:

Rational choice would be present if the actor had sufficient knowledge of the end to be realized as well as the different means apt to succeed. But this postulate implies:

1. Knowledge of the place of the end to be realized within the framework of the plans of the actor (which must be known by him, too).
2. Knowledge of its interrelations with other ends and its compatibility or incompatibility with them.
3. Knowledge of the desirable and undesirable consequences which may arise as by-products of the realization of the main end.
4. Knowledge of the different chains of means which technically or even ontologically are suitable for the accomplishment of this end regardless of whether the actor has control of all or several of these elements.
5. Knowledge of the interference of such means with other ends of other chains of means including all their secondary effects and incidental consequences.
6. Knowledge of the accessibility of these means for the actor, picking out the means which are within his reach and which he can and may set going.

The aforementioned points do not by any means exhaust the complicated analysis that would be necessary in order to break down the concept of rational choice in action. The complications increase greatly when the action in question is a social one. . . . In this case the following elements become additional determinants for the deliberation of the actor. First, the interpretation or misinterpretation of his own act by his fellow man. Second, the reaction by the other people and its motivation. Third, all the outlined elements of knowledge (1 to

6) which the actor rightly or wrongly attributes to his partners. Fourth, all the categories of familiarity and strangeness, of intimacy and anonymity, of personality and type which we have discovered in our inventory of the organization of the social world.

But then, asks Schutz, where is this system of rational choice to be found?

... The concept of rationality has its native place not at the level of everyday conceptions of the social world but at the theoretical level of the scientific observation of it, and it is here that it finds its field of methodological application.

Schutz concludes that it is found in the logical status, the elements, and the uses of the model which the scientist decides on and uses as a scheme for interpreting the events of conduct. But,

This does not mean that rational choice does not exist within the sphere of everyday life. Indeed it would be sufficient to interpret the terms clearness and distinctness in a modified and restricted meaning, namely, as clearness and distinctness adequate to the requirements of the actor's practical interest ... What I wish to emphasize is that the ideal of rationality is not and cannot be a *peculiar* feature of everyday thought nor can it therefore be a methodological principle of the interpretation of human sets in daily life.

Reconstructing the problem of rationality so as to hand it back to researchers consists in the proposal that sociologists cease treating the scientific rationalities as a methodological rule for interpreting human actions.

Procedurally speaking, how would an investigator act once he has ceased to treat the scientific rationalities as a methodological rule?

NORMS OF CONDUCT

When the above-mentioned rational properties of actions are conceived as norms of proper conduct, four meanings of such norms can be distinguished.

First, the norms may consist of the rationalities to which scientific observers subscribe as *ideal norms* of their activities as scientists. Second, the term may refer to rationalities as operative norms of actual scientific work. Empirically, the two sets of norms do not show point for point correspondence. For example, there is a routinization of problem design and solution as well as a trust of other investigators found in actual investigative operations which textbooks in methodology generally ignore. Third, the term may refer to the socially employed and socially sanctioned ideals of rationality. Here the reference is to those rationalities as standards of thought and conduct that remain in accord with a respect for the routine orders of action of everyday life. Such standards are referred to in everyday language as 'reasonable' thinking and conduct. Fourth, there are the rationalities as operative norms of actual activities of daily life.

To use the rationalities as a methodological principle for the interpretation of human actions in daily life means to proceed as follows: (1) The ideal characteristics that scientific observers subscribe to as the ideal standards of their investigative and theorizing conduct are used to construct the model of a person who acts in a manner governed by these ideals. Von Neumann's game player, for example, is such a construction.[1] (2) After describing actual behaviours, one looks to the model for the discrepancies between the way in which a person so constructed would have acted and the way the actual person has acted. Questions like the following are then asked: Compared with the model, how much distortion is there in recall? What is the efficiency of the means that the actual person employed when they are viewed with reference to the observer's wider knowledge, this observer's wider knowledge being typified as 'the current state of scientific information'? What constraints are there upon the use of norms of technical efficiency in the attainment of ends? How much and what kind of information is needed for decisions that are predicted on the consideration of all the scientifically relevant para-

---

[1] Consider his characteristics. He never overlooks a message; he extracts from a message all the information it bears; he names things properly and in proper time; he never forgets; he stores and recalls without distortion; he never acts on principle but only on the basis of an assessment of the consequences of a line of conduct for the problem of maximizing the chances of achieving the effect he seeks.

meters of the problem, and how much of this information did the actual person have?

In a word, the model states the ways a person would act were he conceived to be acting as an ideal scientist. The question then follows: What accounts for the fact that actual persons do not match up, in fact rarely match up, even as scientists? In sum, the model of this rational man as a standard is used to furnish the basis of ironic comparison; and from this one gets the familiar distinctions between rational, non-rational, irrational and a-rational conduct (Pareto, 1935; Levy, 1952).

But this model is merely one among an unlimited number that might be used. More importantly, *no necessity dictates its use*. To be sure, *a model* of rationality is necessary, but only for the task of deciding a definition of credible knowledge and then *only but unavoidably for scientific theorizing. It is not necessary and it is avoidable in theorizing activities employed in coming to terms with the affairs of everyday life.*

It is necessary for scientific theorizing but *not* because of any ontological characteristic of the events that scientists seek to conceive and describe. It is necessary because the rules that govern the use of their propositions as correct grounds for further inference, i.e., in the very definition of credible knowledge, describe such sanctionable procedures as, for example, not permitting two incompatible or contradictory propositions both to be used as legitimate grounds for deducing the warrant of another proposition. Since the definition of credible knowledge, scientific or otherwise, consists of the rules that govern the use of propositions as grounds of further inference and action, the necessity of the model is provided by the decision in the first place to act in conformity with these rules (Kaufmann, 1944, pp. 48–66). The model of rationality for scientific theorizing literally consists of the theorizer's ideal that the meanings of these rules can be clearly explicated.

It is a consequence of the fact that actions of inquiry and interpretation are governed by what to common sense are the outlandish rules of scientific activities that the decision to use a proposition as grounds of further inference varies independently of whether or not the user can expect to be *socially* supported for using it. But in activities governed by the presuppositions of daily life the body of credible knowledge is not subject to such rigid restrictions regarding the use of propositions as legitimate grounds for further inference and action. Within the rules of relevance of everyday life, a correctly used proposition is one for whose use the user specifically expects to be socially supported.

RATIONALITIES AS DATA

No necessity dictates that a definition of rational action be decided in order to conceive a field of observable events of conduct. This result has the important and paradoxical consequence of permitting us to study the properties of rational action more closely than ever before.[1] Instead of using the vision of the ideal scientist as a means for constructing descriptive categories of behaviour—and rational, non-rational, irrational and a-rational are such categories—the rational characteristics of activities may be addressed with the empirical task of describing them as they are found separately in the above list of rationalities or in clusters of these characteristics. The uses, then, would look to the conditions of the actor's make-up and to his characteristic relationships to others as factors that might account for the presence of these rationalities, but without ironic comparison.

Instead of the properties of rationality being treated as a methodological principle for interpreting activity, they are treated only as empirically problematical material. They have the status only of data and have to be accounted for in the same way that the more familiar properties of conduct are accounted for. Just as we might ask how the properties of a status arrangement are relevant to the incidence of striving behaviour, or organized dissent, or scapegoating, or to the chances of occupational mobility or whatever, so we might ask how the properties of a status arrangement are determinative of the extent to which the actions of the actors show the rationalities. Questions such as the following, then, press for answers: Why are rationalities of scientific theorizing disruptive of the continuities of action governed by the attitude of daily life? What is there about social arrangements that makes it impossible to transform the two 'attitudes' into each other without severe disruptions of the

[1] It is through the absence of the 'scientific rationalities' in the actions that constitute the routine social structures that rational action becomes problematical in the ways intended in Max Weber's neglected distinction between formal and substantive rationality.

continuous activity governed by each? What must social arrangements be like in order that large numbers of persons, as we know them in our society today, can not only adopt the scientific attitude with impunity but can for their success in employing it make substantial claims for a living upon those to whom the attitude is foreign and in many cases repugnant? In a word, the rational properties of conduct may be removed by sociologists from the domain of philosophical commentary and given over to empirical research.

It is possible to state a general rule which subsumes innumerable research problems: *Any factor that we take to be conditional of any of the properties of activities is a factor that is conditional of the rationalities.* This rule sets up the claim that such factors, for example, as territorial arrangements, the number of persons in a net, rates of turnover, rules governing who can communicate with whom, timing patterns of messages, the distributions of information as well as the operations for altering these distributions, the number and location of information 'transformation' points, the properties of coding rules and language, the stability, social routines, the structured or *ad hoc* incidence of strain in a system, the properties of prestige and power arrangements and so on, are to be considered determinative of the rational properties of action governed by the attitude of daily life.

The immediate need is for an instrument that can be used to estimate the clusterings of the rationalities and their extensiveness for the actions of persons found at strategically different places in the social structure.

CONCLUSIONS

It has been the purpose of this paper to recommend the hypothesis that the scientific rationalities can be employed only as ineffective ideals in the actions governed by the presuppositions of everyday life. The scientific rationalities are neither stable features nor sanctionable ideals of daily routines, and any attempt to stabilize these properties or to enforce conformity to them in the conduct of everyday affairs will magnify the senseless character of a person's behavioural environment and multiply the anomic features of the system of interaction.

Bold as the statement may be, it does no violence whatever;

and, in fact, it is entirely compatible with current sociological discourse and current sociological theories and findings. Sociologists have long been concerned with the task of describing the conditions of organized social life under which the phenomena of rationality in conduct occur. One of these conditions is continually documented in sociological writings: routine as a necessary condition of rational action. Max Weber, in his neglected distinction between substantive rationality and formal rationality, and almost alone among sociological theorists, used the distinction between the two sets of rationalities throughout his work, although he proposed the distinction on the basis of a keen methodological intuition rather than on empirical grounds.

The relationships between routine and rationality are incongruous ones if they are viewed either according to everyday common sense or according to most philosophical teachings. But sociological inquiry accepts almost as a truism that the ability of a person to act 'rationally'—that is, the ability of a person in *conducting his everyday affairs* to calculate, to project alternative plans of action, to select before the actual fall of events the conditions under which he will follow one plan or another, to give priority in a selection of means to their technical efficacy and the rest—depends upon the fact that the person must be able literally to take for granted, to take under trust, a vast array of features of the social order. In order to treat rationally the $\frac{1}{10}$th of his situation that, like an iceberg, appears above the water, he must be able to treat the $\frac{9}{10}$ths that lies below as an unquestioned and, even more interestingly, as an unquestionable background of matters that are demonstrably relevant to his calculation, but which appear without being noticed. In his famous discussion of the normative backgrounds of activity, Emile Durkheim made much of the point that the validity and understandability of the stated terms of a contract depended upon the unstated terms that the contracting parties took for granted as binding upon their action.

The sociologist refers to these trusted, taken for granted, background features of the person's situation, that is, the routine aspects of the situation that permit 'rational action', as mores and folkways. Among sociologists the mores depict the ways in which routine is a condition for the appearance of rational action or, in psychiatric terms, for the operativeness of the 'reality principle'. The mores have been used, thereby, to show how the stability of social routine is a condition which enables persons in the course of their everyday affairs to recognize each other's actions, beliefs, aspirations, feelings and the like as reasonable, normal, legitimate, understandable and realistic.

REFERENCES

Kaufmann, Felix, *Methodology of the Social Sciences*, New York: Oxford Univ. Press, 1944.

Levy, M. J. Jr., *The Structure of Society*, Princeton, N. J.: Princeton Univ. Press, 1952.

Pareto, Vilfredo, *The Mind and Society*, translated by Livingston, A. & Bongiorno, A., New York: Harcourt Brace, 1935.

Schutz, Alfred, 'The problem of rationality in the social world', *Economica*, 1943, 10, 130–49.

Schutz, Alfred, 'The stranger', *Am. J. Sociol.*, 1944, 49, 499–507.

Schutz, Alfred, 'On multiple realities', *Phil. Phenom. Res.*, 1945, 5(4), 533–75.

Schutz, Alfred, 'Choosing among projects of action', *Phil. Phenom. Res.*, 1951, 12, 161–84.

Schutz, Alfred, 'Common sense and scientific interpretation of human action', *Phil. Phenom. Res.*, 1953, 14, 1–38.

von Neumann, J. & Morgenstern, O., *Theory of Games and Economic Behaviour*, Princeton, N. J.: Princeton Univ. Press, 1947, p. 79.

4 ALAIN TOURAINE

Towards a Sociology of Action[1]

1. INDUSTRIAL SOCIETY AND SOCIOLOGY

From the beginning of the industrial revolution, society has learned to think of itself as the child of its own creative activities. But the violence and novelty of the technical and economic transformations, just as much as the particular features of European industrialization characterized by liberalism, subjected to a very feeble political control, and marked by a very sizeable gap between mass production on the one hand and mass consumption and democracy on the other, have given this self consciousness its own particular character.

Industrial society, as it developed, defined itself first not in social, but in historical terms. More precisely, the philosophy of history tended, of necessity, to confuse the two kinds of analysis during the first period of transformation. Analysis no longer made any reference to 'meta-social' guarantees of the social order, to the physical order of nature or to the laws of providence; nor, on the other hand, did it invoke human nature and human passions, the randomness of events or the accident of personalities. Social action was regarded as a system, but since, even though men made their own history, it was evident, the degree of disorder and uprooting being what it was, that they did not make their own society, the idea of social action remained concealed under that of historical evolution. Whether it was the rise of rationality, or of nationality that received special attention, or

[1] First published as 'Pour une sociologies actionnaliste' in *Archives Européennes de Sociologie*. Translated by Tom Burns.

The translation of the terms *'action'*, *'actionnaliste'* and *'actionnalisme'* has given rise to considerable difficulties. The term 'action' has been retained in the English text, with the proviso that this has a special sense for Touraine. It is especially necessary to stress that Touraine's 'sociology of action' is not to be confused with Talcott Parsons' 'action theory', from which the former specifically distinguishes it.

whether more attention was paid to the social contradictions of accumulation and development, social processes appeared to be no more than belated responses to the questions posed by the growth of productive forces and the social relations of production. In a situation of liberal economic transformation only violence, i.e., a drive mounted outside the traditional social system, is capable of directing society towards a future whose direction remains obscure or appears in the guise of Destiny. The scope and generality of the transformations of society required some recognition of an irreversible tendency, but since this could not be recognized as having any meaning, it seemed no more than some (transcendental) controlling force.

When industrial civilization becomes more solidly established, or when outside Europe, it installs itself in virtually virgin territory, social thought, free from the problems which accompanied the birth of capitalist-industrial society, naturally began to question the conditions under which industrial society exists and functions. It is during what Georges Friedmann calls the second industrial revolution that these questions became more clearly formulated: how can one account for the cohesion of a society deprived of any reference to an absolute, which is founded on change and on its own dynamics? What kind of basis can there be for social norms? How can such norms be 'social' when it is the exigencies of technology, of mechanization, of rationalization, which are imposed on men with implacable force? What kind of basis can participation and solidarity have in such societies, disenchanted as they have become? This kind of questioning, which lies at the core of Durkheimian thought, has had its most striking repercussions in American society, anxiety-ridden about the definition of its existence and its unity over and above its heterogeneity and the incessant transformations which have followed upon its geographical expansion, its economic development and the impact of wave after wave of immigrants. In this kind of situation, society does not view itself any more as its own product but recognizes that it is confronted with problems which are social, and not merely historical. Social problems, criminality, urban disorganization, ethnic conflict, education, law and institutions in general constitute the natural objects of sociological attention, for which virtually the one and only problem is that of integration under conditions of social change.

The fertility of this approach is not limited by the conditions under which it was formed. In any case, it would be fairly easy to discover antecedents for it in historical or philosophical thinking. Nevertheless, there is some usefulness in reacting against the tendency, too frequent today, to regard functional sociology of this kind as inexplicably mixed with sociological analysis altogether, to suppose that, in fact, it *is* sociology proper, as Shils and Kingsley Davis have said in different ways.

Before developing this criticism further and putting forward claims for the existence of another type of sociological analysis, it is necessary to make its purpose more comprehensible by putting it in the context of the evolution of industrial societies. There are two facts which must be taken into account here. First, in Western industrialized countries, economic development is becoming more and more a deliberately chosen objective. Having established some protection against the more disturbing consequences of a market economy, having brought into line with each other the structure of economic institutions and concern for social problems through the concept of full employment, most societies have learnt to define themselves as industrial societies, i.e., societies in which economic development is not only a principal goal, but even more, a principle of legitimacy. The more or less rapid development of democracy and mass consumption has contributed in a decisive manner to free industrialization from its liberal origins and to create societies in which the great majority, participating in some way in the movement towards industrialization, internalize industrialization as a value. Secondly, later arrivals at the stage of industrial civilization have not known the distinction between industrial production and participation in decision-making or sharing the product which characterized industrialization in Britain. In such instances economic development cannot be perceived as a point of departure, but as a consequence of politics, and, still more, of social movements.

In these circumstances, it is impossible to concern oneself solely with society as it functions and changes: necessarily, it is society's development, its will to live, the manner in which it defines and creates its terms of reference for action which have to become the object of study. In the same way, economic thought, so long preoccupied almost exclusively with determining the conditions of equilibrium and the way in which it can be established, has turned its interests more and more to growth and the intervention of organized social forces into economic decision-making. Throughout this evolutionary trend, sociology has progressively separated itself off from history. Not that it can ever be indifferent to the study of history, but because the meaning of social action is less and less sought for in laws of historical evolution. In the first of the phases that we have been considering, the social sciences claim no more for themselves than to analyse the conditions of equilibrium for an economic system; in the second, their field of study is immensely broadened, the concept of social system occupying the central place in analysis. But this functionalist, wholly inward-looking, approach has to be complemented by a certain evolutionary type of thinking, in the absence of which change would have the appearance of nothing more than a disordered series of modifications. The transition from *Gemeinschaft* to *Gesellschaft*, or from mechanical solidarity to organic solidarity, the tendency towards increased differentiation of roles or the expansion of achieved status at the expense of ascribed status, are general characteristics of social evolution which make it possible to give some sociological evaluation of observed changes, but together make up the basic assumptions (the point of departure) for a realistic sociology of action. We are always stuck with the duality between society and its environment even if it is not always desirable to preserve the terminology of social physiology and social morphology.

In the last of the situations to which I have alluded, at the same time as sociology has become more and more preoccupied with what one can call (to adapt a familiar term) 'voluntaristic' history, it has been giving more and more direct recognition to the existence of 'non-social' factors in decision-making—i.e., historical events. This is the significance of Raymond Aron's thesis, conscious first of all of the nuclear peril, the importance of which is such that it can obviously no longer be relegated to the category of historical events. The more societies define themselves as systems of action, the more clear appears to be the importance of what is happening within society, and consequently, the importance of the analysis of strategies. What, then, is the principle of sociological analysis in societies which seek to become industrial societies; or rather, what is the analytical principle which is most specifically appropriate to such societies?

2. ANALYSIS IN TERMS OF THE HISTORICAL SUBJECT

Functionalist analysis, from its earliest manifestations, taught us that sociology was not the study of reality or social phenomena, but of social processes. But to believe that it is the study of ideas, of intentions, of purposes, which should constitute the main principle of sociology would be to return to the most archaic forms of social thought. It can never be said forcefully enough that the very existence of sociology excludes any choice between materialism and idealism—philosophical stances which are foreign to our discipline, the object of study of which is meaningful social action. It is because the significance of such action is not apparent for the actor himself, because in a way sociology is the study of the social 'unconsciousness', that the greatest success has been obtained in the study of the most 'natural' systems—those which are the least self-conscious—those, in short, which are particularly appropriate to ethnographic studies.

In the same way, functionalist analysis has never demonstrated its usefulness better than when it has been used for criticizing (in particular at the hands of R. K. Merton) the naïve and often tautological ideas of Malinowski. The idea of latent function, of unanticipated consequences, points analysis towards the study of the social system and not of the intentions of the actor. To study the equilibrium between roles and expectations, the relationship between social sub-systems, or forms of deviant behaviour, always implies reference to a system of social relations which does not make sense by itself, but serves as a reference point by which processes take on meaning.

Alongside systems of signs and systems of processes there exists, there seems to me, a third type of systematization and a third type of analysis. Alongside the structuralist approach and the functionalist approach, there is one which we propose to call the action approach (*actionnalisme*). This is not to return to a sociology of ideas and intentions by which social action is recognized in terms of a meaning defined in relation to action itself, rather than by relationships with other actors and with other significant elements. Action is by definition the relationship of the subject, the actor, to the object facing him. Let us consider labour: it is impossible to recognize its existence if the products of labour are not observable; impossible, moreover, if those products are considered as 'things' and not as 'products'. This simple, even banal, proposition can lead on to quite a number of philosophical implications, but it is no more philosophical than the notion of the social system, the utility of which one does not ordinarily think of arguing about. For the dialectical nature of labour interests the sociologists only in so far as it contains in itself some social evaluation of activity.

We are not saying that everybody wants to be creative, and to be recognized as a creative person, which would be manifestly false as a statement of fact, but that the two-fold normative orientation towards the creation of 'products' and towards their control by their creators plays the same conceptual part as notions of social norms, collective attitude, or obligation, in functionalist theory.

To avoid any misunderstanding, i.e., to avoid the possibility of construing these analytical principles as statements about the needs and desires of men or about their 'psychology', it might be preferable to speak of development rather than creation. For, if it is true that action can be considered at every level from that of the individual to the societal, the subject is not an empirical reality but a principle of analysis. It is never to be identified with any real actor, individual or collective. The term 'control' might in the same way be replaced by the more abstract term of 'liberty'. But further clarification is necessary. This term ('control') is taken in its English sense rather than its traditional French sense, but this first sense has become of sufficiently common usage in our society, where access to power without possessing it (i.e., control) is a major social phenomenon, to make it worth while being retained. Control is not defined here in terms of institutional means, but in terms of reference back to the subject. This reference back takes different forms. All that needs to be said here is that it relates more or less directly to the subject by way of the personality of the actor and his different social roles. Freedom in work is first of all harmony between the demands of the task and those of the 'human factor'; there is next the feeling of participation in an organization; lastly it is the awareness of belonging to a society which works on behalf of its members and which is democratic in its orientation and functioning. It is necessary to add that the awareness of control is not a simple correspondence between the social situation and a personal sense of just reward, but the comprehensibility of the situation for the subject, the awareness of its own creativeness realized in terms of its works.

Just as there exist marginal men and deviants, there are people who do not behave in conformity with this double normative requirement which I have just defined. In particular, there are actions which one can call either ideological or utopian. The latter endow the creative subject with a special position at the expense of works (objects or work-products) which require him to get outside of himself, to risk losing himself or dirtying his hands. The former (the ideological) by contrast identify the subject with its works, God with his church and the proletariat with its party. There are also several levels of orientation towards creation or control. But this is not the matter of central concern. This kind of analysis is sociological because the connection of the subject to its object is defined in social terms whether we are concerned with individual action or collective action. Labour is not definable except in social terms, i.e., the relationship of the worker to his products is either recognized or denied in social terms. If it departs from this social character, it ceases to be labour and each of us knows that it then becomes either a game, or behaviour only relevant to the understanding of individual personality.

Interposed between the worker and his works are intervening social connections which are also obstacles. It is always possible to regard factories, corporations and societies as systems of social relationships, but this should not prevent one from regarding them at the same time as means, which are interposed between the worker and his tasks. My analysis of organizations, published in this journal in 1962[1] was based on this principle. I shall not repeat it here. It is necessary, however, to remember that it would be wrong to understand the point of view presented here as merely summarizing my previous exposition by saying that action is always oriented towards an ideal, and that it is always the prisoner of the limited means of which it can dispose or in which it is involved. (Every church always deserting the inspiration which gave birth to it!)

At the point that we have reached there can be no question of

[1] Alain Touraine: 'Travail et organisation', *Archives européennes de sociologie*, Vol. 3, 1962.

having recourse to the familiar 'Mertonian' paradigm, which is the clearest and most polished expression of the functionalist perspective on individual modes of adaptation. All we are able to do, in the perspective which, we have adopted, is to deal with the relationship of the subject with itself (*le rapport du sujet à lui-même*). In other words, we shall only concern ourselves with the production of values and not as yet with their utilization; we stop short of their institutionalization. The action approach never leads up to the characteristics of a social system but towards the position of the subject. In concrete terms, the role occupied by the concept of social system in functionalist analysis is occupied in action analysis by social movements. The term social movement denotes all action that involves the historical subject—which is only an agent in so far as its actions are related to the double requirement of control and creation. One is justified in regarding trade union activity as an element in a system of industrial relations; one is no less justified in regarding it as a movement, oriented at the same time towards economic development and social democracy. In neither case is it necessary at all to postulate any hypothesis concerning what the workers 'really' want or concerning the general historical significance of trade union action. In both cases one has to go beyond concrete description and relate social phenomena to some kind of analytical matrix.

The social connections in terms of which we have just defined organizations are not a special case of social relationships. This kind of notion is useful and precise in so far as it is confined strictly to the notion of role—which is fundamental to functionalist analysis because it refers back, through the intervening stage of the complementary notion of role-expectation, to the concept of the social system. Filling a role means doing what others expect of you in the situation in which they perceive you. Social relationships, on the other hand, are established among individual actors in so far as these individuals represent the subject as it becomes a mirror-image or partitioned up in its passage through systems of organization. These are no more to be seen as conflict relationships concerned with authority than functional relationships of complementarity or difference. In this respect my analysis is to be distinguished clearly from that of Dahrendorf. His analysis made a distinct step forward in the sociology of social relationships by breaking with the substantive concept of social class and groups in conflict, by separating the 'positive' from the dogmatic aspects of Marx's analyses, and by stressing that a group in conflict with another is not necessarily a cohesive group with its own norms and locked in a death-struggle with its adversary. But by defining the group only in terms of its relationship to authority—hence restricting himself to organizations and social systems—instead of offering a perspective which can be distinguished from that of functionalism, he (Dahrendorf) condemns himself to giving only a variant of it, ultimately of limited significance; for conflict with authority, as he defines it, can only take place within a system of norms, since such conflicts appear to be concerned with claims in terms of means—not with the goals or with the values of society.

This position conveniently frees us from the primitive conception of classes each being bearers of a total cultural and social model, a conception which makes the existence of society incomprehensible, or, at least, has to resort to explanations as unconvincing as that of 'false consciousness' and eventually to transform all institutions and all social organizations into a vast conspiracy, the existence of which is utterly impossible to prove. But it neglects an essential aspect of social relationships, which is the reference to society in its entirety, implicit in the actions of each one of the groups engaged in conflict. Capitalist employers are not only those who accumulate profit and power, they are also the people who made industrialization work; the workers who oppose them are not just rejecting their authority or the dependent position to which they are subjected; they also want a society which incorporates both justice and abundance.

One is constantly confronted with the sheer impossibility of basing social analysis on conflict. It is a point of departure which can only lead to a Machiavellian type of analysis of truly political, i.e., inter-group relationships, which are established between independent social units. This is just as important for the study of social conflict as for the study of international conflict; but this can only be an essentially political study complementary to sociological analysis. By starting off from conflict one can detect and represent strategies, negotiations, armistices—*not* social relationships, conventions, social systems or systems of action. Sociological analysis is only possible if it poses some principle of structural unity on the field of study with which it is concerned. Since Durkheim, functionalism has found a principle of this kind in the social system, a principle which has obviously proved extremely fruitful. If one wants to move away from this 'classic' sociological position one is obliged to propose another principle of unity that I shall call the subject of action, i.e., the system of normative orientations—more often latent than manifest—involved in the very fact of action; in other words, in the double process that binds the actor to the object of his activity.

It is no accident that labour is the paradigmatic concept used to illustrate the action approach, i.e., the study of the generation of social action by the subject, its emphasis on the dialectical relationship between the subject and the objects of its activities. There is even some temptation to call this approach no more than generalizations of the sociology of work. This point of view is, however, inadmissible. Clearly, work displays in explicit form the dialectical relationship of the self and its products, but why limit a principle of analysis of more general application to the field of work? It has necessary application to two other fundamental themes of sociological analysis. In the first place, a relationship with another does not simply mean inclusion in a network of social relationships. We are so accustomed to consider concepts of status and role as fundamental that we have often, it seems to me, lost sight of certain aspects of social relations, always seized on by literature and philosophy, with which it is unthinkable that sociology should not concern itself. Psychology, happily, has been more venturesome in this respect than sociology. Sociability, i.e., the formation of social relationships, has been a principal focus of interest. As in the case of labour it is a twofold, reciprocal, motion. I place the 'other' over against myself, I recognize him and in return I reappropriate him, defining my relationship to him at the same time. This is what is expressed in daily life when one declares oneself as a member of a group. This would be meaningless if one did not regard the group both as real, existing apart from our desire to belong to it or not, and, on the other hand, as something of our own. Each person projects himself into the group and at the same time incorporates a part of it in his own identity. Once again, the processes may be utopian and ideological. The group can be no more than a hall of mirrors which reflects my image; I, on the other hand, am able to become

absorbed in it and demand from it a *raison d'être*—i.e., in a fundamental sense, to surrender my own being.

There is no intention at all of casting doubt on the importance
of the sociology of groups, already well developed. But the study
of sociability is of a different nature. In the same way, the workers'
movement demands a different kind of analysis from that appropriate to industrial relations, and studying the household cannot
be a substitute for an analysis of love. In the second place, how
can one disregard the fact that the meaning of action is apparent
not only in labour and sociability but just as much in a man's
relationship with his own self, that is to say, the relationship of
consciousness with the body, with human nature, i.e., the physical
aspect of man? The two-way motion of creating and controlling,
defined in reference to labour would be called the dialectic of
feeling and consciousness in this case, or, if one takes a concrete
example, the dialectic of pleasure and tragedy. There is a twofold
movement according to which I both posit the existence of a
biological entity and define myself as its owner. In this case the
ideological process might be called passion and the utopian
process adoration.

These three major themes are independent of each other. In no
sense do they correspond to different levels of social reality. One
might be tempted to say that the theme of labour is situated at the
most macro-sociological level, that of human existence most bound
up with problems of personality, while that concerned with social
relationships would be situated at the micro-sociological level.
But this view would be unsatisfactory, since it would impoverish
sociology in a pointless fashion. For not only is it not possible to
perceive relationships with others as existing at the inter-personal
level, at the group level or at the level of social collectivities, but
it would be utterly absurd to think of man collectively transforming nature outside himself while having as an individual nothing
at all to do with his own material nature, apart from enjoying
himself with it, or holding himself aloof from it. Clearly, in the
century which saw the genesis of psycho-analysis, we must recognize that the personality is built up through effort, and in the
course of a personal history. We have always learned from eth-
nography that human nature is not purely individual and that
societies are capable of producing more and more elaborate social
forms of pleasure and of tragedy.

Each of these three themes may be developed on three levels, individual, collective and social. This is a very elementary classification which in no way prohibits further multiplication of analytical forms. The most important social phenomena are those calling for a multiplicity of thematic developments. Labour is one such case. Even if it has been identified with one of these three themes, one cannot deny that empirical study of labour processes necessitates also the consideration of work groups or solidarity on the one hand, and, on the other hand, of the theme (of which G. Friedmann has been acutely aware) concerned with work, i.e., the relationship between the ergonomic features of work and the worker's personality. Such is also the case with love, which is self-created, is shared and which builds on itself.

3. THE SOCIOLOGY OF ACTION AND FUNCTIONALISM

These remarks, elementary as they may be, are aimed at bringing us back to the subject of action instead of regarding it, in terms of a flabby-minded and tedious empiricism, simply as a response to a social situation. During the nineteenth century, the invocation of social determinants of human affairs was regarded as implicit with values of a somewhat revolutionary kind; this was because, if nothing more, it had some critical force, and was opposed to idealist explanations. Today, only too often, sociology seems to be no more than the depressing study of platitudes, a bleak justification of a petty bourgeois world, lacking any drive or passion, without any sense of tragedy or revolutionary impulse. But to believe that all one has to do is to substitute some other kind of analysis for classical sociology, inspired by functionalism, would be to provide a cure worse than the disease. The notion of such a choice is absurd. The object of a sociology of action is to understand the involvement of the subject in action; it is not a sociology concerned with values, but with action in so far as the latter constitutes the realm of social interaction. The study of social systems and of social processes is obviously complementary to it. The meaning of action in terms of the subject has to be transformed into social values and into institutionalized norms, into which individuals and groups have to be socialized. This transition of action analysis into functionalist analysis cannot be defined in general terms, and its character changes according to the theme and the level under consideration. For the present, I shall confine myself to one of the most familiar points of transition, the idea of social class.

My present objective is not to analyse this idea, but in order to understand the place that has just been given to it, I must at least indicate some of the elements of analysis involved, even if I stop short of a complete justification. The initial problem is how to introduce the idea of class when one takes the needs of the worker as a starting point. I suppose one could say, as I have already done in dealing with organizations, that there exist both managers and managed. To put it this way places the worker, as subject, at odds with the organization; on the one hand, the workers seek some means of participating in the organization, since it serves as a medium for their activity; on the other hand, they set themselves over against it, since, from the fact that it is a particular social collectivity representing special interests and not the fulfilment of the subject, it exists as an obstacle. Managers, on their side, are the innovators, and therefore represent creative labour, but they also are co-ordinators, committed to the 'ideological' defence of a particular collectivity. This total interaction, this double dialectic of organizations can perhaps serve as a model of a double dialectic of social classes. But one must go on to say, and this is the essence of the matter, that we are dealing with a negative dialectic. In pre-industrial society, which is not able to regard itself as the product of its labours, the outcome of its activity, workers are not able to regard themselves directly as creators, and envisage the principles which constitute the social order as lying outside themselves, i.e., outside the society. At the same time, they look for ways of establishing their identity, which is the inverse of their urge to control (their situation). Thus they come to recognize an immense gap between themselves and the world order, a gap occupied by the dominant classes who are partly identified with that order and make use of it in order to legitimate their powers, and partly accumulate goods by means of which the work of creating is carried on. The interaction between classes is not a direct, actual, relationship, but the very expression of the alienation of the workers; acknowledging his master is the only way for the slave to claim any identity as a worker. In this situation, a limiting one, the two-fold requirement of the subject is completely reified in class society and social stratification, the unfair distribution of social goods is no more than the direct institutionalized expression of the alienation of the self. On the other hand, as one advances towards industrial society, the meta-social guarantees of the social order become eroded, and a distinction grows up between what on the one hand tends towards the double dialectic of organizations and, on the other, the unfair distribution of social goods. This latter has become increasingly obvious, a point people like to make when they observe that the submission of the wage earner to the power of the managers of his enterprise is more and more obviously out of alignment with the part he is called upon to play in mass consumption. In a class society, i.e., pre- or proto-industrial society, an analysis of social stratification on functionalist lines is closely bound up with the analysis of class interaction in terms of action sociology. In an industrial society, on the other hand, functionalist analysis is more and more separated from any analysis of power in terms of action; this makes for an increasingly autonomous sociology of institutions concerned with the mechanics of negotiation between systematized inequality, bound up with the existence of power, and the clear hierarchial differentiations required by the func-tioning of industrial production.

All this is abundantly clear when one considers one of the classic issues discussed in contemporary sociology. No society can func-tion properly if the inequality of the different positions in society is not matched by a certain adaptation to that inequality; for example if the occupational or economic aspirations of indi-viduals at the bottom of the social scale are not lower than those of members of superior strata; as everybody knows, this difference in the levels of aspirations has been tested and proved frequently. But at the same time, the managed are constantly making claims against the managers about the dependent situation in which they find themselves placed. And this appeal is made in the name of equality, i.e., in terms of the subject. This last demand can be more or less powerful, or more or less constrained, but it is just as widespread as adaptation to inequality. Everybody says 'things being what they are . . .' at the same time as saying 'the injustices of the present situation . . .'; but it is relatively rare that some compromise is not found between these two opposed attitudes. Consequently, 'the real state of affairs', i.e., the system of stratification, is almost always more or less given recognition as a social order, inequality is accepted in so far as the power of the managers is recognized as legitimate. It is this which assures a certain continuity between action theory and functionalist theory, a continuity which is however always partial and limited.

This continuity is manifest in the existence of scales of occupational prestige. In an industrial society, it is impossible not to admit the superiority of a director as against the worker, or a doctor as against the tradesman. Their inequality is a necessary condition of the functioning of society, but it is only partially accepted, as indeed the significant differences between stratification systems of different industrial societies demonstrates. What makes itself manifest through these different systems is the different modes of the social relations of production. Functionalist theory is therefore only acceptable in so far as it is open to the kind of theory which is logically prior to it, and which I have called action theory. This openness is always preserved by the best of the functionalist sociologists, but often enough one finds people yielding to the temptation to stay within the limitations of the situation 'as it is' and to replace the dynamics of the interconnections of class and power by the set of institutionalized division points which weld together these class and power relations with social stratification. So an arbitrary unity is substituted for this living dynamic, in the 'spirit' of the system of a civilization with the organizations of industrial society, exactly as utopian socialism used to do. In particular, in so far as it relates to models concerned with the purposeful transformation of society, social conflict is frequently regarded as an anachronism, as the manifestation of a system of social interaction implicit with preindustrial values; this kind of perspective reveals itself, in its most usual manifestations, as a kind of neo-liberal utopianism. The endeavour to develop an action theory comes from the desire to provide a militant critique of this kind of approach.

The transition from historical activity to the social system is reflected in the analogous transition at the level of social processes. In the action perspective, different levels of social processes are defined according to the greater or lesser involvement of purposes and values in the system of social interaction. One needs to do no more than refer to the kind of terms used in studies of organizations: the worker can keep himself apart, disengaged, taking refuge generally in the self over against the organization as a whole which he perceives as a hostile and inhuman world; he can pursue individual aims within the organization; if he is more involved, he can feel solidarity in a collective situation, in a group or in a category of workers; finally, at the highest level, he can identify himself with the organization's own ends against the organization, against the management in terms of rationality and progress. This kind of theory is obviously different from any study of attitudes and of statements in any given social situation, and the distinctiveness of the two methods could be demonstrated in plenty of ways. I have myself attempted to illustrate it in connection with processes of social mobility. Many writers have successfully studied the connection between the decision to move, at the point or origin, and the integration of migrants in the place where they end up, thus making clear both the causes and effects of social and personal disorganization, of the anomie of the social system or the marginality of certain social processes. But it is possible to outline another kind of study, which is complementary and not contradictory. Mobility, especially if it is on a large scale, as in the case of internal or external migrations connected with economic development, modifies the situation of the society to which the migrants have to adapt themselves. Thus integration is also necessarily a creative activity, the creation of a new action situation. In those countries which are still at the beginning of industrial development, the question is whether workers coming from the countryside in numbers which are going to swamp the pre-existing nuclei of workers are just an uprooted, disorganized mass, the prey of demagogues and agitators, or do they bring with them a sense, implicit simply in their existence, of the renewal of society, of social interaction and of social movements? The action method corresponds with the second of these two responses.

But here again one cannot emphasize the distance between the two methods without also emphasizing their essential connection. In a study of class consciousness, in a work now in preparation,[1] we have endeavoured to define it in terms of the interaction with the principle of individual rewards—or skills as against profit— and with the principle of totality which emerges with the rational organization of large-scale industry. Working-class consciousness

[1] Subsequently published as *La conscience ouvrière*, Paris, 1966.

is analysed in terms of the given meaning of the work situation. But this idea does not comprehend the whole set of what one conveniently calls workers' attitudes. The individuals we interviewed see themselves confronting a society in which they evaluate their chances or where they seek to improve their conditions, or where they feel themselves close to certain people and distant from others. The relationships between the activity which constitutes a field of social action and the behaviour within a given field are certainly complex, but it is not permissible to be satisfied with distinguishing them and juxtaposing them as two points of view without trying to relate them in some way.

More generally, the two strategies of action theory: the study of social movements and the study of the experience of 'projects', correspond with two approaches of functionalist theory, the study of social systems and the study of decision-making. This transition from one kind of analysis to another is not the only kind of transition possible in sociological theory. We cannot dwell on it here, but it is at least relevant to make the point that action, translated into the system of social relations in this way, has to be made manifest through a system of signs, and that structuralist theory is concerned with revealing the way in which this system is built up. There often seems to be an unbridgeable gap between action theory and structuralism, and in many ways these approaches represent two poles of sociological theory. In its extreme form, structuralism regards the social sciences as being natural sciences concerned with man. The sociology of action always clings to the notions of *Kulturwissenschaft* and of *Wertbeziehung*; structuralism is concerned with signs, the former with meanings. But we do not have to see these differences as leading to a complete break, for this would condemn the first to formalism and the second to a simple-minded study of semantics. Structuralist theory is situated at the point where social sciences and mathematical sociology are most closely linked without having any overlap. However, on the other hand, the closer one gets to the realm of action theory, i.e., the more direct the reference to the subject, the further apart the invocation of the meaning of action in terms of the subject, and the articulation of formal procedures. Economic theory is probably the clearest example of this essential separation, dominated as it is by the constant shifting between the formal structures of econometrics and sociological theory, the idea of an economic subject—'economic man'—coming into play only as a fairly useless and even dangerous link between two kinds of theoretical approach.

The less dense the world of labour, the more manifest the subject becomes in terms of its own being rather than by its practical activity, and the more is the discrepancy between sociological models and the system of formal structure reduced. The greater importance consequently attaches to the notion of structure, the study of the laws according to which the mind works. Man finds himself putting nature into words, in giving names to what he cannot change and in filling the gap between the sign and what is signified. The objectives and methods of structural anthropology has been laid down in the work of Lévi-Strauss. In the realm which belongs to functionalist theory, the dissociation between form and meaning is less pronounced, and the mathematical study of communication networks, or of areas of decision-making, is more closely bound up with the sociological analysis of the social system than, say, econometric analysis is concerned with actual people. One can assume that under industrialism the part played by action theory cannot but expand, simply because of the growing dissociation of the individual from the product of his labour, from 'social problems' and from the ways in which technological systems operate.

But in addition, the growing dominance of the system of work will make the two other fundamental themes of action theory more and more obvious; the problems of relationships with others, and of human existence. Industrial civilization is not merely triumphant, it is also subject to disturbance, and nothing is more foreign to us today than the romantic symbolism of the last century. One no longer finds anthropology being dismissed by the historicist school, but awareness of historical action and of human existence does expel mythologies at the same time as it introduces existential inquiry. The interdependence of the three fundamental approaches of sociological theory—action theory, functionalism and structuralism—of the three forms in which they reach completion—the dialectic of the subject, the cohesion of the system of social relations and the logic of sets of signs—is left as the ultimate principle of the unity of sociology, but this principle is only fruitful if each of these approaches is acknowledged as autonomous in the widest possible sense, and if, sociologists maintain, for as long as possible, a mistrust of any general theory which claims to re-unite them within a single framework of ideas.

4. PHILOSOPHY OF HISTORY OR SOCIOLOGY?

After having attempted to locate the sociology of action in relation to other forms of theory, we must return to its own special territory and make some response to the objections which come quite naturally to mind. The most direct of these concerns the use made of the idea of labour, and levies the charge that action sociology is no more than a new name for a philosophy of history.

At this point, one can hardly review the question satisfactorily by referring to the introductory passage in which the development of sociological theory was presented as a progressive renunciation of the philosophy of history. The easy reply to that would be that we are in love with what we have destroyed. Rather, one has to acknowledge that the sociology of labour is historical in inspiration, simply because labour is that through which man changes his environment and himself. Yet it is not purely historical since it has recourse to theoretical principles which are not found at the level of directly observable facts and of social evolution. In particular, it makes no claim whatsoever to explain the actual data of history; it is concerned only with abstracting a certain number of relationships from reality. This alone ensures that it differs from the philosophy of history. It is absolutely opposed to any attempt at a single and universal systematization of social processes, in that it not only recognizes the plurality of the procedures of sociological theory but also the plurality of the units—the social actors—a fact which maintains the notion of 'the event' in its rightful place.

Combining action, functionalist and structuralist theory, complicated as it would be, would nevertheless not result in the re-creation of the physical actor or in completely accounting for his acts, i.e., his politics. The very good reasons which have induced great historians to separate the history of economic and social structures from narrative history should not lead us to erroneous conclusions. The more profound kind of history is no more than an application of the social sciences to the past, and fortunately, a sociology of historical societies is developing which will broaden the field of social analysis immensely. But this kind of progress ought to lead to the acknowledgement rather than to the denial of the importance of relationships between units of action, individuals, groups or nations which are not located within an overall system of action. The maintenance of this margin between social analysis and events or politics is the best guarantee against any philosophy of history, since it requires social analysis to verify its propositions whatever they are, in a scientific manner, by investigating relationships and then systems of relationships, i.e., structures among certain facts or certain categories of facts so as to form explanatory models, instead of seeking to prove its validity in some direct correspondence between its theoretical constructs and sets of historical facts.

It is true that action theory offers a kind of understanding, at a certain level, which is based not on principles or abstract relations but on a concept of activity, which one knows has not appeared with any clarity except in industrial societies. At first sight this seems to reintroduce one of the most obvious characteristics of the philosophy of history, which is the reinterpretation of the past in terms of the problems of the present. One could put the objection in an even more precise form: by what right are industrial societies taken to be the end of history? Already there are those who speak of post-industrial society, and does not this make the conception of action sociology a little anachronistic, since it composes a Promethean image out of man, an image which is already foreign to contemporary society in which consumption and leisure are becoming the main preoccupations?

In part, these objections are well founded. Action sociology belongs to industrial society, and is even at pains to distinguish this type of society in utterly different terms from those of the previous conceptions, which were more sensitive to Western industrialization as a set of exceptional conditions. In this sense, it is proper to consider Western industrialization as a subject for historical analysis. But where does such an analysis lead? Historians observe one system of values or one kind of direction taken by activity, followed by another. This seems to exempt them from the direct analysis of one central fact beyond the substance of the particular circumstances—that action is subject to normative direction. Philosophy of history only comes into account because of a refusal to deal directly with this essential fact. It becomes involved much more easily in so far as one is compelled to discover the meaning of action in the situation itself, something which makes it obligatory to provide some general conception of man to set against the so-called laws of history. This incessant see-saw between the dialectic of natural forces and the philosophical conception of man is precisely what the whole of sociology is trying to get rid of. This, I suggest, cannot be done more thoroughly than by rejecting this dualism and rediscovering the *raison d'être* of the meaning of action, not in some essence of man but in his activity, i.e., in the relation of the subject to its objects. We leave out of account the reasons why man works, just as we leave out of account the reasons why he speaks. But since he does work, is it possible to avoid the admission that he locates outside of himself the products of his labour, which he claims as his own?

This theoretical principle allows of an infinity of particular theoretical formulations; it also leads to the possibility of an historical definition of systems of action; nevertheless it does not imply any judgement about the direction in which history is going or about the point it has reached. It is evident enough that other societies must succeed industrial societies, and that this term itself may already be an unsatisfactory way of defining those contemporary societies with the highest level of production. Turning from description to imagination, there is nothing to prevent one imagining future forms of organization and of social life of a non-utopian kind—i.e., presenting them neither as a paradise or a hell. Action sociology, in particular, has no *a priori* pronouncement to make on the relative importance of the various themes with which action may be involved, and, so far as it is concerned, there is no objection at all against dreaming up a future society in which labour might not be the central principle of its historic development.

The idea of the historical subject, i.e., the system of normative constraints tied up with labour, is not a conception of man, still less a psychological concept, for this would mean actually to revive a kind of thinking which is not merely pre- or anti-sociological. It would mean putting forward propositions of the type: man wants this, (but) the most important thing for him is that. The historical subject is not a reified personage, even in the sense that France is the central 'personnage' in Michelet's history. It is a theoretical principle, like the concept of society or that of social norms. More precisely, the historical subject is the structure of social relations of labour, the unitary principle of what has been called the double dialectic of classes or of organizations. The principal danger in any theoretical approach in sociology is being trapped in a tide of increasing specificity, which leads to classifications and typologies which interpret observable phenomena but do not explain them, in the sense that they do not take the form of verifiable hypotheses. The only place for typology is at the beginning of a study, in order to align particular analytical instruments; beyond this it has no validity, and it ought to be got rid of as soon as possible. This is not so as to pay proper respect to the variety one finds in observed fact, but, on the contrary, in order to replace it by systematic analysis, i.e., so as to focus attention on a system of action, a system of social relations or a system of signs as a way of organizing a problem defined in terms of the principle by which an analytical procedure is articulated: the historical subject for action theory, the social system for functionalist theory and language for structuralist theory.

This is why the sociology of action, like functionalist theory, is not a collection of concepts which can be developed and elaborated in abstract terms. What interest it has can only reside in its fertility, i.e., in the hypotheses which it can yield for scientific examination. The difficulties faced in establishing it are no different in principle from those which confront any theoretical procedure. In practice, nevertheless, it does meet with one additional obstacle: the more attention one pays to the orientations of activity and thereafter to social movements, the greater difficulty one finds in dealing with the images of themselves which the actors construct, and wish to present. If the meaning of action was clear for the actor himself, the sociologist could be replaced by a tape recorder. The greater the involvement of the actor in voluntary action, the greater his struggle against powerful adversaries, the more he wishes to preserve his threatened power and the more he guards against any interpretations of his acts and of his thoughts. These circumstances have as their consequence a resistance to any sociological probing, which is stronger still when one adopts the action perspective. One is tempted therefore both for political and methodological reasons, to give preference to a descriptive approach, most frequently expressed in statistical form. But action theory is not alone in running sizeable risks in allowing itself to be drawn into this all-too-easy way out, in which sociological explanation loses any chance of producing interesting results. The choice is not between action sociology and quantitative research, but between sociology and blind sociographic survey.

If one bears in mind that action sociology has regard, like any other sociological method, to the construction of verifiable propositions, this does not mean that one disregards its philosophical implications or its historical application, its connections with conscious experience of moral or aesthetic values. More straightforwardly, the closer one feels it to be to all modes of human understanding, the more dissociated it becomes from the pseudo-descriptions behind which lurk ill-disguised ideologies. One would like to define it in terms of 'anthropological sociology' so as to make clear its basic disclaimer in connection with the concept of society and with a particular Durkheimian tradition, despite the value that it has as the basis of functionalist theory. Among the precursors of sociology, the preferred connections are with the social philosophers of industrialization: Saint-Simon, Comte, Marx, in the hope of preserving the more innovative elements of their thought at the same time as replacing them by a perspective more appropriate to sociology.

An even greater justification for its existence lies in the current development of industrial societies—which, in turn, brings up a further objection: to call industrial society that in which the dialectic of creation on the one hand, and control on the other, of economic development and of social democracy is most clearly manifest, is surely to assume the existence of *one* industrial society, and more precisely, *one* general political orientation. Yet what strikes one first of all is the sheer diversity of industrial societies. Behind this objection we detect once more the widespread suspicion of the imposition of a conceptual framework on the whole of historical reality—thus reintroducing a philosophy of history. The first possible response could be that there is no single society which can be called absolutely industrial, and that all observable industrial societies still carry the traces in them of pre-industrial civilizations, of traditional societies or perhaps *laissez-faire* capitalism which accompanied the birth of industrialization in the West. But this kind of reply is obviously insufficient, since one would hardly speak of industrial societies if one could not distinguish certain specific characteristics which are common to all of them. What is needed is simply a declaration that the differentiation of types of industrial societies is not only compatible with our particular point of view but indeed implied by it.

What we are maintaining is that an industrial society is one in which the will to create and to control constitutes the centre of the system of orientation of social movements, and that this will is located above all at the level of the system of production. Yet, in the first place, the will for control is not an undifferentiated totality. It can be developed at the level of the individual's work situation—'job control'; at the level of the firm—industrial democracy; at the level of society—social democracy. In the second place the will for development may be more or less aimed at progress or reform: it can lead the way to a voluntary reorganization of society, or on the other hand merely acknowledge the dynamism of the society under study. The orientation adopted by a society is determined by the character of the obstacles encountered by one or other of these drives. The simplest typology distinguishes between societies where neither of these two drives encounters any obstacle which is regarded as insurmountable, those where one or other type of obstacle appears fairly sizeable and, lastly, those where a double economic *and* social barrier is erected in the worker's path. At a deeper level, the will to create and the will to control the object of creation tend always to be in opposition: a voluntaristic model of development tends to be integrative and authoritarian; a model of control in terms of reward is matched by weak participation by workers in the politics of development. The very definition of industrial society means that there cannot be a single or special type of industrial society; or, to put it more concretely the constant tension between participation and confrontation makes for variety. Once again, the ideas being put forward cannot be assumed to define an ideal type of society, but merely as constituting the terms in which social action may be studied.

It is impossible, if one adopts the method of the sociology of action, to take the view that there exist types of society or of social situation within which, and in terms of which, social processes are formulated. Instead, starting with the general orientation of social activity, it seeks to discover how systems of social relationships are built up, which themselves determine through institutional forms the particular characteristics of a particular historical society. Its main objective is to build models of social action from the basis of forms of commitment adopted by the actual, historical, subject.

It is in this way that it differs quite clearly from the non-sociological study of social movements, which is based on the perception of inherited inequality and on the absence of direct reference to the value aspects of development. Action sociology aims at being the social consciousness of an open society in which systems which have lost their values, and in which consequently, social problems take on an immediate political meaning. Its most obvious limitations derive from the fragmentation of the world today, but here again it is possible for it to take part in a work of innovation and discovery, looking beyond the problems which spring up between societies—which can be regarded as being formed within a universal industrial civilization.

One could therefore define action theory as the sociology of development, as against the sociology of change, which has its origin in functionalism. It looks indeed towards discovering how social movements determine institutional forms and the ways in which societies engaged in industrialization function, instead of outlining the conditions which determine change in a society or which make for integration in a type of social organization conditioned by factors set in motion by economic change. Nevertheless, it is the most industrialized societies above all that are regarded by action theory in terms of societies in the process of development, i.e., in the process of choosing certain forms of appropriation of the means and the results of rationalization and growth. For the ethnographer, it is necessary to detach oneself from one's own society; it is no less necessary for the sociologist of action to penetrate into his own society below the surface of propaganda of all kinds, for him to concern himself with the rationalization of political and moral integration or to get behind the confused uproar at the surface level of mass consumption. It is perhaps even more difficult to escape from this false modernism than from ethnocentricity. There is every encouragement today to close one's eyes when one is at the threshold of a society of abundance, at the point where one's sense of historical development as well as knowledge of the progress of productivity seems to herald the satisfaction of material needs. The advantages and privileges, more and more considerable, which the most economically developed part of the world has at its disposal today tend to discourage belief in social movements and rather to encourage the belief that the only problems are those of reasonable and effective management of a society in which scarcity is about to disappear. The great social movement, the great collective project which industrial societies created towards the end of the nineteenth century and the beginning of the twentieth, the working-class movement—because of its own success as well as because of the transformation of economic conditions—is no longer the medium of profound social changes; negotiation has replaced aspiration. To say this is not to anticipate some nostalgic revival of the great questions of the nineteenth century but to raise questions, theoretical as well as practical, about the nature of the debates and struggles, the forms of power and the conflicts which characterize industrial civilization. In this sense the sociology of action also represents an appeal for the definition and study of new social problems, for the understanding and the orientation of new social movements directed against the seductions of the *affluent society*.

5 JEAN-DANIEL REYNAUD and PIERRE BOURDIEU

Is a Sociology of Action Possible?[1]

The Sociology of Action, by Alain Touraine,[2] is a difficult and baffling work: fiercely critical, it attacks most of the established ideas of sociological theory, claiming at the same time not to replace, but to 'complete' what they have established. The book is conceived to conquer a new field for 'scientific sociology', although it is not based upon generalization from the results of empirical research, nor upon an analytical discussion of how such research might be undertaken, but is written 'rather like a doctrinal work' [15]. Touraine develops and elaborates certain intuitive ideas before showing how they could give birth to a method. With the ambition of constructing an audaciously novel theory, the author gives little definition of his fundamental concepts, and introduces them in the course of his discussion as a means of meeting difficulties and resolving problems. The reader is not led into an intellectual edifice which was built before him *more geometrico*, but thrown from the beginning straight into a complex system of thought, full of retractions, revisions and inuendos, which does not have 'the intellectual rigour of a purely analytical construction' [16].

There are thus two ways of approaching the work. Either one begins from that part given over to industrial civilization (to the political system, the workers' movement and mass culture) in order to grasp from these examples what the author's method contributes; or one first attempts to understand the postulates and propositions from which he begins, to define the logic and aim of his work in the most general terms, perhaps then moving

[1] First published as 'Une sociologie de l'action, est-elle possible?' in *Revue française de Sociologie*. Translated by Anthony Giddens.

[2] Figures in square brackets refer to the page numbers in this work (Paris, 1965).

on to illustrate their implications. It is the second approach which we have chosen, at the risk of appearing to neglect unjustly the rich historical and sociological material which it draws upon; but this has the advantage, we hope, of casting a more systematic light upon it.

'Social action only exists if . . . it is *oriented* towards certain ends' [9], that is to say, towards values. This proposition, as a point of departure, has nothing apparently revolutionary about it. Is it not also that of Talcott Parsons, for whom action is behaviour 'directed towards an end', 'adaptive', 'motivated', 'guided by symbolic processes'? Sociological theory, in Parsons' sense, begins when we reject behaviouristic reductions; when we recognize that what the social actor does has some direction to it, and that 'meaning' is an indispensable category for sociology. The values institutionalized in a social system 'control' that system, because they legitimate the norms in which they are given concrete expression, and because in the last resort they define the orientations of social action.

Alain Touraine would not dispute this. It is, indeed, from this point of view that he begins. In any social system, values are given, and form the centre-piece of the system. But where do they come from? Is it enough to treat them as the elements of a culture which is institutionalized in the system? Should we not inquire into their origin? The individual social actor is oriented towards values, and we can describe how he learns them, through socialization, in infancy as in his adult roles. But is it not necessary to relate these values to 'the action which creates them' [9]?

Thus there appears a second sense of the word 'action'. For the sake of clarity, let us distinguish the Parsonsian sense, which Touraine proposes to translate by 'social conduct', and the Tourainian sense, which reserves the word for that which is not simply the 'response to a social situation', the learning of values which already exist, but involves the 'creation, innovation, or attribution of meaning' [10]. The sociology of action is thus not, as in the case of Parsons, the study of meaningful social conduct; it is, much more, the study of the creation of social values. The former aim belongs to what Touraine calls, in a somewhat loose way, 'functionalism'. We may understand by that term any way of studying social actors which takes social value as given. With a questionable taste for symmetry, Touraine adds to this the study of symbolic systems, which he treats as the object of structuralism. There remains a place for a third major approach, which deals with problems which the two others do not come to terms with: action theory is the science of the creation of values by social action. This third approach does not seek to take over the field of the two others, and installs itself modestly at their side. But these qualities assure that in general it occupies pride of place, and Touraine hardly manages to conceal this behind his pacific declarations. Functionalism and structuralism analyse 'the functioning of "social and cultural systems": action theory seeks to understand "their *raison d'être*" ' [10].

Where is this to be found? Two cautions are given as a preliminary to the answer: we shall not be able to find the *raison d'être* of social values in the conditions of action (this is the naturalist error); nor can we detach these values from society as if they existed in themselves and all that needed to be done was to discover them (this is the idealist error).

Any interpretation which treats values as the result of the response to a situation is naturalist. It is not that situations or stimuli do not elicit responses: in the same way as an individual reacts with fear or love, adoration or mistrust, to the impact of events, we may accept that a society responds to external or internal stresses—that society responds to these in terms of the formulation of choices and orientations. But the occasion of this creation of values must not be taken for their '*raison d'être*': this would be to pass from an historical description, perfectly correct in itself, to a false explanation. What Touraine calls, somewhat vaguely, 'the naturalism of the nineteenth century', is represented by the effort to discover the basis of social values in the economy, in technology, in demography or warfare. These attempt to substitute an economic or technological logic for the internal logic of society, society's own logic—to subordinate social facts to a non-social determinism. Naturalism consists in explaining a meaningful action by a natural situation which, in itself, possesses no meaning. 'It is always impossible to understand how sense is born of non-sense, short of admitting that there exists a dialectic in nature . . .' [124]. Only action creates meaning; and action cannot be reduced to the circumstances in which it occurs, nor explained by them.

Conversely, every interpretation which locates values in some sort of intangible firmament or, more generally, attempts to define them apart from the social action which creates them, is idealist. Doctrinal interpretations which categorize the good and the bad, the just and the unjust *a priori*, or which describe social movements as the progressive discovery or conquest of a pre-determined truth, are all of this sort. The same may be said of philosophies of history which superimpose upon the meanderings of social life a meaning which transcends their immediate reality, whether this is realized by the Hegelian Spirit or by any other transhistorical being. In all of these cases, the interpreter substitutes his values for the real values of social action. He projects upon others that which comes from himself; upon the past that which belongs to the present; or upon other societies that which is characteristic of his own. He puts himself in the place of the social actor, and thinks for him. Instead of paying attention to the operation which creates values, he assumes the existence of a god somewhere who already possesses them and who distributes them at whim. Either to seek meaning in material reality, or to postulate it *a priori*, is equally to betray sociology—to abandon any attempt to understand the social origin of social values. We need, on the contrary, to 'explain values in terms of the process of action itself' [12].

Having avoided these two blind alleys, we must discover the correct avenue of approach to follow. If social values are created socially, who is the subject who creates them? What is the basic experience or situation in which this creation takes place?

For Alain Touraine, this subject cannot be the individual actor. This is not only because there is an evident disproportion between my creative power, as an individual, and the totality constituted by the existing values in my society, but also because the values which are to be explained are not necessarily conscious, let alone present in the behaviour of a single actor. They are collective, not only because they are refracted through many actors, but because they express a collective meaning. The postulate developed by Alain Touraine is that 'men make their own history'; we may understand by this that they participate in an enterprise which has a global meaning, even if it is expressed in a contradictory or dialectical fashion. To seek to understand the creation of values is to attempt to discover, behind the logic of institutions and rules, 'the dynamic of an historical system of action' [125]. Although this dynamic is never embodied in 'an historical unity or epoch, social regime or national society' [121], it possesses its own unity. It is 'the emergent structure of a totalizing activity, the unity of the dialectical movements of historical action' [121].

Consequently the subject of this creation, the actor in this enterprise—the author of this meaning—can only be a super-subject, which Touraine calls the 'historical subject'. This does not entail imagining a collective consciousness, a Great Being or a Spirit which is the agency of this meaning, which would be to relapse into the philosophy of history. The historical subject is not an empirical subject, 'nor an object of empirical studies, a category of social facts, but a tool of analysis' [121]. It must be 'constructed ... on the basis of knowledge of collective representations and actions' [122]. In the same way as functionalism begins from the postulation of a social system, that is to say, hypothesizes a regulated interdependence between the conduct of actors, action theory postulates an historical subject—that is to say, the creative unity [unité totalisante] of a social act.

This subject is present in action which at the same time both faces the world and gives it meaning; such action is labour 'considered as action upon the non-social world and, according to Marx's thought, as the principle whereby man transforms himself while transforming nature' [10]. We should not understand by this merely the techniques or relations of production. 'Labour', as Touraine speaks of it, is conceived of in as broad a sense as the Marxist Praxis, and perhaps even in a broader one since, since in developing his argument in relation to the explanation of symbolic systems, he states that 'it is not material activity or the tangible results of labour which must be considered at the outset, but rather that organizing thought or intelligence which always places man over against nature at the same time as he is in nature' [132]. In any case, whether it is material transformation or organizing intelligence, labour creates values at the same time as it embodies them. 'Through labour, man constructs, out of nature and against nature, a social world; he creates a universe of human products and becomes conscious of himself in his relation with these works' [120]. It is therefore the source of products and of social relations; it provides 'the raison d'être' of symbolic and social systems.

Labour is hence not only the meeting or opposition of man and nature. Through labour, the subject creates his products and while these products have an existence of their own, whereby they may escape from him, he seeks to regain his mastery over them, to control them. 'There is no labour without the will to create products, without the will of the producer to control, to decide how his product is to be used . . . The very definition of labour implies a double exigency of creation and control' [10]. It is not simply a matter of the right of the producer over his products, but much more generally of the operation by means of which action becomes externalized in a product and attempts to retrieve its own exteriority. This 'necessarily twofold relation of creation and dependence' [120] is the general form of the connection between man and his products. It is, by its very definition, dialectical in origin.

In itself, this dialectic is transhistorical; it is the very nature of the historical subject, the source of its creative capacity. But, on the other hand, the situations in which labour takes place are historical: the forms of creation and the possibilities of control vary, according to the degree of dependence of man in relation to nature, and the complexity of the productive framework which man brings into being. It is characteristic of industrial societies that social action no longer appears as confined and constrained by the presence of material necessity, nor even by that of economic laws. Because these societies are more capable of self-direction, their problems are those of 'the voluntary organization of social life' [13]. At its limit, 'social action relates to itself alone' [13]. Otherwise expressed, if action analysis is valid in principle for all societies, certain forms of society lend themselves to it more easily, or rather, particularly call for it. 'The more industrialization is voluntary, the more it calls for the consideration of historical systems of action' [14]. 'The more historical are the societies studied, that is to say, the more possible it is to follow the progress of their labour, the more direct is the relevance of action analysis . . .' [131].

This analysis must not, however, reify the historical subject. Its task is to grasp, from the point of departure of the unity of meaning, the meaning of the modes of conduct of individual actors. No individual actor, or, more precisely, no specific actor, embodies the historical subject. But he participates in it: to the degree to which

it is oriented towards this totality, his action has a '*charge subjectale*';
all conduct which is socially regulated can be considered '. . . as a
manifestation of the historical subject' [137]. 'Every specific
actor, at least in principle, participates in the historical subject,
in the sense that his action has a certain *charge subjectale*' [148].
His action can be explained by his interests or situation. But at the
same time it has a meaning and, by this token, is a 'project':
that is, 'a level of implication of the actors in the system of
orientations that defines the historical subject' [149]. The project
is thus not an intention of a specific actor. It is not a psychological
fact, nor even an empirical datum. It is that which is identified by
action analysis in intentions and conduct, which it constructs out
of these: the 'projection' of the historical subject which it manages
to discern.

These principles established, action theory can be put into
practice, to show how an organization manifests a dialectic
between those who command and those who are commanded,
via different levels of action, or how the working-class movement,
simultaneously an expression of discontent, negotiation and
political objectives, develops. With great regret we leave aside
these chapters. But if we accept that the question posed as fundamental and legitimate (how are social values created?), are we
committed to accepting the postulates upon which the given
answer rests? Should we not examine them one by one in order
to test the validity of this answer?

First of all, it is necessary to clarify the very notion of labour.
We have already noted that it is not, in principle, the only source
of normative orientations. If the relationship between man and
his works serves to define an 'historical consciousness', it is
theoretically possible to look for the source of other values in the
relationship of man to other men—in 'sociability'—and also in
the 'existential or anthropological consciousness': 'nature is
also in man, as a biological being who is born, reproduces,
and dies, whose very existence manifests the perennial contradiction between nature and culture . . .' [57]. In other words,
at least two other situations or themes also appear in action
analysis.

But the terms 'sociability' and 'anthropological consciousness'
are perhaps misleading. Anthropology does not study the 'agony'
born of the clash of nature and human culture—or, rather, the

contradiction between the given being and its movement towards a 'beyond' [57]. However much one might draw such a description from certain of the reflections of Lévi-Strauss, it is quite simply characteristic of existence, such as philosophers from Kierkegaard to J. P. Sartre have interpreted it. It is the theme of philosophical rather than anthropological thought, and to speak of 'existential or anthropological consciousness' is to introduce a confusing element. 'Anthropology' figures here only to provide a scientific aura for existential thought. Similarly, it is not the problem of sociability which Touraine considers, but simply that of 'otherness', and it is no accident that the examples he mentions are those of love and friendship, 'communication through the subject' [65]. The two other themes of action analysis are in fact the already classic themes of philosophical deliberation about existence.

From this point of view, the symmetry between the three themes is an artificial one. Only labour gives rise to an 'historical consciousness'. More than this, it is the 'relation between man and his products' which defines 'culture' [66]. But does not this definition singularly restrict the scope open to the other normative orientations? It is not a matter of chance, or a result of the specific fields of competence of the author, that only labour is treated in the work. It enjoys a privileged place because it alone allows for the construction of the collective subject which forms the historical subject that corresponds to the aim of the enterprise.

But what is 'labour'? It is the generality of the definition, or rather the continual oscillation between a very general and a very narrow definition, which allows everything to be built upon this foundation. Transformation of nature, but also 'organizing intelligence', labour is sometimes equated with the universal characteristics of any effort to overcome some resistance, any intentional striving for an objective. In this case, we should not say that social action is labour, but rather that labour is action. It is creation and control, because every mode of action has an objective result and seeks to retrieve and master whatever part of that result escapes it. But at the same time labour is sometimes treated as productive activity: the role of 'producers' and their consciousness in the analysis of classes or the working-class movement illustrates this sufficiently. This oscillation between labour as action and labour as production is one of the major ambiguities of the work.

The ambiguity is not without consequence, because it makes it possible to move directly from a philosophical notion to a concrete situation. To define labour as creation and control is to define the general characteristics of action in a transhistorical manner (on this level, one could say just as relevantly: exteriority and recovery by the self, or even the dialectic of the for-itself and in-itself). But to consider situations of labour in which the producer depends upon natural forces is to identify an historical situation, defined by technical means and organization. The 'submissive consciousness' which prevents men from thinking of society 'as a product of human labour' is tied to the fact that 'the storm engulfs the merchant ships', 'the hail ruins the harvest', or that 'ignorance precludes the measurement of space, time or production' [128]; but what liberates us from the storm, the hail and from ignorance are maps and clocks, meteorology and assured knowledge. Labour is therefore defined in terms of an historical condition of knowledge and means of action. What is there here which proves, then, that labour thus understood is the essential source of normative orientations—that it is not one situation among others?

On a deeper level, the confusion between a transhistorical definition, which may usefully serve to delineate a method, and an historical definition, which specifies an object of analysis, involves a confusion of method and object. There is action analysis, but there is also, as we have seen, societies to which it is particularly relevant, which lend themselves to it. In the abstract labour is creation and control, and this is universally true; but, in industrial societies, because it is less dependent upon natural constraints, labour is creation and control in a more direct sense. In other words, from the abstract definition, we can establish a hierarchy of societies. Moreover, the abstract definition allows us to define values in relation to others in such a way as to measure not only societies but also modes of conduct. In an organization, for example, instead of resting upon general commands, creation and control become translated into 'development' and 'democracy'. From then onwards, every organization 'appears in the action perspective as a mediation . . . between historical actors . . . and the values of development and democracy' [183]. One can thus describe 'low' or 'high' 'levels' of action. By reference to such considerations, we may classify and assess modes of conduct in terms of a normative scale.

Action is the source of values, but, in its universal definition, the origin of all values. Labour, in its historical situation, is the source of certain values. The confusion between the two definitions makes it possible illegitimately to attribute to the latter the universality of the former. If creation and control can be correctly translated by development and democracy, they are too specific in connotation for a general definition of action and we must reject this definition. On the other hand, if we accept the notion in its most general sense, it is not legitimate to slip from one to the other. This is to confuse a method of analysis and a normative assessment. It is justifiable to inquire into the *'raison d'être'* of social values, but on condition that we do not profit from the ambiguity of the term in order to transform a sufficient reason into a means of justification, to pass from explanation to legitimation. Moreover, if creation and control have a directly concrete content, which we can locate in diverse situations, it is easy to see that this involves the postulation of transhistorical values in which we find a new form the idealism which was previously condemned. This pre-established harmony between action analysis and industrial societies transforms a method into a theory of the evolution of our societies, and turns action analysis into that philosophy of history from which it was supposed to escape.

The difficulty perhaps goes even deeper. It undoubtedly derives from the manner in which Alain Touraine has conceived his aim of accounting for social values. Social values are meanings. They have a meaning for the social actor because they orient his behaviour, and motivate him in terms of external sanctions and the internalizations he makes of these. But they also have a significance which escapes him: he is not the author of them, even if he takes them over and modifies them. They are already there, in the roles he plays; he discovers them before reproducing them on his own account. Moreover, his intentions only take on meaning within an already given scale: I desire justice, but justice such as I represent it within a political context, and the positions I defend are those of a union, party or movement. Lastly, what finally decides the meaning of an individual action is the response of others to it. The objective meaning results from a sum of individual intentions. The relation of the individual actor to the objective meaning is thus an ambiguous relation, because he constructs his own meaning before creating it, and his creation escapes him. The objective meaning always exists prior to the meaning intended by the actor, and becomes modified through the successive interventions of other actors. Alain Touraine assumes that we can explain this objective sense by relating it to a collective actor which would stand in a directly creative connection with it. The historical subject is thus the hypothetical author of objective meaning.

Here there is a second postulate, directly tied to the former: although we have identified partly opposed, partly contradictory meanings in the complex game of actors, Touraine presumes that behind these there is ultimately *one* meaning. 'Men make their own history.' We are led to understand, not only that the conjunction of their heritage and their projects create, whether they know it or not, new meanings; but that there is *one* historical dynamic underlying these projects, *one* meaning at work in them all. 'Sociological analysis makes no sense unless it accounts for the totality of social changes, unless it connects each of them, in a dialectical way, to a moment or situation of the historical subject' [127].

To give an account of the totality is to find a common meaning for it—not, to be sure, a static meaning, given at the outset, but the logic of a multiple becoming: a process whereby particular meanings come to form a totality. The unity of this process is given by the historical subject, the universal subject, which we can identify in its moments and situations, but which is the very expression of the formation of the totality: that is to say, which gives a common meaning to individual actions. It 'implies totality, as the foundation of a social and cultural situation considered as a whole, including its conflicts and contradictions' [127].

The historical subject is thus something quite other than a principle of explanation. Or rather this ambiguous term must be understood as setting out a methodological requirement, as establishing a first principle. The parallel between the notion of social system in functionalism and the notion of the historical subject in action sociology is misleading: the former is certainly a heuristic postulate which points to the analysis of the interdependence of actors; the second is a substantive postulate which affirms, over and beyond empirical data, the existence of a unique meaning.

This is proved by the fact that the recognition of the historical subject is not accompanied by any sort of description of the method which would allow us to get to grips with it. Specific actors have 'a *charge subjectale*' or 'projects': by what criteria are these to be identified? What procedure or mode of analysis can be used to distinguish them, and to transpose them into an historical dynamic? The historical subject is 'constructed' from social institutions and social relationships. But the mode of construction is nowhere described. Let us agree that action analysis 'is more of a point of departure than a method' [92]: nowhere is it made explicit how we can advance from this starting-point, step by step. In fact, the book gives us no guidance as to this difficult and perilous enterprise. It nowhere indicates the way in which we are to move from concrete actors to their postulated unity.

Is this accidental, or the result of the author's negligence? It appears to us that, on the contrary, it could not be otherwise: to postulate a unity in the dynamic of history, a unity in the meaning of social action, is in fact to turn one's back upon any empirical approach. This single meaning cannot be present for all the actors, and neither is it given objectively in their acts. It necessarily has the arbitrary character of an interpretation. To assume an historical subject, the author of objective meaning and to emphasize the unity—even in the form of the creation of totality —of this meaning, is to found a philosophy of history, not to make a scientific advance. The historical subject secularizes the Hegelian Spirit, or matches the determinisms of the dialectical reason of J. P. Sartre, but the fundamental objective is the same.

Hence it can only be grasped by intuition, by an intellectual operation. Far from moving from specific actors to the historical subject, the book proceeds in the obverse direction. It asserts, by inspiration, the existence of the historical subject, and deduces from it the *charge subjectale* of specific individuals. It proceeds from the higher to the lower level and, having recognized a collective author of meanings, examines to what degree real actors share in them. For they share in somewhat the same way as the objects of the mundane world share in Platonic ideas and the step involved in deducing them is even stated explicitly: 'The principle of analysis in relation to the individual subject is simple:

he always represents a level of diminution of the historical subject' [149].

No one will dispute the illuminating character of this work, with its sensitivity to change and creativity, and the attention which is given to the modes of origin and genesis of values. And, all things considered, nothing could be more unjust than the methodological critique we have given of a work of such insight. But how does it adhere to the initial aim of widening the field of scientific sociology? Seeking to renew a tradition of social philosophy and historical thought, Touraine gives as the ultimate aim of his analysis the discovery of an agency which is a global creator and carrier of meaning. 'The study of the historical subject is, above all, a sociology of freedom' [123]—of freedom in history, or rather of the freedom which makes history. There is a sociology of the forms of social determinism, which has insisted with good reason upon the plurality and diversity of these forms of determinism. But in seeking this total freedom, how can we do otherwise than to set up a metaphysical construction?

6 ALAIN TOURAINE

The Raison d'Être of a Sociology of Action[1]

I

The intention underlying the sociology of action can first of all be best understood if it is related to the *raison d'être* of 'classical' sociology. This is primarily concerned with social order.

The functioning of society rests upon the voluntary application of operative rules. Some of these are conventions, others express technical and scientific knowledge, but what we call 'social norms' are those which define the adaptation of conduct to a social order —that is to say, to a more or less institutionalized system of positions or statuses. Each of us finds himself placed in a framework of norms, which is neither always clear nor always coherent, but which must be sufficiently visible and integrated for the behaviour of others towards ourselves to be predictable, such that most of our actions do not impose upon us an exhausting effort of analysis and choice.

Certain social groups have developed very strongly this control of modes of behaviour, which always involves a certain formalism and which ensures the integration of individuals within the collectivity. It is easy to understand why sociologists, who have almost always studied societies in upheaval, dominated by industrialization, urbanization, changes in forms of work and modes of life, should have constantly interested themselves in the conditions of the existence and maintenance of social order, in the integration of migrants, national, ethnic or religious minorities, or the working-class—all those who, not being recognized as members of the society, seek to make a place for themselves within it, to have their rights recognized as well as their obligations, and to become citizens. A leader of the N.A.A.C.P., the

[1] First published as 'La raison d'être d'une sociologie de l'action' in *Revue française de Sociologie*. Translated by Anthony Giddens.

American association for defending the rights of blacks, said to me more than ten years ago: 'We are not reformists but conformists. I, the grandson of a slave, wish to enforce upon the descendants of those who invented Anglo-Saxon law the recognition of its tenets.' He wanted equality, the observance of the law and civic rights. He believed in justice and education, in the court and the school, in institutions.

But the approach which allows us to study the functioning of institutions and organizations, the transmission of cultural norms and the adaptation to change, does not suffice to analyse the formation of a polity, of a social movement, class relations or the transformation of customs.

I am certainly prepared to admit that the country in which I live, and in those which resemble it in their recent history, the most striking development today is the decline of those great economic conflicts stimulated by capitalist accumulation. Social rights develop, negotiation replaces authoritarian command and violence diminishes, at least in the sphere of labour. But does this justify turning away from the study of the demands and movements which lead to social transformation, seeing nothing but the re-establishment of order and the rule of law, and asking only about the adaptation to change—as if the forms of social life were controlled only by the level of economic development associated with forms of consumption, human relationship and organization?

Those who interest themselves only in the functioning of society must exclude from their field of study the determination of normative orientations of action. They think of industrial civilization, therefore, as a highly differentiated form of organization, in which each individual relates to others in a multitude of statuses and roles, conjoined by the rational demands of the division of labour and of rationalization. Individual or collective strategies are grafted upon a system of social stratification, which itself essentially reproduces the exigencies of production. The organization of society is that of a market, in which pressure groups confront each other, and negotiate among themselves within the framework of institutions which serve to ensure compromise and social equilibrium. Struggles for power and ideas are replaced by the defence of standards of living and life-chances, and by the capacity to bargain.

Our society would seem thus to have two faces: on the one side it is a social market, on the other it is a set of organizations whose functioning does not proceed without difficulty, but which, from whatever aspect one considers it, is a system within which actors conduct the defence of their particular interests, respecting or using the rules of the game, without ever opening a debate about the ends of the society. In other types of industrial societies, totalitarianism or centralized bureaucracy appear as social obstacles; in our own, they appear as an inheritance of the past, of the rigidity of societies strained by their efforts to drag themselves out of underdevelopment. The more production develops, the richer society becomes, the more its system of decision-making must diversify, arbitration expand, and empirical rationalism become substituted for the authoritarian definition of aims.

Is there not a certain naïveté in this unfailing belief in the good, the great, the new society? Is it not possible to criticize, just as stringently as the brutality of the state apparatus and the constraints of ideological conformism, the degeneration of social action, the corruption or irresponsibility, the rigidity of the system of stratification and general tendency to segregation, and the feeling which individuals have of the absurdity of social change? American society seems to have passed through the period of self-satisfaction that marked its entry into abundance; social criticism, social conflicts, forms of personal rebellion reappear in abundance, and force observers to take stock anew. The East-European societies, which are beginning to become more wealthy, at the same time as they abandon their international responsibilities, gradually shed their ideas and slogans of the turn of the century, but become dulled by a petty-bourgeois torpor.

II

I did not write my *Sociologie de l'action* in order to return to the debates of yesteryear, but to focus attention upon social movements and the necessity of knowing how the actor, collective or individual, forms his social being through his involvement in disputes, conflicts and strivings. The principal danger here is that of opposing to the social game the purity of a moral or ideological absolute, of singing the praises of spontaneity as the antidote of bureaucracy; or of the permanent revolution, social and cultural, as the contrary of order. It is natural that these orientations come to be expressed in social practice, that thousands of students at Berkeley sing with Joan Baez, 'We shall overcome', and launch campaigns of civil disobedience. These new utopias are no less important than those of the beginning of the nineteenth century, but we must not confuse analysis and sentiment; we have to construct an explanatory tool which explains these social facts and is not simply content to accept them at their face value.

A sociology of action is not a social philosophy, and its strength can only become apparent when its subject-matter is identified; that is to say, the totality of forces acting towards, and the forms taken by, the dislocation of the game—or, as we more usually say, the social system. The workers' movement is not only an element in a system of social relations, it is also a demand for workers' control; a group discussion is not only social integration and dialogue, it also creates a charismatic affirmation of ends; a factory or an office are not only organizations, they are also enterprises and centres of power; love relations are not merely companionship but also at the same time eroticism and a personal encounter; political society is not simply a system of pressure and arbitration, it is also the medium of choice of a particular type of social organization.

III

None of these problems is unique to industrial society, but it is the formation of the latter which impels us to newly define the principles of an action sociology. The most general characteristic of this type of society is that the legitimacy of social action no longer rests upon the respect for a traditional or meta-historical order, but upon the putting into practice of rationalized schemes. The union of moral and political principles with socio-economic action becomes weakened. The church separates from the state, the state no longer imposes its law upon civil society. Economic growth and its social corollaries become self-justifying. By the same token, social action no longer seems directed by familiar and institutionalized values. Man in industrial society lives in a world of objects and signs, not of principles and symbols.

From then onwards, how is it possible to look for the *raison d'être* of orientations of action outside of action itself, outside of the tension between the actor and his works? In choosing this point of departure, we say nothing about the content of action; we do not have recourse to any specific picture of Man and the Good. Nor do we suppose a unity of meaning in all observable phenomena. We wish only to illuminate a new body of factors, which others dismiss too easily as the result of a natural evolution that leads to organic solidarity, to universalistic norms, or to the generalization of the social market. The real point of departure of action sociology is not in the identification of its most general principle of analysis. It is in the recognition of the fact that, in our type of society, the rationalizers, enamoured of growth in general, and the categories of consumers, are not separate from one-another, each struggling to improve their particular situation. Such a separation, if it were complete, would undermine the possibility of social movements, since social demands would no longer bear upon the orientation of society, but only upon the distribution of benefits. But this is an extreme situation, and the ruling groups are not only interested in rationalization, but are also a power elite, pursuing power or profit as much as growth, which leads them from their side to act in the name of rationality of development at the same time as in defence of their interests.

These observations define concretely what I have called the historical subject. It is not a principle that guides the conduct of the actor, the system of values which dominates the culture of a society: it is, in an industrial society, the meaning of the relations established between the process of development and claims for control of the instruments of production, and the results of this development. It cannot therefore be identified with any particular being. No actor, individual or collective, acts exclusively by reference to the problematic of the historical subject. It is not a descriptive concept, but an instrument of analysis.

Those who rule and are ruled, like capitalists and proletarians, are neither angels nor beasts. To the degree that the ruling groups ensure growth, those who are subordinate to them can do more than defend their own particular interests; to the degree that the latter struggle against the opaqueness of the economic system, the ruling groups may defend the particular interests of the state as a planning agency, an instrument of power politics, or those of the great corporations building their empires without paying attention to a broader economic rationality. There are two ways of eliminating the historical subject. The first consists in affirming the existence of a unified social and cultural system, within which there exists a division of labour and status differentiations, and which does not operate without problems, but which does not place institutionalized values in question; the second consists in contrasting the private versus the public interests as a social war, which does not proceed without truces and compromises, but which excludes any form of social unity of a system torn from top to bottom by a struggle between good and evil.

In these varying degrees, all actors participate in the historical subject, that is to say in the social debate. It is not necessary, in this analysis, to define the historical subject 'psychologically', as if it could be grasped directly, by responses to questions, as if it were a conscious principle and consciously isolated from the orientation of conduct.

The role of the sociologist is to construct a structure of action: that is to say, to isolate within a totality of social relations a system of social connections defined by a twofold reference to the collective creation and the control of the specific actor over his conditions of labour.

IV

It is evident that the situation of the historical subject is not to be confused with labour problems. Labour normally is entered into in the context of an organization, and this latter must first of all be considered as a social system possessing its own established rules and procedures, stratification and social mobility, its pressure groups, its methods of negotiation or, sometimes, arbitration. The worker is also a man who budgets, organizes his career or looks for a better job, is a member of primary groups on the shopfloor, etc. It would be as dangerous—and false—to say that action sociology is a sociology of work as to limit its field of application to a particular category of aspects of labour. More concretely, it is even more indispensable than hitherto not to limit the analysis of social relations of labour (an expression that I use distinguishing it from the functional motion of social relations) to the scope of the enterprise. This limitation might in some part be justified in a purely capitalist economy, where the private firm constitutes an independent agency of production and decision-making largely separated from the intervention of social forces other than that of capitalist power and organization itself.

Today it is not the enterprise but the economy which is more and more the key level of analysis, to the extent that the enterprise itself takes on a new importance as an organization, rather than as a system of roles and statuses. Planning or programming, the politics of public investment and revenue, the controls of consumption by fiscal measures and social security, are more central terms in the analysis, and more illuminating than those of property and profit. At the same time, the problems posed by social relations in work extend into new areas, marked by mass production, etc. From one context to another the problems and their definition differ greatly, but the game of social creation and control appears everywhere. I readily admit that the notion of labour seems in my book sometimes to have archaic connotations, as the legacy of a situation in which the creative and transformative effort of nature was more directly apparent than today, since productivity is more significantly determined by the influence of organizations. But it is easy to free oneself from this too specific picture of labour. The real problem is elsewhere, and J. D. Reynaud and P. Bourdieu have clearly formulated it. Is there not a constant confusion, in the *Sociologie de l'action*, between a philosophical notion of action-labour, objectification of products, the effort to recover or maintain the control of these products, and an historical notion of labour-production, modifying the relations of man and nature and the forms of the division of labour?

My answer first of all is that the latter definition is not mine. It defines an historical situation, a level of productivity, perhaps a technical division of labour and also a general standard of living; it does not explain the social division of labour, class relationships and the nature of social movements, for the simple fact that it does not introduce the fundamental idea of normative orientations of action. The first definition is certainly more in conformity with my intentions. What therefore is at fault with it? That it is philosophical? I willingly accept this. The historical subject can be grasped philosophically, in its two-fold action, in separation from its dissolution among concrete social actors. The task of sociology only begins when direct observation is replaced by an indirect analysis; the central figure in the *Soulier de Satin* is not the Jesuit who speaks directly to God, but Rodrigues, who takes the long, indirect and obscure road.

This is why the notion of the historical subject first enters into sociological analysis as the foundation of that system of action, the most simple form of which is the contradiction between rulers and ruled. Labour only becomes a sociological notion from the moment that transforming and organizing action, which initially is the search for power or profit, the need for subsistence or for experimentation, is grasped as production: that is to say, when this gives birth to a social product, the object of a more or less complex system of appropriation. Class conflict is not only a theme of sociological analysis; it is the primary object of a sociology of the historical subject, the condition of its existence.

V

It would be risky to stop at this point in order to return to general principles of analysis. The historical subject, defined in terms of labour, that is to say by the creation of material works, by a product open to definite forms of appropriation is only one modality of subjective existence (*n'est qu'une modalité d'existence du sujet*). The absence of concrete analyses concerned with sociability in the *Sociologie de l'action* is merely a reflection of my professional limitations, but one can easily envisage an analysis of communities founded upon the same principles as my analysis of organizations. It is even very possible that in the future an action analysis of forms of sociability will prove more important in sociological discussion than the re-analysis of problems by labour, which I have devoted myself to because these touch most directly upon the field of social relations. A group is not merely a network of interpersonal relations; it only exists because it acts, and the connection of the individual with the group is not fundamentally different from that with his labour. The conflicts between rulers and ruled, the role of charisma in the leadership of the group, make manifest that it is a system of action: that is to say, the sudden emergence of a common endeavour among diverse actors. The same applies to what I have called the anthropological consciousness and which is dependent upon sociology to the extent to which collectivities—the family above all—are organized around the great social and biological experiences of birth, reproduction and death.

VI

In all these cases, the sociology of action takes the form of placing the actor before, rather than in, a given situation. This is not because it treats a collective situation in terms of individual action, but because this situation is an involvement, which only has meaning if it is considered as a drama and not as a fixed setting. This appears most clearly when an actor does not play the game, opposing the flexibility of systems of social relations that always tend towards a moving equilibrium by new demands; as where the faith of the believer breaks out from the life of the Church, where the beliefs of the militant overturn political strategy, where the conviction of teachers goes beyond pedagogic communication. This is not to say that these cases are simpler, but only that the necessity of analysing the subjective component (*champ subjectal*) of conduct is more visible when the project of the actor is more elevated. This psycho-social analysis of projects no more governs the analysis of the historical subject than it is governed by it; the two points of view stand in the same reciprocal perspective as the study of the institution and socialization, or society and the individual.

But let us return to our point of departure, let us accept the idea that action analysis is most easily undertaken wherever a system of social relations is dislocated, which creates, in the void that has thus been opened up, a new system of social ties that in its turn becomes organized and institutionalized, leading again a life of its own that will sooner or later be shattered by a new crisis. Perhaps we should begin from there—from the experience of the upheaval, the charismatic appeal, the call of the absolute. But the whole effort of the sociologists must be directed towards re-creating, around the break, the unity of a system of action. This unity is not that of a concrete situation, that for example of occupational relations in a firm or an industry. In the same way, the unity of a social system is not the totality of actions of a given mass of actors, but the structure of a system of roles. Sometimes the social debate becomes organized, and the analysis becomes simpler, because the concrete limits of observation can be more easily traced, but sociology has learned to consider political opinions and not simply parties and votes at elections; similarly, it is possible to construct an action system even when it does not take on the organization and the ideologies of labour conflicts in our societies.

VII

The objective of this undertaking is not exorbitant. Everyone recognizes that there exist systems of signs and systems of social relations. Why not recognize in the same way that there can be action systems, that behind the exchange which nourishes discussion it is possible to analyse the content of a confrontation, that behind the complex game of negotiation there is revealed a social conflict, which is first of all a misunderstanding in the sense that the actors communicate without replying to one another? The unity of a system of action is not that of a social movement, which is the construction of an actor or plurality of actors, but is also not that of an institutionalized system of social relations. To take the example which I have frequently used, it is neither that of the workers' movement nor that of the system of occupational relations, but that of class relations.

It is much less concrete than the former, and one of the most recurrent tasks of action analysis is to explode these entities which confuse social phenomena whose significance is very diverse. The colonizer and the colonized, the capitalist and proletarian, the technocrat and the employee, are opposed to each other by their interests and their strategy, but together they form a system of action in so far as there exists what I have called the double dialectic of social classes or organizations—that is to say, in so far as their relationship is one of forces of development which are at the same time two systems of appropriation. It is the sudden appearance of the historical subject (*éclatement du sujet*) among the actors, such that the subject cannot be apprehended, does not exist, apart from their relationships, which makes it the case that the behaviour of the particular individual never represents the conduct of values in pure form; at the same time, there always exists a certain overlap between the normative orientations and the interests of historical actors opposed within a system of action.

This zone of overlap constitutes the area which can become institutionalized, in which social norms and mechanisms of integration of the social system emerge. Action analysis is very far from representing society as torn by a fundamental force; and it is equally dissatisfied with the view which presents society as a social play within a system of institutionalized and internalized norms.

VIII

The practical aim of the sociology of action is to reintroduce into sociological analysis the vast areas which seem too often excluded from its preoccupations. It seems to me that sociology has only succeeded in constructing a system of analysis at the cost of abandoning to the descriptive social history of contemporary industrial societies an important part of its observable subject-matter. Sociologists speak of 'organization' and leave to economists the study of the enterprise; they define the forms of adaptation or maladaptation to change, and abandon to political science the study of social movements which channel development; they interest themselves in urban stratification, but leave the study of urban politics to geographers and town-planners; they are well aware of cultural diffusion, but less so of movements of national or racial liberation; they leave the study of the workers' movement to historians, while they preoccupy themselves with occupational relationships.

I do not wish, in any of these cases, to condemn the efforts that have been made, so long, at least, as they are not accompanied by a legitimizing ideology; but I believe it to be possible and certainly desirable to stretch the sociological task to encompass the totality of phenomena or moments in social life in which, through conflict, institutions are created and society is born.

Such an approach is not only warranted in the study of industrial societies, but it assumes a particular importance in relation to these, since such societies, although undoubtedly burdened by various forms of inheritance from prior ages, are more defined by their anticipations for the future than by the influences of their past. Does this mean to say that industrial societies are treated here as superior to others—as if others represented merely a dim foreshadowing of a social form which could only see the light of day when societies emerged capable of consciously directing their own growth? Certainly not, and I am wholly opposed to the evolutionism to which functional analysis has recourse as its necessary complement. But there is nothing shocking in recognizing that a new type of society makes possible the appearance of a new type of knowledge, and that it is in the most active societies that an action sociology naturally comes into being.

IX

When we speak of the historical subject, of systems of action and projects, we do not construct a philosophy of history, but an historical sociology (*une sociologie de l'historicité*) and, beyond this, an understanding of the formation of social systems—which others study from the functional point of view. The historical subject is not a concrete totality, like feudal or industrial society; it is thus not an interpretation of an observable entity, but the basic principle of a type of analysis, a mode of analysing the normative orientation of conduct.

To be sure, at any given moment a consciousness of obligation is created by the recognized existence of a norm, but at each moment also the norm is placed as a value or rejected as a scandal; it is judged, and it is this appeal from norms to values, this putting on trial of the rule and the game, which must first of all be considered. Some may seek to grasp it directly, as it is experienced by the individual or group; others, who are sociologists, look for it first in the controversies, dislocations and inventions which manifest, beyond the interaction, the drama unfolding.

There can be no question of explaining the historical future by means of the adventures of the historical subject; the task to be accomplished is that of demonstrating, in each specific instance, the existence of a structure of social relations, the notion of historical subject being no more than the formal expression of this structure. In actual fact I rebel against the reduction of sociology to the study of modes of social determinism considered as the influence of the situation upon behaviour. Any proper understanding of determinism consists, not in repeating that *le mort saisit le vif*, but in penetrating to the inside of systems of social conduct themselves and understanding their organization and the grounds for their existence, instead of describing environmental constraints. We should not say: things being what they are, nor even: men behaving as they do, but should follow, as in the theatre, the movement and ever-present visible flow of the drama. We cannot therefore make an immediate transition from the concrete actors to their unity; we must grasp directly their relationships, what ties them without harmonizing them, makes them both indissoluble and strangers to each other.

What seems to me to be virtually certain is that this task cannot be undertaken in terms of a progressive extension of descriptive methods, although these have played a very great role in the progress of sociological knowledge. What I am calling for is a new sociology attached to the study of the flux of social relations or cultural action in conditions that are closely controlled, and manipulated, in separation from the excessive complexity and false unity of social problems. Sociology should follow the path opened up by social psychology, freeing itself more and more from the charms of the concrete. I hope for more today than descriptive generalizations from the experimental imagination, for what we have to do is not to uncover the meaning of history, but to analyse the process of the transformation of the field of action by action itself.

7 ERNEST GELLNER

The New Idealism—Cause and Meaning
in the Social Sciences[1]

Anthropomorphism is not a live issue in the natural sciences. On the whole, the freedom of natural scientists does not need to be protected from people insisting that the picture presented by the results *must* conform to some human image—that it must resemble man, make room for him, underwrite his purposes, be compatible with his self-image, or with some doctrine concerning these matters. There are notorious exceptions to this generalization, such as for instance the interference with Soviet biologists or even physicists in the interests of supporting an extrapolated version of a social theory: but these are, happily, exceptions. In an important and extended sense, the Copernican revolution is well established: humanity is known not to be at the centre of things; human requirements are not allowed to limit, or even create presumptions in, the sphere of scientific theory. (Moral philosophers are proud of the autonomy of ethics: this is one point on which a large proportion of professional practitioners of the subject are agreed. They do not quite so often note that the autonomy of ethics only followed on the autonomy of science, the exclusion of the argument from morals to fact, *from* 'ought' *to* 'is', of the form 'This must be true, otherwise our life would not make sense', or 'This cannot be true, otherwise our life would make no sense'.)

In social or human studies or sciences, however, the question of anthropomorphism—though not under this name—is by no means dead. The plea for a *humanist* psychology or sociology is frequently heard. The philosophy of mind has recently witnessed a sustained and interesting attack on the view that individuals have 'privileged access', cognitively, to their *own* minds. But there has been no corresponding attack on the view, which might at least superficially seem parallel, that we have, *collectively*, a privi-

---

[1] First published in *Problems in the Philosophy of Science*.

leged access, through our shared human concepts, to the understanding of the social life and institutions of humanity. On the contrary: philosophers associated with the school responsible for the attack on the *individual* 'privileged access' view, have at the same time been prominent in putting forward versions of what I call the collective privileged access theory—that we understand social life through human concepts.

The general motive or attraction of anthropomorphism, in any sphere, is fairly obvious. Anthropomorphic doctrines enlist the world on the side of our values or aspirations. If, to take an example with which I am familiar, the deity or supernatural beings arrange floods, droughts or other disasters in a way such that these sanctions strike perjurors and their lineages, this provides a convenient underpinning for a legal system. A centralized and effective state may have neither the need, nor indeed be willing to tolerate, the handing over of punishment to the supernatural: but where such a centralized law-enforcing agency is absent, and Nature apparently allows itself to be used in so moral a manner, this makes possible trial by collective oath—a very common institution in anarchic or semi-anarchic tribal contexts. The rain does *not* fall on the just and the unjust alike.

Those concerned with defending anthropomorphism, in any sphere, can do so positively or negatively, or perhaps one should say in an offensive or a defensive spirit. A positive anthropomorphism, one that is on the offensive as it were, puts forward a specific doctrine, a doctrine which if true restores a 'meaningful moral order' to the area which it is meant to cover.

A negative or defensive anthropomorphism is not concerned with putting forward a specific positive picture, but merely with demonstrating that theories which necessarily make the world 'meaningless', which inescapably exclude meaningful visions, *cannot* be true. How can this be shown? Most commonly, perhaps, we show that a class of theories is false by establishing that some other theory, incompatible with all the members of that class, is true. But negative or defensive anthropomorphism (by definition) does not put forward any specific theory of its own. It has an alternative way, and one which we may (in accordance with the terminology of its propounders, I think), call epistemological. It argues that the very nature of knowledge, in the sphere in question, is such that no non-anthropomorphic theory can possibly be true. This leaves the field open for anthropomorphic theories, without however at the same time positively singling out any one of them.

The present argument will be concerned with these negative or defensive, epistemologically based anthropomorphisms. It would be an exaggeration to say that positive anthropomorphic theories are absent from the intellectual scene. They do exist, in social theory, on the fringes of medicine, in psychotherapy and perhaps elsewhere. One of the appeals of psychotherapeutic techniques is, I suspect, precisely that they restore a kind of moral order: people find it more tolerable to believe that the fault is in themselves, than that they have been struck arbitrarily, accidentally, for no purpose whatever. In the joke, the psychiatrist tells the patient: 'The reason you feel inferior is that you *are* inferior. That will be 20 guineas.' In fact, he does not say anything as brutal. He tells the patient that his suffering is the corollary of something else, has its roots within him. The manifest advantage of this is that it makes the suffering manipulable, but the latent, and perhaps more important advantage, one which survives the possible failure to manipulate and remove the misery, is that it makes it meaningful, and at least quasi-deserved. I think we prefer to be guilty, rather than the objects of entirely accidental 'punishment' which, somehow, is *more* humiliating.

In brief, positive, moral-order-preserving anthropomorphic doctrines do exist, even in the field of 'modern' theories, i.e., those formulated in our time and in a contemporary idiom. But within philosophy we find more commonly the negative, defensive versions, which defend a whole class of meaningful visions against a whole class of, as it were, inhuman ones. The 'meaningfulness' defended need not be a crude picture in which sinners are punished and virtue prevails. It is rather a world in which things happen and are understood in human terms, in some sense to be clarified further. These thinkers are not concerned or able to demonstrate that the human world is a *moral* tale, with justice and truth vindicated and some noble purpose attained: but they are concerned to show that it is, at least, a *human* tale. They wish to defend *the anthropomorphic image of man* himself.

This aspiration is by no means self-evidently absurd. The requirement that human activities and institutions should be interpreted in human terms does not have the offensiveness which nowadays immediately attaches to the requirement that *nature* be seen in human terms. *That* requirement offends both our tacit autonomy of nature principle, and our rejection of a-priorism. (These two might be considered in conflict, but anyway, I think we hold them both.) Hence modern anthropomorphism is doubly transformed, it has undergone two shifts: it has shifted its area (from nature to man), and its grounds (from substantive to epistemological). The *in*human interpretations against which the negative, defensive anthropomorphist guards us may be various, but some of their forms are very notorious: materialistic, mechanistic, deterministic, 'external' causal explanations.

Anthropomorphic or idealistic thought (as we may call it with reference to its contrast, and in order to bring out a certain continuity) has undergone another interesting development, in addition to the shift from nature to man and from substantive to epistemological considerations. This development concerns the *terms* in which the contrast with matter, to mechanical causation, etc., is conceived. Roughly: idealism has moved first from stuff to subject, and then from subject to meaning.

Throughout, the requirement is always to establish a *dis*continuity, between the area abandoned to mechanism or what have you, where anthropomorphism is abandoned, and the redoubt area where the human is to be preserved. But the redoubt is conceived differently at the various stages. Descartes' thinking substance is conceived as substance, in the image of extended substance, and somehow parallel to it and co-ordinate with it. Kant has no truck with a substance-self (a paralogism, this), but for him it is the cognizing and acting subject who provides a bearer for those crucial human characteristics (freedom, responsibility, validity of thought), for which there is no room in nature.

The recent form of idealism with which I am now concerned does not attempt to reassure us by telling us that, as cognizers and agents, we may be allowed a kind of inner emigration from nature: it tells us, instead, that meaningful action, as such, is exempt from nature, in the sense that it is not susceptible to the kind of explanation held to be appropriate in nature, with its attendant moral inconveniences. The outstanding and most uncompromising formulation of this view is found in the work of Mr. Peter Winch, notably in *The Idea of a Social Science*.[1]

[1] London, 1958.

This book is, and is intended to be, the working out of the implications of L. Wittgenstein's mature philosophy for the social sciences. It is in fact meant to be more than this, in as far as Winch believes that these implications are not something marginal or tangential to that philosophy, but on the contrary are altogether central to it. (In that I think he is entirely right.) Likewise, he does not consider these implications to be marginal or tangential for the social sciences either: on the contrary, he believes that they reveal the central and most important features of those sciences. Winch's book has certainly made an impact on those concerned with the philosophy of the social sciences.

All this gives it a double interest. The central part of what he has to say about social sciences and hence (whether he intends this or not) about actual societies, seems to me profoundly and significantly wrong. Hence it has the interest of an influential and well-formulated expression of an (in my view) mistaken theory. But it also has another interest. It constitutes the best, most elegant and forceful, if quite unintended, refutation of Wittgenstein—one far more forceful than any stated by a deliberate critic. If WM is to stand for 'Wittgenstein's mature philosophy', and ISS for the position argued in Winch's book, the situation is roughly as follows:

$$WM \rightarrow ISS \qquad (1)$$

$$\text{but } \underline{ISS \text{ is absurd}} \qquad (2)$$

$$\text{therefore WM is absurd.}$$

When I say that ISS is absurd, I mean that it stands in blatant and manifest contradiction with obvious and salient features of both human societies and the practices of social scientists.

Mr. Winch does not think that he is doing methodology at all, and would deny that he is interfering with the specific methodology of social scientists. He would, on the contrary, maintain that he is merely clarifying what the social sciences in general amount to, something they share at an abstract level, and that this does not affect the specific research strategies which may be adopted locally in this or that subject, or for this or that problem. This image of his own position and its implications seems to me quite mistaken. For one thing, Winch does say harsh things about some, at any rate, methods or aspirations of social scientists, e.g., the use of the comparative method or the pursuit of causal explanations. A theory cannot be all at once a condemnation of some methods, *and* methodologically neutral.

What underlies Winch's wrong assessment of his own position at this point is simply a preconception, an *a priori* philosophic idea that one can clarify what social knowledge is in general without prejudice to its specific tools. But this preconception has no intrinsic authority: it must be judged in the light of whether in fact Winch's position does or does not have methodological implications, and if it does, the preconception must be withdrawn. The preconception must not be invoked as a reason for why the methodological difficulties must be based on a misinterpretation of his position! In fact, methodological implications, negative and positive, do follow. And more than this: not merely a mistaken methodology, but also quite mistaken substantive beliefs about concrete societies, do follow from Winch's position.

If this is so, and if proposition (1), on which he and I agree, be granted, one should have thought that only a critic of Wittgenstein would have gone out of his way to establish that WM entails ISS. But this, interestingly, was not Winch's case. He is anxious to establish (1).

The steps condensed into (1) are, however, of some interest.

Wittgenstein's central doctrine was the account of meaning in terms of use. Meaning was not reference to an entity, be it transempirical (various forms of Platonism), be it a range of actual or possible sensations (various forms of empiricism): it was, on the contrary, the employment of an expression in diverse concrete contexts. These contexts were endlessly diversified, and were parts of 'forms of life'.

This is the form in which the doctrine first made its impact, and, as indicated, it was in this form aimed primarily against rival theories of meaning, notably those contained in either transcendentalism or empiricism. It does not in this form *seem* to have any particular relevance to the social sciences.

Winch's interest is that he was the first, at any rate from within the movement, to read the doctrine in the reverse direction and work out fully its implications. If 'meaning = use', then 'use = meaning'. Of course, no one actually formulated the first equation *as* a formal equation (which would give us the premise for the second, reverse order reading), and in any case, it is not very clear what the thing means when formulated in reverse order. Nothing in the present argument hinges on this: I use this merely as a kind of expository device, to bring out the underlying pattern of Winch's argument.

The inference obtained by inverting the order, as it were, reads roughly as follows when expanded into more intelligible English: if the meaning of expressions is their employment, then, in turn, it is of the essence of the employment of expressions (and by an independent but legitimate extension, of other social behaviour), that it is meaningful. This gives us a kind of mnemonic device for understanding the genesis of Winch's position. We can see why, all at once, he can claim (rightly, in my view), to be following the Master, and yet find in a hitherto apparently un-sociological doctrine, *the* 'Idea of a Social Science'. Where Witt-genstein taught philosophers not to ask for the meaning but for the use, Winch advises social scientists not to look for the cause, but for the meaning. Social behaviour is essentially meaningful: to understand it is to understand its meaning. It cannot but have meaning: the fear that understanding might reveal it to be the slave of antecedent causes (thus being 'explained' by them) turns out to be an error, and one demonstrably such in *all* cases: one, it appears, arising from a fundamental error concerning the very nature of social understanding. This is where the idealism comes in: remove this one error, and we are freed forever, by an omnibus proof, of the bogies of determinism, mechanism and so on.

'One appears to be attempting an impossible task of *a priori* legislation against a purely empirical possibility. What in fact one is showing, however, is that the central concepts which belong to our understanding of social life are incompatible with concepts central to the activity of scientific prediction' (ISS, p. 94).

What, incidentally, *is* it for an action to 'have meaning', or, in as far as this is meant to be a defining characteristic of an 'action', for an event to become an action through possessing meaning? I think it corresponds roughly to what we would, in unself-conscious unsophisticated moments, describe as 'being lived through consciously from the inside, as it were'; but Winch, of course, in accordance with the principles and customs of his movement, does not operate with notions such as 'consciousness', 'inside', etc. Instead, an event acquires meaning through the fact that it is conceptualized by the agent with the help of shared concepts—and for Winch all concepts are necessarily shared[1]—and that the conceptualization is essential to the very recognition of the event. Example: a man 'gets married' not merely by going through certain motions in church or registry office, but by possessing the concept of what it is to be married. If the concept were lacking, the same physical movements, in the same places, simply could not be classified as 'marriage'. For Winch, it follows from the fact that an event 'has meaning' that it cannot be caused.

The manner in which this position is extracted from Wittgensteinian premises is interesting and throws light both on those premises and on Winch's idealism. One crucial step has already been stressed: it consists of reading backwards the tie up between meaning and social behaviour, and instead of invoking this connection to destroy both platonic and empiricist theories of meaning, using it instead to establish that 'meaningfulness' is an essential attribute of social conduct, *and* that this excludes causal, mechanical explanation. But there are other crucial steps.

Winch himself highlights these crucial Wittgensteinian premises. On page 40 of his book, he quotes from Wittgenstein's *Philosophical Investigations*: 'What has to be accepted, the given, is —as one could say—forms of life.' The first wave of Wittgensteinians, including the Master himself, using this perception merely to beat rival theories of language, did not worry much about the fact that 'forms of life' (i.e., societies, cultures) are numerous, diverse, overlapping, and undergo change. Which of them is to be accepted? All of them? Or each of them, on the principle 'When in Rome do as the Romans do'? But what happens when these 'forms' are in conflict, or when one of them is in fundamental inner conflict?

These questions, obvious though they be, did not seem to have been raised in the course of what I called the first wave of the movement. The significance of Winch is that he has pondered on the fact that others (i.e., social scientists) have also taken an interest in 'forms of life', and tried to bring their concern in contact with the invocation of 'forms of life' in philosophy. The oddity of Winch is that he has used this connection not in a *reductio ad absurdum* of Wittgenstein, but in an attempt to set right

---

[1] In a sense, Wittgenstein went beyond Durkheim: for Wittgenstein *all* representations are collective.

the social sciences. Because: the multiplicity, conflict (inner and outer) and change, all undergone by 'forms of life', present a crucial, indeed on its own terms insoluble, problem for a philosophy which would treat them as something 'to be accepted', as 'the given'. For the point about forms of life is that they do not always, or even frequently, accept themselves as given, as something to be accepted. On the contrary, they often reject their own past practices as absurd, irrational, etc. Hence the recommendation of acceptance becomes internally incoherent. It has the form —'Accept whatever X says as true', when, in fact, (*a*) there is a number of mutually inconsistent sources called X, and (*b*) some Xs say: 'What I have said in the past is false.' (There are interesting historical precedents for this incoherence. In the seventeenth century conflict between the Papacy and the French Crown, the Papacy in the end ordered its French supporters to accept the authority of the Crown. Hence the acceptance of the authority of the Papacy entailed . . . its rejection. During the Second World War, the leader of the American Communist Party instructed the members to 'embrace capitalism'. Hence the acceptance of the authority of Moscow entailed its rejection. Similarly, the acceptance of the ultimacy of 'forms of life' has just this paradoxical consequence.)

Both the argument from plurality and the argument from self-rejection or self-criticism is disastrous for the general position. The early Wittgensteinians simply did not think about societies and social change, and *given* this, it is at least in some measure understandable, why they did not notice this decisive weakness in their position. (What is not intelligible is how any man, in the mid-twentieth century, can be oblivious of social diversity or change.) The oddity of Winch is, as stated, that he is aware of both—and in particular of diversity—and still holds on to the initial premises.

Let us take the problem of plurality first. Like the other problem (of social self-criticism), it imposes a dilemma on anyone holding the initial premises, a dilemma neither of whose horns is acceptable. But Winch is clearly aware of this particular dilemma, and firmly embraces one of the available alternatives. Hence to explain the dilemma is also to explain the genesis of Winch's position.

The initial position is: 'forms of life' are ultimate, they cannot be criticized from some external viewpoint, by some independent standard. There is not such a standard. There is no external reality in terms of which forms of life, 'languages', could be judged, for the distinction between that which is real and that which is not only occurs within a language, a form of life.[1]

The first dilemma is this: does this acceptance embrace *all* cultures, or only one?

Either answer entails intolerable consequences. Suppose that only one (or, for that matter, a limited set) is 'accepted': it necessarily follows that it must be selected by some principle of selection. This must be stateable and some reasons should be available for preferring it to other principles or selections. There is of course nothing absurd about this position as such (and I happen to believe that something like this is true), but it is in blatant contradiction with that central Wittgensteinian doctrine, taken over by Winch, to the effect that one cannot seek external and general criteria for the validation of linguistic or conceptual custom. If *selection* is to take place, then it follows that some principle is being employed. This means, in turn, that philosophy must return to the place which in my view it should never have left—the attempt to formulate and defend criteria which are more than mere descriptions of *de facto* custom.

Winch firmly commits himself to the other alternative. The trouble with this branch of the fork is quite different from the first: it does not, at least immediately, lead us to the implicit assumption of extra-cultural norms and hence the contradiction of the initial assumption. It leads us to recognize a multiplicity of 'forms of life', each with its own criteria of distinguishing the real from the unreal, and none of them competent to judge the others. Repeatedly, this is the picture Winch sketches and to which he commits himself. In other words, he commits himself to a profound conceptual relativism: contrary to what, for instance, Sir James Frazer and most of us think, scientific language is not superior to the witchcraft language of (say) the Azande, even when they appear to be explaining the same type of phenomenon. 'Reality is not what gives language sense. What is real and what is unreal shows itself *in* the sense that language has' (italics Winch's). Later, in the same article,[2] the Wittgensteinian premise is made

---

[1] Cf. the formulation of this position in P. Winch, 'Understanding a primitive society', *American Philosophical Quarterly* (1964).

[2] 'Understanding a primitive society', op. cit.

very clear: 'Oracular revelations (among the Azande) are not treated as hypotheses and, *since their sense derives from the way they are treated in their context*, they therefore *are not* hypotheses' (first set of italics mine, the second Winch's).

Winch does, it is true, reject *individual* relativism (quite consistently with his position—indeed his position strictly requires this): '. . . it is *within* the religious use of language that the conception of God's reality has its place, though, I repeat, this does not mean that it is at the mercy of what anyone cares to say . . .' (italics Winch's). A use of language, it appears, does convey reality, though not through the agency of 'anyone', i.e., not, presumably, through any one individual. (We shall have very significant trouble with the question of how many individuals, or under what conditions of differentiation, constitute *a* use of language. A single atheist—or, to strengthen the case, a single logico-positivist —denying that the term 'God' has any meaning, makes no difference. But how about the Soviet Union?)

He also rejects, more obscurely, 'an extreme Protagorean relativism, with all the paradoxes that involves'. No indication is given how such an 'extreme' kind differs from the kind he actually puts forward (without claiming the name, though I do not believe he would repudiate the title 'conceptual relativism'). The paradoxes certainly are not avoided.

There can be no doubt about this relativism itself. Concerning the Zande acceptance of witchcraft and the European rejection of it, Winch says '. . . it is clear . . . that (Evans-Prichard) would have wished to add . . . the European is right and the Zande wrong. This addition I regard as illegitimate . . .'[1] In other words, witches or the processes alleged to occur according to witchcraft belief, are, like the deity, though not apparently at the mercy of *individual* belief, at the mercy of a whole style of thought. For the Azande they exist, as scientific entities exist for us, and no one is entitled (or rather: no one can meaningfully) judge between the two!

As Winch does not surreptitiously return to some hidden standard by which to sort out valid language from invalid, but accepts all languages as valid—by their own lights, and there are for him no others—we must consider why such relativism is untenable. It is worth noting that it is intuitively repellent to

[1] 'Understanding a primitive society', op. cit.

pretend that the Zande belief in witchcraft is as valid as our rejection of it, and that to suppose it such is a philosophical affectation, which cannot be maintained outside the study. I should not myself urge this point against a position—at least, not in isolation. But it ought to worry Winch, who belongs to a tradition which the fact that a given belief can be held by the philosopher in the study, but not in life, is held to be a serious, or crucial, or indeed *the* crucial, objection to a belief. Such a state of philosophic schizophrenia is held to be an indication that the philosopher in question divorces, in his study, some terms which he uses, from their real (and hence authoritative) use in his real life, and is of course incapable of carrying this divorce over into his real life. Had he but remembered the real use, *and* the fact that this is what gives those terms sense, he would not have embraced the schizophrenia-engendering doctrine. There is thus a pragmatic contradiction within Winch's position.

There is another objection which is frequently urged against any kind of relativism, and that is that it leads to a paradox when applied to itself.

This objection is not applicable to Winch, or at any rate not immediately, for he gives us no warrant to apply his relativism to his own argument. He makes an exception, not merely for himself, but for philosophy in general. (Presumably for sociology as well, in view of its near-identity, in his view, with philosophy.) This view involves its own and very considerable difficulties, but it does at any rate exempt Winch from the conventional and facile charge to which relativists are often exposed.

We are arguing that Winch's account of the social sciences is incompatible with certain conspicuous and important features both of the methods of social sciences, and of societies themselves. The latter class of objections—the contradiction between what Winch says and social reality itself—can be made very concrete. Here again there are two subclasses: the contradictions which arise from certain features internal to individual societies, and those which arise from the existence of a multiplicity of societies and their mutual relations.

Let us take the former. Consider certain crucial events/ideas/forces in Western history, events without which quite obviously no adequate account of Western society can be given: Christianity, the Reformation, the Enlightenment. All these have something in common with each other and with other movements or systems of ideas which could be added to the list: they are inherently, essentially, committed to proselytizing and to a kind of exclusiveness. In this they may be wrong, intellectually or morally: but there can be no doubt about the beliefs themselves. These are not, as it were, tribal deities, willing to accommodate tribal deities of neighbouring communities on terms of tolerance and equality. On the contrary, they contain a claim to unique, exclusive and absolute truth.

For Winch, philosophical theories of meaning, and substantive beliefs of concrete societies, are as it were at different levels and do not, cannot, come into conflict. In fact, however, absolutist and exclusive and proselytizing faiths do come into conflict with his contextualist theory of meaning and its appendage, the contextualist theory of truth. Take the example of a Reformer. He says, in substance, that the Divine Will is revealed and accessible in a set of Scriptures, and that its meaning is accessible to the individual conscience. If social practice, the ongoing tradition which claims allegiance to those scriptures, the organized church, is in its real activities at variance with the content of the independently knowable Word—well, then those practices, that church are in error and must be reformed.

That, at any rate, is what the Reformer claims. My argument does not require the Reformer to be right: it merely requires Reformers to be an important social phenomenon—and this can hardly be denied. And what is true of Reformers is, *mutatis mutandis*, true of proselytizers of Christianity itself, of believers in Natural Law, of rationalists of various kinds, and of many of the more radical kinds of secular reformers.

An agent of the Counter Reformation, equipped with philosophic prescience, might have replied to our ideal-typical Reformer as follows: but your insistence on the independent meaning of Scripture and its alleged divergence from the actual practices of the Church betray, on your part, an illusion concerning the nature of meaning. If the sacred formulae seem to you in conflict with practice, ought you not to remember that what gives formulae meaning is the real social context in which they occur? It is *your interpretations* of the formulae, and not reality, which is at fault! Thus, an infallibility of the real social context, of, e.g., the concrete church, could easily be deduced from a theory of meaning . . .

I do not know whether any of the theoreticians of the Counter Reformation employed variants of this argument. But the secularized descendants of the Reformers, the thinkers of the Enlightenment, certainly encountered it from romantic and conservative political theorists. Rationalist rejection of superstition had the same logic, in this respect, as Protestant rejection of idolatry.

In brief: a very important segment of the *subject matter* of the social scientist, (i.e., certain civilizations, broad movements, etc.) holds beliefs which are themselves in contradiction with the principles which, according to Winch, must guide the social scientist. If whole societies believe that what they believed in the past is profoundly absurd, then Winch, who is committed to excluding the possibility of a whole society being wrong in its belief, is caught out, either way: either the pagans were wrong, or the Christians were (*in supposing the pagans to be wrong*); either the pre-Reformation Church was wrong, or the Reformers were, in supposing *it* to be wrong; either those addicted to superstition were wrong, or the rationalists were wrong . . . One way or the other, *someone* must be wrong!

It is instructive to observe Winch's attempts at coping with this question, crucial for his position, and in my view quite insurmountable. He makes a number of attempts:

(1) A shift from a descriptive or analytical position to a normative or prescriptive one. He says, in effect: Yes, there are proselytizers, missionaries, who attempt to interfere in the customs and beliefs of other societies, and remould them in the image of an abstract ideal. But they are *wrong*. They *ought not* to do this.[1]

It is difficult to see how this shift to a normative viewpoint can be either justified or squared with the general purpose of Winch's argument. That he should consider this possible at all is connected with his assumption of a philosophical vantage point outside and above all concrete societies and their beliefs. The fact that from this vantage point certain social trends—notably missionaries, proselytizers—should become open to a supposedly neutral, dis-

---

[1] Cf. for instance, a statement of Winch's in a broadcast on the Third Programme, *Men and things*, of 2 May, 1961: '. . . this is a way of thinking which I wouldn't support at all . . . I am not generally in favour of missionary activities . . .' These are his comments on the universalist claims of some faiths, claims not mindful of cultural boundaries.

passionate condemnation, makes one suspicious of the alleged neutrality of that viewpoint. This Instant Olympus looks rather like a camouflage for one of the concrete beliefs (for a certain romantic traditionalism), and its neutrality is quite spurious.

One could deal with his whole argument here in summary fashion and say that the social sciences are just as concerned with intolerant exclusive beliefs as with tolerant tribal ones, with reformers as much as with traditionalists, with rationalists as much as with believers: a methodology which cannot explain one side of this antithesis, and turns into an ethic, is useless.

But we need not be quite as summary as this. A small dose of normativism might be tolerable even in an analysis or a methodology.[1]

Above all, this would be in total harmony with Winch's general Wittgensteinian position.

That position can be summed up as follows: men speak and live their lives and pursue their manifold interests in the context of 'forms of life', cultural/linguistic traditions, and the concepts they employ derive their validity from, and only from, possessing a place in these forms of life. It is not the task of philosophy to interfere with these traditions. But from time to time misguided philosophers (of the old kind) arise, who, under the mistaken and generally tacit belief that concepts are all of some simple kind, and that they can possess a universal and as it were extra-cultural justification, try to judge, and in effect misinterpret, those actually used concepts, in terms of those supposed external norms. It *is* the task of philosophy to neutralize this error, to protect actual traditions from such misguided interference.

Given such a picture, a small amount of normativism does indeed follow: the philosopher is neutral *vis-à-vis* cultural traditions proper (and indeed, this is Winch's view), but he is professionally entitled, or obliged, to castigate that small minority of transgressors, e.g., missionaries, who would interfere with other cultures, or their own, in the name of a supposed universal norm, of a kind of validity which is more than the recognition of a place of a concept in a culture.

---

[1] Hume was guilty of precisely this in his ethics. He gives a certain account of the basis of moral valuation—roughly, in terms of human convenience—and when he comes across *ascetic* values, which contradict this account, instead of modifying the account, he *condemns* the 'monkish virtues'.

The trouble is, however, very simple: *these transgressors are not a minority*. They are the majority. They are not deviants. They are the mainstream of at least one important tradition. Missionaries are not foolish and redundant excrescences from, e.g., the Christian tradition: they are of its essence. It is not a contingent, but an essential feature of Christianity, that the Gospel should be spread!

In other words, the normativism does not come in a small dose, but is, in effect, overwhelmingly large. Think away the missionaries who spread Christianity over Europe, the Reformers who reformed it, the Rationalists who secularized it—and what is left of the European tradition?

(2) A second, and equally desperate way out for Winch is to claim that the offensive doctrines—the absolutism, exclusiveness, universalistic claims—whose proscription would, absurdly, exclude most of the European tradition from the European tradition, are not really part of it at all, but 'about it': that, for instance, the belief that some god is the only true god is not part of the belief in him, but a belief *about* the belief—a philosophical accretion, as it were: something which only occurs to the theoretician looking at the belief from the outside, not to the real, practising believer.[1]

There may well be tribal religions concerning which something of this kind is true. The believer subscribes to certain ritually consecrated formulae which, interpreted naturally—i.e., on the assumption that the words employed here have the same meaning: for instance, that the deity created the first man X, where X is also known to be the general tribal ancestor, descent from whom defines membership of the tribe and the moral community. Taking this belief literally, it has certain strange consequences: either, that all men are descendants of X, as the first and only created man, and hence that all men are also members of the tribe—which in fact is in contradiction with the practice of treating foreigners as non-members—or, alternatively, that foreigners are non-human. In fact, and in contradiction of the implications of the

---

[1] In the same broadcast, Winch says: '. . . the idea that these beliefs are universally valid is a view *about* the nature of these beliefs . . .' (Italics mine.) The contrast is, of course, with the *content* of the beliefs. The universalist claims are, according to Winch's view at least at that time, no part of the content of the belief!

legend, the actual practice of the tribe recognizes foreigners as humans who at the same time are not members of the tribe.

In this case, it could certainly be false to credit the tribe with holding the manifest implication of its proclaimed belief (i.e., that either all humanity can lay rightful claim to its tribal membership, or that some beings normally considered human are not really such). The context in which the initial belief is asserted is one which does not lead the believers to ask themselves which of the alternative implications they accept. Hence they cannot really be credited with holding either implication.[1] Only an outsider to the usual practice would ask the question. He might, I suppose, be a member of the tribe acting in, as it were, a different capacity, but the question and its answer cannot really be credited to the tribesmen themselves. (But, as we have noted in connection with Winch's device (1), if the questioner is also a member of the tribe, the supposition that the questioning is only done in a kind of external capacity, as an honorary outsider, as it were, becomes quite absurd when the inner questioners become numerous, a real force within the society, or even the majority!)

But while the treatment of theoretical questions concerning the belief—concerning, to take the crucial example, its exclusive validity, for instance—can generally be credited to a real or honorary 'outsider' in the case of *some* tribal religions, it becomes quite absurd to do so in the case of the literate, scriptural world religions. Consider the following news item:

Pope Paul's ruling on Eucharist.

. . . Pope Paul yesterday published an encyclical letter upholding traditional Catholic doctrine on the Eucharist. . . . the Pope reasserted . . . that the body and blood of Jesus Christ 'are truly and substantially present' in the consecrated bread and wine during Mass. The 6500-word document is believed to be the Pope's reply to a group of West European Catholic theo-

---

[1] It would however be disastrously wrong to conclude from this that what the members of the tribe do believe, does not have the implications in question at all, and must be interpreted as meaning something quite different, something more innocuous. The world is full of beliefs with unacceptable implications which are ignored for the time being, till the moment comes when either the implication becomes attractive, or when its unacceptability can be invoked against the initial belief.

logians who expressed the view that the bread and wine of the
Eucharist were purely symbols . . .

(*The Observer*, 12 September, 1965)

At a pinch, one might perhaps allow Winch to say that the
views of the group of 'West European Catholic Theologians'
were 'about', and not 'within', their faith. But Pope Paul's encyclical letter, while as a reply to the theologians it must be on the
same logical level as their error, is manifestly also an event, a
pronouncement, *within* the Faith itself. This merely illustrates
something terribly obvious, but something also in blatant contradiction with Winch's position: in the Western tradition (among
others), a dialogue between the 'beliefs *within*' and the 'theories
about' religion has become part of religion and belief itself.

Or take another example, crucial for Winch: the exclusiveness
of the Muslim deity. The stress on Its exclusiveness, the classification of un-believers, the prescriptions for their treatment, all
this is manifestly *part* of the religion itself, not a piece of speculation added on from outside by theoreticians.

(3) Winch's third device for coping with the fact that cultures
themselves indulge in self-correction and self-condemnation is to
assert that the corrections themselves *emanate from inside*, from
the practice of the tradition itself, and thus do not lead to the
paradoxes with which his critic would saddle him.[1]

But the paradox cannot be avoided where the self-correction
also involves the view that the previous practice was radically
irrational—the view, roughly, which the Reformers have of the
medieval Church, or the Rationalists of the preceding periods
of religious faith. The point of Winch's claim that the corrections
somehow arise from within the practice is meant to be that each
tradition still fails to rise above that collective solipsism, that
private enclosure, with which in his view they are all credited.

But the view that the correction and its norms arise from inside
is ambiguous and, on either of two possible interpretations, untenable. The two possible interpretations are: (*a*) that the correc-

---

[1] 'Do not the criteria appealed to in the criticism of existing institutions
equally have a history? And in whose society do they have that history?'
Thus Winch, in 'Understanding a primitive society'. The answer he offers
to these rhetorical questions is that it *must* be inside the society itself: '. . .
outside that context we could not begin to grasp what was problematical'.

tions or their norms arise from within the society, *as opposed to other societies*, and (*b*) that they arise from within society as such, *as opposed to some extrasocial realm which houses norms of rationality*.

Taking interpretation (*a*): as a generalization, this is simply false in the most straightforward, empirical sense. Sometimes, indeed, social change and new standards are endogenous. But, for instance, the diffusion of Christianity in early medieval Europe, or the diffusion of industrial-scientific society throughout the world in the modern period, to take two events which have made the world what it is, have, both of them, meant the transformation of societies by ideas and standards which were in no way the fruits of an inner development, but which, on the contrary, arrived from outside.

But let us interpret Winch's point here in the second sense. There is, I suppose, no way of forcing Winch out of that strange collective subjectivism, if he is determined to hold it. Some criteria of rationality seem to me quite independent of any social tradition, but I don't quite see how I could go about establishing this. But here we return to device (2) and the paradox to which Winch finds himself committed: societies themselves, when reforming their previous practices and beliefs, believe themselves to be acting under the guidance of an external, independently valid principle of rationality, and not merely externalizing something emanating from their own nature. So—either they were systematically wrong in their earlier, rejected belief, or they are wrong in their new stance and their belief in its absolute justification. Either way, they contradict Winch. His only way out here is to claim that they speak with a different voice when they claim absolute justification, from the healthy voice in which they assert what are, in Winch's account, more basic, first-order beliefs. But this doctrine of the Two Voices and its total inapplicability to the major literate traditions has already been discussed.

Winch's theory can be destroyed either by appealing to the way in which the major and most interesting traditions actually view themselves, as in the above arguments, or equally by appealing to the multiplicity of existing traditions. This second line of attack, however, calls for some elaboration. Winch's theory and attitude would be, for practical purposes, an acceptable one, *in a certain kind of world*. (It would still be, in an ultimate sense, false, in as far as even in a world designed to fit it, our actual world would remain a possibility.) But it is instructive to sketch out such a world. Ironically, it is a world in which there would be no room for Winch. But no matter: let us nevertheless imagine this world, Winch-less but observed and recorded by a for-the-sake-of-the-argument-Winch. What would this world look like?

Imagine a world populated by a set of fairly small tribes, discontinuous enough to have fairly little to do with each other and —here is an important characteristic of this imaginary world— of roughly equal cognitive power. Not one of these small, fairly discontinuous tribes possesses an understanding of its environment which would, numerically or in power, put it at a decisive advantage *vis-à-vis* the others.

For the sake of the argument we must now imagine at least two philosophers in such a world. One of them is a bad, pre-Wittgensteinian thinker. The other is a kind of proto-Winch. The bad one has succeeded, by luck, accident or endeavour, in travelling from one of the tribes to another, and his reflections have been stimulated by the differences he has observed. He tries to judge the practices of one tribe by the standards of another; or he tries to attain speculatively some standards independent of either; or he tries to combine premises drawn from diverse traditions, or to convert members of one tradition to the beliefs of another, etc.

At this point, he encounters the Ur-Winch, who expostulates: 'My dear friend—you are quite misguided. You are doing nothing but mischief by trying to convert tribe A to the rituals and doctrine of tribe B. The doctrines and rituals of tribe B developed in the natural and social context of tribe B, where they make good sense and perform a valuable role. But transplanted into the quite different social context of A, they make no sense at all. There is no one reality and one set of norms, for all tribes: there are different forms of life, and each of them generates, or contains as an essential part of itself, its own way of distinguishing the real from the unreal, the good from the bad. And do not be misled by the fact that the traditions themselves change! They do, under the impact of new norms emanating from their own practice; but it would be a total misunderstanding to infer from this to suppose that they can or should change under the impact of some outer standard.'

In an ultimate and fundamental sense, the Ur-Winch is still mistaken—because, as indicated, even in this hypothetical world, our real world remains a possibility—but for most practical purposes, *in that kind of a world*, he would be right.

But it is a fact of very considerable interest, that our world is quite unlike this imaginary world. The world we do live in is one of countless, overlapping, interacting traditions—so much so that, for sociological purposes, it is extremely difficult to decide which units are to be isolated for purposes of comparison. (This is, notoriously, one of the crucial problems of the 'comparative method'.) Not small, discontinuous and roughly equal (in size and in cognitive and real power) tribes: but overlapping civilizations of quite unequal cognitive and technical power.

We have seen how the Winchian collective solipsism, derived from the Wittgensteinian treatment of 'forms of life' as ultimate and not susceptible to external validation, is refuted through the fact that some forms of life themselves refuse to treat themselves as ultimate. It is equally refuted by the fact that, in the world as it is, we simply do not have—and have not had for a very, very long time, if indeed we ever did have—those self-contained units, which could be their own standards of intelligibility and reality (and of everything else). What we do have is a set of traditions so complex, so differentiated internally, that we do not know how to delimit our units—indeed any delimitation is largely arbitrary; and these traditions are so sophisticated, so systematically aware of conceptual and moral alternatives, so habituated to interaction, that it is quite meaningless to advise them to turn inwards.

Winch's philosophy illuminates the world we really do live in by sheer contrast; the real contemporary world illuminates Wittgenstein's position by drawing out its crucial implications. These two illuminations are closely connected. It is useful to approach them through considering the strange role of relativism in Winch and Wittgenstein.

For most modern thinkers, relativism is a *problem*: for Winch and Wittgenstein, it is a *solution*. Other thinkers start from the fact of the diversification of belief and morals, and try to find the touchstone of correct belief, etc. This, I think, is the general form of the mainstream of modern Western thought. (For instance: empiricism is, essentially, a theory of the touchstone of truth, or, in later forms, of meaning itself. Materialism is used in a similar way. The various forms of evolutionism claim to have a touchstone which grades degrees of validity, and which is moreover as it were democratically elicited from the specimens to be graded, instead of operating on the material from outside.)

But Wittgenstein and Winch *arrive* at relativism, they don't start out from it, and they arrive at it as a solution to quite another problem, the problem of meaning. Meaning, they say, is not an echo, a reduplication, a structural mirroring of the thing meant, aided perhaps by the struts of a formal framework (*this* was the rejected theory of Wittgenstein's youthful *Tractatus*): it is the possession of a place, a role, in a 'language', a 'form of life', a culture. Wittgenstein arrived at this solution in too exhausted a state to perceive that it raises further enormous problems, given the kinds of complex, interlocking, competing, internally diversified and rapidly changing cultures which in fact make up our world. Nor did he seem to perceive the terribly obvious truth that *this* problem provides most of philosophy with its content: for had he noticed this, he could not have seen his own particular arrival at a position, which is a solution to him and a problem for almost everyone else, as *the* paradigm of philosophy, or as its euthanasia.

It is both characteristic and profoundly revealing that, despite the enormous importance which the notion of a 'form of life' plays in his philosophy, Wittgenstein in *The Philosophical Investigations* gives *no* example of it. Is *English* a form of life? Or only subcultures within the great world of English-speakers, such as, for instance, that of Cambridge dons, of the Gorbals, of West African patois? Or must we, on the contrary go to some larger *Kulturkreis*? Or would only self-contained tribes do?

As far as Wittgenstein himself is concerned, it is quite manifest from his writings that he did not bother to ask himself this obvious question. He had found a solution to his particular problem, the problem of how words come to have meaning: this solution was in terms of a highly abstract model, i.e., the possession of a role in a 'form of life', and although 'forms of life' were the cornerstone of this model, he felt no need to provide examples of them. In this, he was entirely true to himself. In his youth, he had elaborated a philosophy of meaning in terms of an abstract model in which notions such as that of a 'fact' or 'thing' played crucial parts. No examples at all were given: and the philosophy collapsed when he and others tried to find some examples, failed and had the grace to ask themselves why they failed. The philosophy was then replaced by a new model, that of 'forms of life'. But once again—no examples! It is deeply ironic that Wittgenstein's general diagnosis of faulty philosophy is the conceptual intoxication with an abstract model, unchecked by comparison with real examples. His diagnosis certainly has at least one correct application.

The importance of Winch lies in the fact that he does try to relate the abstract model which he has inherited, to concrete examples.

If what matters is cultures, and these are the objects of the studies of social scientists, it follows that philosophy and social sciences have the same subject matter, and that the correct method in the one field is also the correct method in the other. From this, he tries—quite mistakenly, in my view—to inform social scientists of the correct method in their field, by deduction from what he considers the correct method in philosophy; while the proper procedure is, it seems to me, to argue the other way, and conclude to the mistaken nature of the method in philosophy, from its inapplicability to the concrete objects of the social sciences.

The importance of Winch lies in his attempt to relate the abstract model to reality; his error lies in doing great violence to reality in the process, instead of correcting the model by reference to reality. Some of the features of the real world which are incompatible with the model have already been stressed. One crucial one which remains to be stressed is this: in the world as we know it, cultures are extremely unequal in cognitive power. Some possess concepts and methods which enable them to attain some degree of understanding of their environment, and some possess such an understanding only to a minimal degree. To deny this cognitive inequality is an affectation, which can at most be sustained in the study, but not in real life. (Here is another profound irony of Wittgensteinianism: it fails the philosophic test which it has itself popularized, namely, whether a view can really be held, in the business of living, as opposed to being held merely in the special conditions of a kind of philosopher's licence. This is closely connected with the irony mentioned above: the reason why a view cannot be held outside the context of real life, is of course connected with a failure to look at real instances of the abstract model.) No one, least of all those who are deprived of it, has any doubts about the superior cognitive effectiveness of the 'scientific outlook'.

Similarly, no one really has any doubts about the cognitive inferiority of the pre-scientific outlook. It is in this obverse form that the situation comes to the notice of the anthropologist, of course: he frequently has to report beliefs of the form 'ox equals cucumber', 'wine equals blood', 'witchcraft causes death', etc. Are beliefs of this kind to be described as false and inferior?

Winch, quite consistently with his symmetrical relativism ('symmetrical' in the sense of being egalitarian as between cultures, refusing to judge any of them in terms of another or in terms of a supposedly external norm), rejects this condemnation. In the context of the practices and institutions in which they occur, these assertions—he holds—are *not* absurd. It is the interpretations which find them so which are at fault.

The first thing to note about this is that this 'principle of invariably benevolent interpretation' is in conflict both with the actual practice of social scientists, and with *any* possible practice on their part. In fact, they continue to translate or give account of the belief of distant cultures in terms which often make them plainly absurd. Cucumbers are not oxen, the laying-on of royal hands does not have any therapeutic effects, etc., etc. Why do we not admonish anthropologists, historians, etc., who come back with such reports, for translating so badly (or, perhaps, for translating at all!) as to give us the impression of absurdity? It is supremely noteworthy that Winch himself does not admonish Professor Evans-Prichard, whose account of Azande witchcraft he uses, for misdescribing, or mistranslating, Azande beliefs; he merely criticizes him for his tendency to suppose those beliefs false. Yet *if* Evans-Prichard is basically at fault in being tempted to suppose Azande beliefs to be false (as we are all tempted, including, I believe, contemporary Azande), then surely his mistake occurred earlier—in his account of the beliefs, which seems to imply that Azande have faith in the causal connectedness of magical practices and certain consequences.

But, in fact, one cannot avoid these translations, which give the game away and highlight the strangeness of the belief. Many things over and above the belief in a causal connection may be involved—and, indeed, generally are—but that belief is *also* involved. Evans-Prichard's account, which is left unchallenged by Winch, consists in large part of showing how these beliefs survive falsification. This would be redundant and irrelevant, if they were not in fact frequently falsified! The anthropologist's account, far from being committed to respect the truth, in its context, of the belief, as Winch claims, is in fact based on a recognition of its falsehood. Anthropologists do not generally give complex accounts of how a tribe manages to sustain the faith in fire burning, wood floating, etc.: indeed, it would require an anthropological account if the tribe managed to sustain a *denial* of these.

Nor is the anthropologist at liberty simply to seek some other, non-absurd translation. It is part of the role of witchcraft beliefs that it is held possible to *cause* harm in certain ways. Winch's 'principle of universal benevolent interpretation' would exclude, quite *a priori*, important social phenomena such as the social use of absurdity, ambiguity, etc. An absurd formula may, for instance, be used to highlight the solemnity of an occasion. A translation which emptied it of its absurdity, treating it, for instance, simply as the announcement of impending solemnity, would miss the fact that the absurdity is used as a means of conveying that something special is happening, and hence must be present, *as* absurdity.

The example of trans-substantiation is instructive and useful, particularly as it is drawn from the local culture and thus does not call for specialized knowledge for the appreciation of the issues involved. As we have seen, the recognized authority within the religion himself solemnly excludes 'symbolic' interpretations of it, such as the benevolent-anthropological one. Perhaps Winch would not accept the papal ruling, holding it to be an event *within* the 'form of life', and as such not binding on an outside philosophic observer. But surely any adequate account of the Catholic form of life must include a recognition of the fact that, whatever subtleties are present in the interpretation of a Catholic intellectual, to a peasant the doctrine means just what it says, which is highlighted by the fact that, as the papal letter stresses, the simple believer is distressed when encountering the sophisticated interpretations within the fold itself.[1] And let us remember: the point

---

[1] I have argued the case against the Principle of Universal Sympathy in anthropological interpretation, at greater length in 'Concepts and society', *Proceedings of the Fifth World Congress of Sociology*, Washington, 1962.

about miracles is that they are *miracles*. They are such not merely to the unsympathetic observer but also, and above all, to the participants.

Let us return to the interesting and illuminating question of relativism. For Wittgenstein, as indicated, it was a solution and not a problem. It was a rather special kind of relativism, with as it were only one term: in the abstract, a general relativism of 'forms of life' was formulated, but in application, only one form of life was considered—that of the academic philosopher himself, and his disciples. (This was the main basis of the appeal of this philosophy: it provided a justification for a 'form of life' which in fact was threatened by the implication of scientific revisions of our world-view. The philosophy in question provided an omnibus justification of the old view, and facilitated the discounting of the new implication by calling them 'metaphysical', and maintaining that they had the same root as quite artificial, genuinely 'meta-physical' revisions which were re-invented, as straw men, for the purpose.)

Winch has considered other forms of life and the implications of their existence and investigation (though not the implications of the fact that they live non-isolated lives and interact intensely and violently with each other and with our own 'form of life', however that is to be delimited). Consequently he *does* face rela-tivism as a problem, not merely as a solution. He accepts it. This acceptance can be usefully considered a kind of solution. It is— and this is important for the purposes of my argument—a most *symmetrical* solution. It does not favour one form of life over another. It treats them all as equal.

My main contention here is that *no* symmetrical solution of this problem is acceptable. (The evolutionists had a symmetrical solution, which was the main source of the appeal of their doc-trine: it 'overcame' relativism by seeing various forms of life as members of one great series, such that later or superior mem-bers of the series incorporated all or most of the merits of earlier members, while adding something more. In this way, all forms of life had some validity, but there was some over-all yard-stick all the same. This solution is no longer available, if only because forms of life cannot be arranged into any neat and unique series in this manner.) Winch's solution is not merely symmetrical, like that of the evolutionists, but also rather static; all forms of

life are equal. Even if they are credited with change, they all go
their own ways. The starting point of one is not the terminus of
another, they form no grand series.

When formulated in a very abstract manner, I doubt whether
the problem of relativism has a solution. In this it may resemble
the problem of solipsism, of which indeed it may be seen as a
special variant, one in which cultural collectivities replace individual islands of consciousness. But if one considers the world as
it really is—something which Winch refrains from doing—we see
that there is a kind of solution.

The philosophical significance of the scientific-industrial 'form
of life', whose rapid global diffusion is the main event of our time,
is that for all practical purposes it does provide us with a solution
of the problem of relativism—though a highly unsymmetrical
one. (It is for this reason that no symmetrical solution can be
entertained.) The cognitive and technical superiority of one form
of life is so manifest, and so loaded with implications for the satisfaction of human wants and needs—and, for better or worse, for
power—that it simply cannot be questioned.

If a doctrine conflicts with the acceptance of the superiority of
scientific-industrial societies over others, then it really is out. This
point must not be misunderstood.[1] The cognitive and technical
superiority does not imply or bring with it superiority in any other
field. What it does do is to bring along the *possibility*—no more—
of a certain material liberation. On any moderately realistic estimate of human nature, as long as the price of decent behaviour
was, in effect, total self-sacrifice (which was the case in the conditions of scarcity which characterize pre-industrial society), the
prospects of decent behaviour were negligible. But thanks to the
cognitive and technical effectiveness of industrial society, the
possibility, though no more, is now present.

This effectiveness of scientific industrial civilization and its
diffusion are the central facts of our time. It must be accepted,
but it does not uniquely determine the other aspects of our existence. The first task of thought is to understand and perceive

[1] I hope it is not necessary to guard against the misunderstanding that
what is being claimed is some version of a 'racialist' superiority of the societies
in which the scientific-industrial form of life emerged. The form of life
occurs, and is manifestly independent of the 'genetic' composition of the
populations involved.

the limits within which we operate, and the alternatives they offer.

For this reason, any symmetrical solution of the problem of relativism—which automatically ignores the crucial asymmetry of our situation—is erroneous and harmful. If in addition it obstructs social understanding by making sympathetic acceptance an obligation for all interpretation, by excluding the very possibility of false consciousness, in a quite *a priori* manner, then so much the worse. Wittgensteinianism proper led to a narcissistic and sterile observation of the alleged conceptual customs of one's own 'form of life'—sterile because, in fact, philosophic questions are *not* generated by misunderstandings of the working of concepts. The more thorough and realistic—but not realistic enough —application of this philosophy by Winch leads to a misunderstanding both of the real social situation—of the way real 'forms of life' are related to each other in history and notably in the twentieth century—and of the methods really employed by social scientists.

8 HANS ALBERT

The Myth of Total Reason: Dialectical Claims
in the Light of Undialectical Criticism[1]

1. DIALECTICS VERSUS POSITIVISM

The problem-area of the connection between theory and practice has repeatedly aroused the attention of philosophers and social scientists. It has led to the debate which persists even today, concerning the significance and possibility of *value-freedom*, a debate with whose commencement and first critical phase the name of Max Weber is particularly linked. On the other hand, it is has given rise to the discussion on the meaning of *experiment* for the social sciences whereby the methodological claim to autonomy of a cultural-scientific [*geisteswissenschaftlich*] character was placed in question, as is still the case with these disciplines. It is not surprising that such questions represent a point of departure for philosophical reflections into the problems of the sciences.

In recent times, the social sciences have developed to a considerable extent under the influence (direct and indirect) of positivistic trends. The social sciences have positivistically determined solutions to these problems, and have worked out new forms of corresponding methodological conception. However, one can in no way claim that these views have prevailed everywhere today. This is not even the case in the English-speaking world where one would most readily expect it. In the German-speaking world it is difficult to clarify the situation in view of the influence of various philosophical currents in the social sciences. In any case, the newer positivism seems to have had only a minor effect here, possibly no stronger than historicism and neo-Kantianism, or than phenomenology and hermeneutics. Finally one should not underrate here the

---

[1] First published in *Der Positivismusstreit in der deutschen Soziologie*. Translated by Glyn Adey and David Frisby.

influence of the Hegelian inheritance, either direct, or mediated through Marxism, an inheritance which has, moreover, asserted itself in other ways too. Recently, an attack directed against positivistic trends has been made from this side and analysing it can be fruitful since it leads to the heart of the above-mentioned problem-area.[1]

We see in this attack the view that certain difficulties which emerge in the course of the realization of the scientific programme advanced in such positivistic trends can be overcome if one is prepared to revert to ideas which stem from the Hegelian tradition. We might first of all confront this attempt at a dialectical overcoming of so-called positivistic weaknesses of the social sciences, with the question of the *problem-situation* from which the author sets out. More specifically, we should consider the question of the difficulties inherent in this problem-situation; namely, in what respect and to what extent, in the opinion of Habermas, a science of the 'positivistic' type must fall down. A further question would then be that of the *alternative* which he develops, of its usefulness for the solution of these difficulties and its tenability; and finally perhaps one could go beyond this and raise the question of *other possible solutions*.

The problem situation from which Habermas sets out can be characterized in roughly the following manner: In so far as the social sciences develop in a manner that brings them closer to the positivistic scientific ideal—and today this is already to a large extent the case—then they grow more like the natural sciences. This is particularly true in the sense that in both types of science a purely technically-rooted cognitive interest dominates,[2] and theory

---

[1] In connection with the controversy between Karl Popper and Theodor W. Adorno at the internal working session of the German Sociological Association in Tübingen in 1961 (see Karl R. Popper, 'The logic of the social sciences', and Theodor W. Adorno, 'On the logic of the social sciences') Jürgen Habermas published (under the title 'The analytical theory of science and dialectics. Postscript to the controversy between Popper and Adorno') a critical contribution to Adorno's *Festschrift*. Soon afterwards *Theorie und Praxis: Sozialphilosophische Studien*, Neuwied/Berlin, 1963, appeared which merits interest in the same connection. (Ed. note: *Theory and Practice* has now been published Boston and London, 1974.) What was hinted at in Adorno appears to become clearer in Habermas.

[2] This notion has central significance for the understanding of Habermas's thought. It is constantly reformulated in his work; see *Theory and Practice*, loc. cit., pp. 60 f., p. 75, p. 114, pp. 254 ff., pp. 263 f., pp. 267 f., and

is then carried out 'with the attitude of the technician'. Social sciences which are orientated in this way are no longer in a position to offer normative viewpoints and conceptions for practical orientation. They are only able to give technical recommendations for the realization of pre-given ends: that is, they are only able to influence the selection of means. The rationalization of practice which they make possible only refers then to their technical aspect. Thus we are dealing with a restricted rationality in contrast to that produced by earlier doctrines—namely by those which continued to unite normative orientation and technical direction.

The usefulness of a social science orientated in this way is thus in no way in itself denied by Habermas. But he sees the danger of its limitations not being recognized when a simple identification of technical and practical use takes place, and when thereby an attempt is made to reduce the more comprehensive practical to narrower technical problems, as would seem to be the case given the perspective of the 'positivistic' theory of science. The restriction of rationality to the use of means which is legitimized by this view, entails that the other aspect of the practical problematic, the realm of ends, falls prey to pure decisionism, the whim of mere decisions not directed by reason. The *decisionism* of unanalysed, arbitrary decisions [*Entscheidungen*] in the realm of practice corresponds to the *positivism* of the restriction to pure value-free theories in the realm of cognition, where technological problems are not at issue. 'The price of the economy of the selection of means is an unconstrained decisionism in the choice of the highest goals.'[1]

Through rational reflection the images of mythological interpretations of the world can penetrate unhindered into the realm which is liberated through the reduction of rationality. Thereby positivism provides, de facto, not only for the rationalization of the technical but, over and above this—even if unintentionally—

---

passim; further: 'The analytical theory of science and dialectics', pp. 161 f., pp. 166 ff., pp. 184 ff. and *passim*.

[1] Habermas, *Theorie und Praxis*, loc. cit., p. 265; see also pp. 46 f. Similarly expressed metaphorically: 'A disinfected reason is purged of all moments of enlightened volition; external to itself, it has externalized—alienated—its own life. And life deprived of spirit leads an existence of arbitrariness that is a ghostly spirit indeed—all under the name of "decision" ' (p. 263).

it provides for the remythologizing of the ungrasped aspect of the practical problematic. This is a consequence from which of course the representatives of these views recoil. They respond with a critique of ideology which does not serve the shaping of reality, but instead the elucidation of consciousness, and for that reason does not really seem intelligible in terms of the conception of science upon which it is based, and which is directed towards technical rationality. Here it becomes apparent, in Habermas's view, that positivism tends to transcend the limitations which it places upon rationality, in the direction of a more comprehensive conception, one which involves the convergence of reason and decision.[1] But this tendency can only achieve a breakthrough if the limitations of positivism themselves are broken down, if its restricted reason is overcome dialectically by a reason which brings about the unity of theory and practice and thereby the transcendence of the dualism of cognition and evaluation, of facts and decisions and the abolition of the positivistic division consciousness. Apparently only this dialectical reason is in a position to transcend both the decisionism [*Dezisionismus*] of mere deciding [*Entscheidung*] and the positivism of pure theory, in order 'to comprehend society as a historically constituted totality for the purposes of a critical maieutics of political practice'.[2] Basically Habermas is concerned with regaining the lost realm by recourse to the Hegelian inheritance preserved in Marxism: that is, with regaining practice-orientated dialectical reason for rational thought.

[1] The term 'positivism' is used very widely here—even, for example, for Karl Popper's view which differs from orthodox positivistic view on basic points. Popper himself has therefore constantly protested against his inclusion in this group. It also becomes clear that such imputation can lead to misunderstanding precisely in view of the problems which Habermas deals with.

[2] The passage is taken from the chapter 'Between Philosophy and Science: Marxism as a Critique' in the above quoted book by Habermas, p. 205. It stands, therefore, in the context of an analysis of Marx, but in my view it represents very clearly what Habermas himself expects of dialectics, namely, a philosophy of history with practical intent, as he writes elsewhere. This also explains his uneasiness concerning the analysis of Marxism which failed to take into account the unity of the object: society as *totality*, its *dialectical* interpretation as a *historical* process and the relationship of theory *to practice*. On this reference to practice see also Habermas, loc. cit., pp. 78 f.

The basic lines of his critique of the 'positivistic' conception of science in the social sciences have now been described as have the claims which he associates with his dialectical supercession of this conception. We must now examine his objections and propositions in detail in order to see to what extent they appear tenable.[1]

2. ON THE PROBLEM OF THEORY FORMATION

In his confrontation with the analytical theory of science Habermas takes as his starting point the distinction between the *functionalist concept of system* and the *dialectical concept of totality* which he regards as basic but difficult to explicate. He assigns to each concept one of the two typical forms of social science with which he is concerned—analytical and dialectical social science—in order to discuss the difference between them. As regards the former, he discusses four problem-areas, namely: the relationship between theory and object, between theory and experience, between theory and history and between science and practice. The last of these four problem-areas is then analysed again in more detail in the three following sections of his essay and here the problem of value-freedom, and the so-called basis-problem, come to the fore.

It is well known that the dialectical concept of totality which forms the starting-point of Habermas's discussion constantly recurs in theoreticians who follow in Hegel's footsteps. Apparently they look upon this concept as being in some way fundamental. It is therefore all the more regrettable that Habermas makes no attempt to clarify this concept, which he strongly emphasizes and frequently uses, more precisely. He merely says of it that it is to be understood 'in the strictly dialectical sense which prevents one from approaching the whole organically according with the statement: that it is more than the sum of its parts'. Nor,

---

[1] Here it is useful to refer to the above-mentioned postscript to the Popper–Adorno controversy in which he formulates his objections to Popper's critical rationalism in a precise form. Even with reference to this view he regards his arguments against 'positivism' as sound.

he claims, is totality 'a class which might be determined in its logical extension by a collection of all the elements which it comprises'. From this he believes he can conclude that the dialectical concept of the whole is not affected by the critical investigations of the concepts of wholeness such as, for example, were carried out by Ernest Nagel.[1]

Nagel's studies, however, are in no way restricted to a concept of the whole which one could simply dismiss in this context as irrelevant. Rather, he analyses various concepts which, one would imagine, might be worthy of consideration for a theoretician concerning himself with totalities of a social character.[2] Habermas, however, observes that the dialectical concept of the whole exceeds the limits of formal logic, 'in whose shadowy realm dialectics itself cannot appear as anything other than a chimera'.[3] From the context in which this statement appears one may conclude that Habermas wants to challenge the possibility of logically analysing his concept of totality. Without closer elucidation one will no longer be able to see in such a thesis how to protect both the expression from an 'arbitrary decision' [Dezision]—to use this term again which has proved its worth

[1] See Ernest Nagel, *The Structure of Science*, London, 1961, pp. 380 ff., an analysis to which Habermas refers explicitly. One could also consult Karl Popper, *The Poverty of Historicism*, London, 1957, pp. 76 ff. and *passim*, a study which he surprisingly did not take into account, although it refers precisely to the historical-philosophical holism which he himself represents; further, Jürgen v. Kempski, *Zur Logik der Ordnungsbegriffe, besonders in den Sozialwissenschaften*, 1952, reprinted in *Theorie und Realität*, edited by H. Albert, Tübingen, 1964.

[2] Nagel asserts that the vocabulary of wholeness is rather ambiguous, metaphorical and vague and therefore can hardly be judged without clarification. This would also apply to Habermas's 'totality'. Even if Adorno's somewhat vague remarks about totality, with which Habermas begins his article, in no way permit a firm classification of his concept. I would still assume that if Habermas had read Nagel's presentation more carefully he would have come across at least related concepts which could have further assisted him. For example, pp. 391 ff. In any case, his short reference, which creates the impression that Nagel's analyses are irrelevant for his own concept of 'totality' is completely inadequate especially since he himself has no equivalent at his disposal. It is unintelligible that the rejection of the alternatives 'organic whole' and 'class' can be sufficient to exclude the question of a possible logical analysis.

[3] Habermas, 'The analytical theory of science and dialectics', p. 155.

against the positivists—and the concept from the analysis. Anyone possessing sufficient mistrust will detect in this an immunization strategy which is based on the expectation that what ever recoils from analysis will escape criticism. Be that as it may; for Habermas the non-explicability of this concept seems particularly important since from it apparently stems the non-explicability of the distinction between 'totality' in the dialectical and 'system' in the functionalist sense, a distinction which he seems to regard as basic.[1] This distinction is particularly concerned with his comparison of two types of social science since he fosters the problematic notion that a *general* theory must 'refer to the social system as a whole'.

With respect to the relationship between theory and object he explains the distinction between the two types of social science in the following manner. Within the framework of empirical-scientific theory the concept of system and the theoretical statements which explicate it remain 'external' to the realm of experience analysed. Theories, he says, are here mere ordering schemata *randomly constructed* in a syntactically binding framework, utilizable if the real manifoldness of an object-domain *accommodates* them; but this is in principle fortuitous. Here then the impression of randomness, whim and chance is evoked through the mode of expression selected. The possibility of applying strict testing procedures, whose result is largely independent of subjective will, is made ridiculous and this is presumably connected with the fact that it is later ruled out for dialectical theory. The reader is made to think that the latter theory, on the other hand, is *necessarily*

---

[1] He says of it that it cannot be directly signified, 'for in the language of formal logic it would have to be dissolved, while in the language of dialectics it would have to be transcended'. But it may be possible to find a language which would not be overtaxed. What grounds are there for this idea which so quickly establishes itself, namely, that it is not possible at any cost? And incidentally, to what extent is the language of formal logic supposed to 'dissolve' something? Habermas seems to imagine here that with its help one can make a distinction disappear which is present in the actual usage of two concepts. That is certainly possible—in an inadequate analysis. But where does the idea originate that there cannot be an adequate analysis? Here one may assume a certain connection with the unfortunate relationship which Hegelians in general are wont to have with logic which, on the one hand, they underestimate in importance and on the other hand, they overestimate in its ('falsifying') effect.

and internally[1] in accord with reality and thus does not require factual validation.[2]

But for dialectical theory, on the contrary, the claim is made that it does *not* proceed so 'indifferently' in the face of its object domain as is the case in the exact natural sciences where, it is admitted, this is successful. It 'must, in advance, ensure' of the 'appropriateness of [its] categories for the object, 'because ordering schemata, which co-variant quantities only accommodate by chance, fail to meet our interest in society' which, in this case, is apparently *not* a purely technical one, an interest in the domination of nature. For, as soon as the cognitive interest is directed beyond this, says Habermas, 'the indifference of the system in the face of its area of application changes suddenly into a distortion of the object. The structure of the object which has been neglected in favour of a general methodology condemns the theory which it cannot penetrate to irrelevance.'[3] The diagnosis is: 'distortion of the object'; the suggested cure: one must grasp the social life-context as a *totality* which, moreover, determines research itself. In this way, however, social science forfeits its alleged freedom in the choice of categories and models. Theory 'in its construction and in the structure of its concept has to measure up to the object' (*Sache*), and 'in the method the object has to be treated in accord with its significance', a demand which by its nature can 'only be fulfilled dialectically'. The *circle*, produced when one claims that it is only the scientific apparatus that reveals an object whose structure must nevertheless *previously* have been understood to

[1] At this point agreement with the typical arguments of social scientific essentialism is blatant; see, for example, Werner Sombart, *Die drei Nationalökonomien*, München and Leipzig, 1930, pp. 193 ff. and *passim*; also my critique 'Der moderne Methodenstreit und die Grenzen des Methodenpluralismus', in *Jahrbuch für Sozialwissenschaft*, Band 13, 1962; reprinted as chapter 6 of my essay collection, *Marktsoziologie und Entscheidungslogik*, Neuwied/Berlin, 1967.

[2] The section closes with the sentence, 'Reflection which is not satisfied with this state of affairs is inadmissible.' In the next section this 'lack of satisfaction' is claimed for dialectical theory. The word 'satisfy' suggests a restriction. It will not be so easy to produce evidence that Karl Popper—who is presumably the addressee of these objections—wishes to exclude the possibility of speculation. On the contrary, however, it is precisely the dialecticians who frequently seem to desire to 'satisfy' themselves with theories whose unverifiability they believe they can take for granted.

[3] Habermas, loc. cit., p. 158.

some degree is 'only to be explored dialectically in conjunction with the natural hermeneutics of the social life-world', so that here 'the hermeneutic explication of meaning' will replace the hypothetico-deductive system.[1]

The problem which Habermas here takes as his starting point is apparently connected with the fact that in analytical social science a *one-sided technical cognitive* interest leads to distortion of the object. At this point we come to the thesis, already mentioned, which provides him with one of his most basic objections to current procedures in the social sciences. In so doing he adopts an *instrumentalist* interpretation of the empirical sciences and ignores the fact that the philosopher of science, to whom presumably his objections are basically addressed, has explicitly dealt with this interpretation and has attempted to demonstrate its dubious nature.[2] The fact that informative theories of a nomological character have proved themselves to be technically utilizable in many spheres is in no way a sufficient index of the cognitive interest upon which they are based.[3]

An unbiased interpretation of this state of affairs can be geared to the fact that from a deeper penetration into the structure of reality one can expect insights which are also of importance for the orientation of action, for a form of intercourse with real factors (*Gegebenheiten*). The methodology of the theoretical empirical sciences seeks, above all, to grasp law-like connections,

[1] Habermas, loc. cit., p. 158.

[2] In Popper's view it is as dubious as the earlier essentialism which above all remains active in cultural scientific thought; see Karl Popper, 'Three Views Concerning Human Knowledge' (1956), reprinted in his essay collection, *Conjectures and Refutations*, London, 1963, and also other essays in this volume; further, his article, 'Die Zielsetzung der Erfahrungswissenschaft', *Ratio* I, 1957, reprinted in *Theorie und Realität*, loc. cit.; further, Paul K. Feyerabend, 'Realism and Instrumentalism', in *The Critical Approach to Science and Philosophy*, Glencoe, 1964. In fact, Habermas's instrumentalism seems to be more restrictive than the views of this sort that have been criticized in the above-mentioned essays.

[3] It appears superfluous to point out that the personal interests of the researchers are largely not directed towards technical success. Habermas presumably does not wish to dispute anything of the sort. Apparently he is thinking more of an institutionally anchored or methodically channelled interest from which the researcher, despite other personal motives, can in no way withdraw. But he does not provide sufficient evidence for this. I shall return to this point.

and to suggest informative hypotheses concerning the structure of reality, and thereby the structure of actual events. Empirical checks and, connected with these, predictions are made in order to ascertain whether the connections are as we presume them to be. Thus our 'prior knowledge' of course can at once be placed in question. Here a fundamental role is played by the idea that we can learn from our mistakes by exposing the theories in question to the risk of destruction at the hands of the facts.[1] Interventions into real events can serve thereby to create situations which make the risk relatively high. Technical successes produced in connection with research can be attributed to the fact that one has in part drawn closer to the real connections. To a certain extent, then, this is rephrased by Habermas 'dialectically' in the idea that a one-sided cognitive interest is present here. The most conspicuous consequences of scientific development, which moreover can easily be interpreted realistically, are made the occasion for reinterpreting the cognitive efforts accordingly and 'denouncing' them—as one would presumably have to express it in neo-Hegelian terms—as purely technical.[2]

Let us for the present take the alleged dominance of technical cognitive interests for granted. As long as it is present, says Habermas, theory remains indifferent towards its object domain. But if interest is directed beyond this then this indifference changes suddenly into the distortion of the object. How can a change of interest achieve this? Does the type of proposition perhaps or the structure of the theory change? How may we conceive of this? Habermas gives us no indications. In any case, he robs the social scientist who proceeds analytically of any hope of altering his desperate situation in any way through an

[1] See the works of Karl Popper.

[2] The instrumentalistic interpretation of the natural sciences seems to be endemic among Hegelians as is the notoriously poor acquaintance with logic. One finds both, for instance, well developed in Benedetto Croce's *Logik als Wissenschaft vom reinen Begriff*, Tübingen, 1930, where the natural sciences in principle are accredited only with 'pseudo-concepts' without cognitive significance (pp. 216 ff.), formal logic is devalued as being rather meaningless (pp. 86 ff.) and philosophy and history are identified with one another in a curious manner as genuine knowledge (pp. 204 ff.). See Jürgen v. Kempski, *Brechungen*, Hamburg, 1964, pp. 85 f. In Habermas one finds the tendency to link together both the technical rationality of science with the 'logic of subsumption' and the universal rationality of philosophy with dialectics.

appropriate alteration of his interest unless he goes over to dialectics and in so doing relinquishes his freedom to choose categories and models.[1] The naïve advocate of analytical modes of procedure will be inclined to adopt the view that he can most readily guarantee the appropriateness of his categories by subjecting the theories in which they play a role to rigorous attempts at validation.[2] This appears insufficient to Habermas. He thinks that he can guarantee the appropriateness of his categories in advance. This seems to be prescribed for him by his cognitive interest, which is of a different nature. What he has written in this connection points to the fact that he would like to start out from everyday language and from the stock of everyday knowledge in order to gain a mode of entry to correct theory formation.[3]

I am not aware of any objection which one could make against recourse to everyday knowledge unless it is linked with any false claims. Even the natural sciences have distanced themselves from the empirical knowledge of everyday life only with the help of methods which rendered this knowledge problematic and subjected it to criticism—partially under the influence of ideas which radically contradicted this 'knowledge' and were corroborated in the face of 'common-sense'.[4] Why should things be different in the social sciences? Why should one not here too be able to draw upon ideas which contradict everyday knowledge? Does Habermas wish to exclude this? Does he wish to declare common sense—or somewhat more sublimely expressed 'the natural hermeneutics of the social life-world' to be sacrosanct?

[1] If this freedom is greater in the type of social science which he criticizes then one must still presume that the theories preferred by the dialectician are included in this margin of freedom so that, at least by chance, he can stumble across the essential. Against this only the thesis concerning the distortion of the object seems to help.

[2] See, for example, my article 'Die Problematik der ökonomischen Perspektive', in *Zeitschrift für die gesamte Staatswissenschaft*, 117, 1961, also my introduction 'Probleme der Theoriebildung', in *Theorie und Realität*, loc. cit.

[3] It is interesting to see here how Habermas approaches not merely the hermeneutic-phenomenological trends in philosophy but at the same time those of the linguistic bent whose methods lend themselves to a dogmatization of the knowledge incorporated in everyday language. On both one finds relevant critical analyses in Jürgen v. Kempski's interesting collection of essays, *Brechungen. Kritische Versuche zur Philosophie der Gegenwart*, loc. cit.

[4] See the essays of Karl Popper in the volume quoted, *Conjectures and Refutations*.

If not, then wherein does the specificity of his method lie? To what extent is 'the object' (*Sache*) treated more in accord with its own significance than in the usual methods of the empirical sciences? It seems to me that certain prejudices are being underlined here. Does Habermas perhaps wish to deny *a priori* his assent to theories which do not owe their emergence to a 'dialectical exploration' in conjunction with this 'natural hermeneutics'? Or does he wish to present them as being inessential? What can be done if, after empirical examination, other theories stand the test better than those with a better pedigree? Or should these theories be so constructed that they cannot be destroyed in principle? Many of Habermas's statements suggest that he wishes to give preference to pedigree over performance. In general the method of dialectical social science makes at times a more conservative than critical impression just as this dialectic looks, in many respects, more conservative than it pretends to be.

3. THEORY, EXPERIENCE AND HISTORY

Habermas accuses the analytical conception of tolerating 'only one type of experience', namely, 'the controlled observation of physical behaviour which is set up in an isolated field under reproducible conditions by subjects inter-changeable at will'.[1] Dialectical social theory opposes such restriction. 'If the formal construction of theory, of the structure of concepts, of the choice of categories and models is not able to follow blindly the abstract rules of a general methodology, but rather ... must, in advance, measure up to a preformed object, then theory cannot merely be united subsequently with an experience which is then of course restricted.' The insights to which dialectical social science has recourse, stem from 'the fund of pre-scientifically accumulated experience', apparently the same experience as that to which reference was made in connection with natural hermeneutics. This prior experience, which relates to society as a totality, 'shapes the outline of theory' which 'cannot clash with an experience however restricted it may be'; but, on the other hand, it need not forego thought which cannot be checked empirically either. Precisely its central statements are not to be 'wholly resolved by empirical findings'. This seems however to be compensated for

---

[1] Habermas, 'The analytical theory of science and dialectics', p. 159.

by the fact that, on the one hand, even the 'functionalist concept of the system' cannot be checked while, on the other hand, 'the hermeneutic anticipation of totality' . . . must 'in the course of the explication establish itself as correct'. The concepts which are otherwise 'merely' analytically valid must 'be legitimated in experience', whereby of course the latter is not to be identified with controlled observation. Here the impression of a more appropriate, if not even a more rigorous validation procedure is created than is otherwise normal in the empirical sciences.

In order to judge these objections and proposals one has to be quite clear what is the problem under discussion here. That the conception which Habermas criticizes tolerates 'only one type of experience' is, as it stands, simply false, no matter how familiar to its critics who are orientated to the cultural sciences, the reference to a too narrow concept of experience may be. Rather, for theory formation, this conception needs to make no restrictions in this respect—in contrast to the conception which Habermas upholds which commits one to a recourse to natural hermeneutics. The 'channelled' experience to which he alludes[1] becomes relevant for a definite task—namely, that of checking a theory on the basis of facts in order to ascertain its factual verification. For such a check it is essential to find situations which discriminate as much as possible.[2] The result of this is merely that one has occasion to favour such situations if it is intended to attempt a serious examination. Stated differently, the less a situation discriminates with regard to a certain theory the less it is useful for testing the theory. If no relevant consequences result from the theory for the situation in question then this situation is useless in this respect. Can the dialectical view raise objection to this? We should bear in mind that according to Habermas even a dialectical theory cannot clash with experience, however restricted it may be. Up to this point his polemic against the

[1] I do not intend to discuss at this point whether he has characterized it adequately in detail but instead I wish to indicate the possibility of utilizing statistical methods in order to perform non-experimental checks and further draw attention to the fact that the whole realm of symbolic and consequently also verbal behaviour is to be classified along with 'physical' behaviour.

[2] See Karl Popper, *The Logic of Scientific Discovery*, London, 1959, *passim*, as well as his essay 'Science: Conjectures and Refutations', in his above mentioned essay collection where the risk of destruction at the hands of facts is stressed.

narrow type of experience seems to me to rest largely on misunderstanding.

The further question of whether one must forego 'thoughts' which are not verifiable in this way can be answered negatively without further ado. No one expects such a sacrifice of the dialectician; not even for example in the name of the modern theory of science. One can simply expect that theories which claim to make statements about social reality are not so constructed as to admit random possibilities, so they make no allowance for actual social events. Why should the thoughts of the dialecticians not be convertible into theories which in principle are verifiable?[1]

As far as the derivation of dialectical insights from 'prescientifically accumulated experience' is concerned we have just had the opportunity of discussing the question of emphasis upon this connection. The advocate of the view which Habermas criticizes has, as we have said, no occasion to overrate such problems of derivation. In principle he has no objection to 'previous experience' guiding theory formation even if he will point out that this experience, as it is sketched out by Habermas, among other things contains the inherited mistakes which can to a certain extent help to 'shape' theory formation. There would be every reason then to invent strict tests for theories with this derivation in order to escape from these and other mistakes. Why should it be merely this derivation which guarantees the quality of the categories? Why should not new ideas similarly receive a chance to prove themselves? It seems to me that at this point Habermas's methodology becomes restrictive for no pur-

---

[1] Habermas cites in this context Adorno's reference to the unverifiability of the dependence of each social phenomenon 'upon the totality'. The quotation stems from a context in which Adorno, with reference to Hegel, asserts that refutation is only fruitful as immanent critique; see Adorno, 'On the logic of the social sciences', pp. 133 f. Here the meaning of Popper's comments on the problem of critical verification is roughly reversed through 'further reflection'. It seems to me that the unverifiability of the Adorno assertion is basically linked with the fact that neither the concept of totality used nor the nature of the dependence asserted is advanced even to a modest clarification. Presumably there is nothing more behind it than the idea that somehow everything is linked with everything else. To what extent any view could gain a methodical advantage from such an idea would really have to be demonstrated. In this matter verbal exhortations of totality ought not to suffice.

pose—in fact, as already mentioned, in a conservative direction —while the conception which he accuses of demanding that theory and concept formation be 'blindly' subjected to its abstract rules makes no substantive prohibitions, because it does not believe it can presuppose any uncorrectable 'previous' knowledge. The extended concept of experience which Habermas invokes appears at best to have the methodical function of making respectable mistakes which belong to so-called accumulated experience difficult to correct.[1]

Habermas does not explain how the 'hermeneutic anticipation of totality' proves itself to be correct 'in the course of the explication as a concept appropriate to the object itself'. It is clear, however, that he is not thinking here at any rate of a verification procedure along the lines of the methodology which he criticizes. After such methods of validation have been rejected as inadequate there remains a claim supported by metaphors which is linked to the supposed existence of a method which is not described in more detail but which is, none the less, better. Previously Habermas had drawn attention to the unverifiability of the 'functionalist concept of system' whose appropriateness for the structure of society apparently seems problematical to him. I do not know whether he would accept the answer that this concept too could establish itself to be correct in the course of explication. Rather than such a boomerang argument I prefer to question all the overstressing of concepts which one finds in Habermas, as in almost all the cultural scientific methodologists, as being the Hegelian inheritance of which they are apparently unable to rid themselves.[2] Here that essentialism finds its expression which Popper has criticized and which has long been overcome in the

[1] In contrast, the methodology which he criticizes also includes the possibility of theoretical corrections to previous experiences. In this respect it is apparently less 'positivistic' than that of the dialecticians.

[2] Recently Jürgen v. Kempski has drawn attention to this point; see his essay, 'Voraussetzungslosigkeit. Eine Studie zur Geschichte eines Wortes' in his *Brechungen*, p. 158. He points out that the shift of emphasis from the statement to the concept which took place in post-Kantian German idealism is closely connected with the transition to *raisonnements* whose logical structure is difficult to penetrate. German philosophers, as another critic has rightly stressed, have learned from Hegel above all darkness, apparent precision and the art of apparent proof; see Walter Kaufmann, 'Hegel: Contribution and Calamity', in *From Shakespeare to Existentialism*, Garden City, 1960.

natural sciences. The view which Habermas is attacking is not concerned with concepts but statements and systems of statements. In conjunction with these the concepts used in them can either be corroborated or not. The demand that they should be judged in isolation independently of their theoretical context lacks any basis.[1] The overtaxing of concepts practised by Hegelians which reveals itself above all in words like 'totality', 'dialectical' and 'history' does not amount, in my opinion, to anything other than their 'fetishization'—that, as far as I can see, is their specialist term for such—it merely amounts to a word-magic in the face of which their opponents lay down their weapons—unfortunately too early in most cases.[2]

In his discussion of the relationship between theory and history, Habermas opposes prediction on the basis of *general laws*, which is the specific achievement of empirical-scientific theories, with the *interpretation* of a historical life-context, with the aid of a definite type of *historical law-like regularities*. The latter is the specific achievement of a dialectical theory of society. He rejects the 'restrictive' use of the concept of law in favour of a type of law which claims 'a validity which is at the same time more comprehensive and more limited', for the dialectical analysis which makes use of this type of historical law of movement apparently aims to illuminate the concrete totality of a society undergoing historical development. Such laws then are not then generally valid, they

[1] Otherwise too Habermas's comments on concepts are quite problematical. He concludes the section on theory and object (loc. cit., p. 159), for example, with the statement that in dialectical social science concepts of a relational form 'give way to concepts' which are 'capable of expressing substance and function in one'. From this stem theories of a more 'flexible type' which have the advantage of self-reflexivity. I cannot think in what way logic is enriched here. One should really expect a detailed explanation. At least one would like to see examples for such concepts—preferably of course a logical analysis and a more precise discussion of where its special achievement lies.

[2] Analysis instead of accentuation ought to be recommended here. It is certainly very refreshing when, for example, Theodor W. Adorno reveals the word magic of Heideggerism with well-formulated ironical turns of phrase; see his *The Jargon of Authenticity*, (Evanston/London, 1973). But does not the language of dialectical obscurantism which goes back to Hegel sometimes appear to the unbiased very similar? Are the efforts which bear the characteristic of strained intellectual activity and which attempt to 'reduce the object to its concept: always so far removed from the exhortation of existence'?

relate rather 'to a particular concrete area of application, defined in terms of a process of development which is, in its totality, unique and, in its stages, irreversible; this means that it is defined not merely analytically but through the knowledge of the object itself'. Habermas accounts for the fact that its realm of validity is at the same time more extensive with the usual reference to the dependence of individual manifestations upon totality, for such laws apparently express their fundamental dependent relations.[1] At the same time however, they seek to 'articulate the object meaning of a historical life-context'. Dialectical analysis then proceeds hermeneutically. It gains its categories 'from the situational consciousness of the acting individuals' and takes up, through 'identification and critique' the 'objective spirit of the social life world', in order to open up from this standpoint 'the historical totality of a social context' which is to be understood as an objective meaning context. Through the combination of the method of *Verstehen* with that of casual analysis in the dialectical approach, the 'separation of theory and history' is transcended.

Once again then the methodological view of the analysts apparently proves to be too narrow. In its place the outlines of a more grandiose conception are indicated which aims at grasping the historical process as a whole and disclosing its objective meaning. The impressive claims of this conception are clearly recognizable, but so far there has been no trace of a reasonably sober analysis of the procedure sketched out and of its components. What does the logical structure of these historical laws look like, which have been accredited with such an interesting achievement, and how can one verify them?[2] In what sense can a law which relates to a concrete, historical totality, to a unique and irreversible process as such be anything other than a singular statement? Where does the law-like character of such a statement lie? How does one manage to identify the fundamental relations of dependency of a concrete totality? What procedure is available in order to proceed from the subjective hermeneutics, which

[1] See Habermas, loc. cit., pp. 163 ff.

[2] What differentiates them, for example, from the law-like regularities of a historicist character which Karl Popper in *The Poverty of Historicism*, loc. cit., has to some extent effectively criticized? May one presume that Habermas assumes this criticism is irrelevant just as earlier he characterized Nagel's investigations as being irrelevant to his problems?

has to be transcended, to the objective meaning? Among dialecticians these might all be questions of lesser importance. One is acquainted with this in theology. The interested outsider, however, feels over-taxed in his credulity. He sees the claims which are produced with superior reference to the limitations of other views but he would really like to know to what extent these are well-founded.[1]

4. THEORY AND PRACTICE: THE PROBLEM OF VALUE FREEDOM

The next topic which Habermas deals with is the relationship between theory and practice, a problem which is of basic importance for him, since what he strives for is apparently nothing less than a practically orientated, scientifically based philosophy of history. Even his transcendence of the division between theory and history, by means of a dialectical combination of historical and systematic analysis goes back, as he stresses earlier, to just such a practical orientation. This has to be clearly distinguished from merely technical interest from which undialectical empirical science springs. This opposition, to which reference has already been made, becomes central to his investigation in this context. Apparently we have now reached the core of his argument.[2]

His basic concern here is to overcome the already criticized restriction of positivistic social science to the solution of technical problems, in favour of a normative orientation. This is to be accomplished, in fact, with the help of that total historical analysis whose practical intentions 'can be released from pure arbitrariness and can be legitimated for their part dialectically

---

[1] It is well known that even the so-called method of subjective understanding has met with strong criticism for some time within the social sciences and this cannot be simply brushed aside. A hermeneutics, which alleges to break through to an objective meaning, may be far more problematic even if it does not become immediately conspicuous, of course, in today's German philosophical milieu. On this see Jürgen v. Kempski, 'Aspekte der Wahrheit', in above-mentioned collection of essays, *Brechungen*, especially 2: 'Die Welt als Text', where he tracks down the background to the interpretive model of knowledge referred here.

[2] To this problematic he devotes not only a considerable section of his contribution to Adorno's *Festschrift* but also the systematic parts of his book *Theory and Practice*.

from the objective context'.[1] In other words, he is looking for an *objective justification of practical action derived from the meaning of history*, a justification, which a sociology with an empirical scientific character cannot, by its nature, produce. But in all this he cannot ignore the fact that Popper too concedes a certain place in his conception for historical interpretations.[2] Popper, however, sharply attacks historico-philosophical theories which in some mysterious manner seek to unveil a hidden objective meaning in history that is to serve a practical orientation and justification. He upholds, rather, the view that such projections usually rest on self-deception and that we must decide to give history itself the meaning which we believe we can uphold. Such a 'meaning' can then also provide points of view for historical interpretation which in each case involves a selection which is dependent upon our interest yet without the objectivity of the connections chosen for the analysis having to be excluded.[3]

Habermas, who wishes to legitimate practical intentions from an objective total historical context—a desire which is usually relegated by his opponents to the realm of ideological thought—can make little use of the type of historical analysis which Popper concedes, for various historical interpretations are possible according to the selective standpoints chosen in each case. Habermas, on the other hand, for his purposes, requires the *single* superior interpretation which can be drawn upon for legitimation. For this reason he plays off against Popper the '*pure arbitrariness*' of the particular viewpoints selected, and apparently claims for his interpretation, which relates to totality, and which reveals the real

---

[1] Habermas, 'The analytical theory of science and dialectics', p. 168; see also *Theory and Practice*, loc. cit., pp. 114 ff.

[2] See the last chapter of his book *The Open Society and its Enemies* (1944), Princeton, 1950: 'Has History any Meaning?' or perhaps his essay 'Selbstbefreiung durch das Wissen', in *Der Sinn der Geschichte*, edited by Leonhard Reinish, München, 1961.

[3] Popper has repeatedly drawn attention to the selective character of each statement and group of statements and also to that of the theoretical conceptions in the empirical sciences. With reference to historical interpretations he says expressly 'Since all history depends upon our interests, *there can only be histories, and never a "history"*, a story of the development of mankind as it "happened".' See *The Open Society and its Enemies*, loc. cit., p. 732, note 9. Similarly Otto Brunner in 'Abendländisches Geschichtsdenken' in his essay collection *Neue Wege der Sozialgeschichte*, Göttingen, 1956, pp. 171 f.

meaning of events—the aim *of society* as it is called elsewhere[1]—an objectivity which can only be achieved dialectically. But the supposed arbitrariness of an interpretation in Popper's sense is not particularly damaging for such an interpretation does not make any of the claims which are to be found in Habermas. In view of his criticism, however, one must ask how he, for his part, avoids such arbitrariness. Given the fact that one finds no solution in his writings to the legitimation problem which he himself raises, one has every reason to assume that arbitrariness is no less problematical in his case, the only difference being that it appears under the mask of an objective interpretation. It is difficult to gauge to what extent he can reject the Popperian critique of such supposedly objective interpretations and the critique of ideology of the 'superficial' enlightenment in general. To some extent totality proves to be a 'fetish' which serves to allow 'arbitrary' decisions to appear as objective knowledge.

As Habermas rightly asserts, this brings us to the problem of the so-called *value-freedom* of historical and theoretical research. The postulate of value-freedom rests, as he says, on 'a thesis which, following Popper, one can formulate as a dualism of facts and decisions'[2] and which can be explained on the basis of the distinction between natural laws and norms. He regards the 'strict separation' of these 'two types of law' as problematic. With reference to this he formulates two questions, the answers to which allow us to clarify the issues involved; namely, on the one hand, whether normative meaning resists a rational discussion of the concrete life-context from which it emerged and upon which it still reacts and, on the other hand, the question of whether knowledge reduced positivistically to an empirical science is in fact released from every normative bond.[3] The manner of posing the questions in itself shows that he appears to interpret the dualism mentioned in a way that rests upon misunderstanding for that which he places in question here has little to do with the meaning of this distinction.

The second of the two questions leads him to the investigation

[1] Habermas, *Theory and Practice*, loc. cit., p. 321, in connection with an analysis of a discussion of Marxism which is, in other aspects too, extremely interesting.

[2] Habermas, 'The analytical theory of science and dialectics', p. 170.

[3] Habermas, p. 175.

of Popper's suggestions concerning the basic problem.[1] He discovers in them unintended consequences which allegedly involve a circle and he sees in this evidence for the embedding of the research process in a context which is only explicable hermeneutically. The problem revolves around the following: Popper, in opposition to the advocates of a protocol language, insists that even basic statements can on principle be revised since they themselves contain a theoretically determined element of interpretation.[2] One has to apply the conceptual apparatus of the theory in question in order to obtain basic statements. Habermas detects a circularity in the fact that to apply laws one needs to have previously established the facts: but this can only be achieved in a process in which these laws are already applied. There is a misunderstanding here. The application of laws—and that means here the application of theoretical statements—demands the use of the relevant *conceptual apparatus* to formulate the conditions of application which come into question, and to which the application of *the laws themselves* can attach itself. I do not see what circularity is involved here nor especially how in this case Habermas's *deus ex machina*, hermeneutic explication, would provide further help. Nor do I see here to what extent 'the detachment of methodology from the real research process and its social function' takes its revenge—whatever he means by this.

The reference to the institutional character of research and the role of normative regulations in the research process which Habermas makes in this context is in no way suited to solving previously unsolved problems.[3] As far as the 'fact' is concerned which Popper is supposed to 'persistently ignore', namely, 'that normally we are in no doubt at all about the validity of a basic statement' and that as a result the logical possibility of infinite

[1] We are concerned here with the problem of the character of basic statements—statements which describe observable states of affairs and of their significance for the verifiability of theories; see Karl Popper, *The Logic of Scientific Discovery*, loc. cit., ch. 5.

[2] This point of view is even more strongly expressed in the later works of Popper; see, for example, the essays in his above-mentioned collection.

[3] In any case Popper himself has already analysed such connections. In his book *The Logic of Scientific Discovery* he criticized naturalism with regard to methodological questions and in his major social philosophical work *The Open Society and its Enemies* he deals explicitly with the institutional aspects

regress no longer comes into question de facto, one can only reply that the factual certainty of a statement in itself can only with difficulty be considered as a criterion of the statement's validity. This apart, Popper himself solves the problem of regress without resorting to problematic states of affairs of this sort. His concern is not an analysis of factual behaviour but rather a solution of methodological problems. Reference to unformulated criteria which are applied de facto in the institutionally channelled research process is no solution to such a problem. The assertion that the problem really does not arise in this process in no way serves to eliminate it as a methodological problem. One only has to recall that for many scientists the problem of information content—incidentally a connected problem—does not present itself, and this frequently has the result that under certain conditions they tautologize their systems and render them devoid of content. Problems must present themselves to the methodologist which other people often do not think of.

The norms and criteria upon which Habermas reflects in a very general manner in this section of his essay are generally treated from the perspective of the sociologist as social states of affairs, as aspects of the research process based on the division of labour, a process embedded in the division of labour in society as a whole. This is a perspective which can certainly be of great interest. For methodology, however, it is not a question of the acceptance of social data but rather of the critical elucidation and the rational reconstruction of the relevant rules and criteria with reference to possible aims: for example the aim of more closely approximating to the truth. It is interesting that the dialectician becomes, at this point, the real 'positivist' by imagining he can eliminate problems of the logic of research by reference to factual social data. This is not a transcendance of Popperian methodology but rather an attempt to circumvent its problems by drawing upon what one is wont to disavow in other contexts as 'mere facticity'.

As far as the sociological aspects are concerned one must likewise doubt whether they can be adequately treated in the way which Habermas suggests. Precisely in this respect—that is, with

---

of scientific method. His *distinction* between natural laws and norms in no way led him to overlook the role of normative regulation in research.

respect to the so-called life-references of research—one must take into account that there are institutions which stabilize an independent interest in the knowledge of objective contexts, so that there exists in these spheres the possibility of emancipating oneself to a large extent from the direct pressure of everyday practice. The freedom for scientific work made possible in this way has made no small contribution to the advance of knowledge. In this respect the inference of technical utilization from technical rootedness proves to be a 'short circuit'.[1]

In connection with the treatment of the basis problem Habermas, as we have seen, introduces the question of the normative regulation of the cognitive process and from this can return to the *problem of value-freedom* which formed his starting point. He can now say that this problem testifies 'that the analytical-empirical procedures cannot ensure for themselves the life-reference within which they themselves objectively stand'.[2] His succeeding comment suffers, however, from the fact that at no point does he formulate the postulate of value-freedom whose questionability he wishes to emphasize, in such a way that one can be sure with which assertion he is actually concerned. One can understand in a variety of ways the value-freedom of science. I do not suppose that Habermas thinks that anyone upholding such a principle *in any* sense of the word could any longer form a clear picture of the social context in which research stands.[3]

Modern advocates of a methodical value-freedom principle are in no way wont to overlook the normative references of research and the knowledge-directing interests.[4] Generally they

---

[1] Albert here makes a pun of *Rück*schluss (inference) and *Kurz*schluss (short circuit). Unfortunately this cannot be rendered into English.

[2] Habermas, p. 186.

[3] As far as the reference, which he makes at the start of his essay (p. 156), is concerned, that positivism has abandoned the insight 'that the research process carried out by subjects itself belongs to the objective context which is to be recognized by means of the acts of cognition' one only needs to refer to the relevant works, above all Ernst Topitsch, 'Sozialtheorie und Gesellschaftsgestaltung' (1956) reprinted in his volume of essays *Sozialphilosophie zwischen Ideologie und Wissenschaft*, Neuwied, 1961. There one also finds critical material on the dialectical processing of this insight.

[4] Such an objection could also hardly be made against Max Weber. Similarly such objections could not be applied to Karl Popper who has ex-

propose more detailed solutions in which various aspects of the problem are distinguished.

Similarly Adorno's remarks on the problem of value, to which Habermas refers, will scarcely take us further. When he points out that the separation of evaluative and value-free behaviour is false in so far as value, and thus value freedom, are themselves reifications, then similarly we may ask who such remarks refer to. Who would relate the above-mentioned dichotomy so simply to 'behaviour'? Who would take up the concept of value in such a simple manner as is implied here?[1] Adorno's judgement that the whole value problem is falsely posed[2] has no relation to a definite formulation of this problem and can therefore hardly be judged; it is an assertion which sounds comprehensive but carries no risk. He alludes to antinomies from which positivism cannot extricate itself without even giving an indication of where they might lie. Neither the views criticized nor the objections raised against them can be identified in such a way that an un-biased person could judge them.[3] In a very interesting manner Habermas too talks of value-freedom as the problem of reification, of categories of the life-world which gained power over a theory which devolves on practice, and similar things which presumably have escaped 'plain enlightenment, but he does not condescend to analyse concrete solutions of the value problem.

---

plicitly distanced himself from the demand for an *unconditional* value-freedom (see his paper 'The logic of the Social Sciences', pp. 103 ff.) nor to Ernst Topitsch. I have frequently expressed myself on these problems, most recently in 'Wertfreiheit als methodisches Prinzip', in *Schriften des Vereins für Sozialpolitik*, Neue Folge, Band 29, Berlin, 1963.

[1] See, for example, the study by Viktor Kraft in his book *Grundlagen einer wissenschaftlichen Werttheorie*, 2. Auflage, Wien, 1951, which can serve as a starting point for a more differentiated treatment of the value-freedom problem. There can be no talk of 'reification' or of a value-concept which can be criticized in this way. If one speaks of value concepts, value-freedom and similar terms as if they were platonic essences which everyone can see then the ambiguity of such terms is inadequately represented.

[2] Adorno, 'On the logic of the social sciences', p. 139.

[3] The passage to which Habermas refers: 'What was subsequently sanctioned as a value does not operate externally to the object . . . but is rather, immanent to it' suggests an interpretation of Adorno's position which one presumes would hardly please him, that is, an interpretation along the lines of a naïve value-realism which is still to be found in the Scholastics.

In connection with the problem of the application of social-scientific theories he then discusses *Myrdal's critique of ends–means thought*.[1] The difficulties to which Myrdal draws attention in connection with the question of value-neutrality lead him to attempt to demonstrate that one is forced into dialectical thought in order to overcome them. His thesis concerning the purely technical orientation of empirical scientific knowledge plays a role here; this de facto has to be guided by 'programmatic viewpoints not reflected upon as such'.[2] Thus technically utilizable social scientific theories could not 'despite their own self-understanding satisfy the strict demands of value-neutrality'. 'It is precisely the domination of a technical cognitive interest which is hidden to itself,' he says, 'which conceals the veiled investments of the relatively dogmatic total understanding of a situation with which even the strictly empirical sociologist has implicitly identified himself before it slips through his hands in the initial stages of a formalized theory under the claim of hypothetical universality.' He then concludes that if these interests which de facto guide knowledge cannot be suspended then they must 'be brought under control and criticized or legitimated as objective interests derived from the total societal context'; this, however, forces one into dialectical thought.

Here the fact that dialecticians doggedly refuse to dissect the complex value-problematic and to treat its particular problems separately apparently takes its revenge in the fear that 'the whole', which they, as if spellbound, seek never to let out of their sight, could slip through their fingers. In order to reach solutions at all, one has, now and again, to avert one's gaze from the whole and to bracket off totality, at least for a time. As a consequence of this thought directed to the whole, we find a constant reference to the connection of all details in the totality, which compels one to dialectical thinking, but which results in not a single actual solution to a problem. Studies which show that precisely here

[1] These are thoughts which Myrdal published in 1933 in his essay, 'Das Zweck-Mittel-Denken in der Nationalökonomie', in *Zeitschrift für National-ökonomie*, Vol. IV; English translation in his essay collection *Value in Social Theory*, London, 1958. I am pleased that this essay to which I have been constantly drawing attention over the last ten years is gradually receiving general attention.

[2] Habermas, 'The analytical theory of science and dialectics', p. 189.

one can make progress without dialectical thought are, on the other hand, ignored.[1]

5. CRITIQUE OF IDEOLOGY AND DIALECTICAL JUSTIFICATION

It can hardly be doubted that Habermas sees the problem of the relation between theory and practice mainly from the perspective of the justification of practical action, and that he understands it as a *problem of legitimation*. This perspective also explains his attitude towards a critique of ideology which provides no substitute for that which it disavows. In addition, there is his *instrumentalist interpretation* of pure science which makes more difficult his own access to the understanding of such a critique of ideology. He links both with modern *irrationalism* which makes plausible his demand for a dialectical transcendence of 'positivistic' limitations.

He believes that the restriction of the social sciences to 'pure' knowledge—whose purity seems to him, in any case, problematical—eliminates from the horizon of the sciences the questions of life-practice [*Lebenspraxis*] in such a way that they are henceforth exposed to irrational and dogmatic attempts at interpretation.[2] These attempts at interpretation are then subjected to a

[1] In my view Habermas does not sufficiently distinguish between the possible aspects of the value-problem. I will not bother going into details here in order not to repeat myself; see, for instance, my essay 'Wissenschaft und Politik', in *Probleme der Wissenschaftstheorie. Festschrift für Viktor Kraft*, edited by Ernst Topitsch, Wien, 1960, as well as the above-mentioned essay 'Wertfreiheit als methodisches Prinzip'. I have written on the problem of ends–means thought discussed by Myrdal in *Ökonomische Ideologie und Politische Theorie*, Göttingen, 1954; 'Die Problematik der ökonomischen Perspektive', in *Zeitschrift für die gesamte Staatswissenschaft*, 117, 1961, reprinted as the first chapter in my *Marktsoziologie und Entscheidungslogik* and the section 'Allgemeine Wertproblematik' of the article 'Wert' in *Handwörterbuch der Sozialwissenschaften*. For a critique of the Myrdal book mentioned in note 1 on the previous page see 'Das Wertproblem in den Sozialwissenschaften', in *Schweizer Zeitschrift für Volkswirtschaft und Statistik*, 94, 1958. In my view, my suggested solutions for the problems in question render the leap into dialectics unnecessary.

[2] See the section 'The positivist isolation of reason and decision' in his essay 'Dogmatism, Reason and Decision', in *Theory and Practice*, loc. cit., pp. 263 f.; further his contribution to Adorno's *Festschrift*, pp. 172‡ f.

'positivistically circumscribed critique of ideology', which is basically indebted to the same purely technically-rooted cognitive interest as is the technologically utilizable social science; and consequently like the latter, accepts the dualism of facts and evaluations. Since a social science of this type, as is the case with the natural sciences, can only guarantee the economy of the choice of means while action over and above this demands normative orientation; and since ultimately, the 'positivistic' type of critique of ideology is in a position to reduce the interpretations which it criticizes merely to the decisions upon which they rest, then the result is 'an unconstrained decisionism in the choice of the highest goals'.[1]

Positivism in the realm of knowledge is matched by decisionism in the realm of practice; a too narrowly conceived rationalism in the one realm matches irrationalism in the other. 'So it is, then, that on this level the critique of ideology involuntarily provides the proof that the progress of a rationalization limited in terms of science empirical to technical control, is paid for with the corresponding growth of a mass of irrationality within the realm of practice itself.'[1] In this context Habermas is not afraid to relate quite closely the diverse forms of decisionism represented among others by Jean Paul Sartre, Carl Schmitt and Arnold Gehlen as in some degree complementary views to a very broadly conceived positivism.[2] In view of the irrationality of decisions accepted by positivists and decisionists alike, the return to *mythology* is understandable, Habermas believes, even as a last desperate attempt 'to secure institutionally a socially binding precedent for practical questions'.[3]

[1] Habermas, *Theory and Practice*, loc. cit., p. 265.

[2] One finds a certain analogy to Habermas's complementary thesis in Wolfgang de Boer's essay, 'Positivismus und Existenzphilosophie', in *Merkur*, Vol. 6, 1952, 47, pp. 12 ff., where the two intellectual currents are interpreted as two answers to the 'same tremendous event of the constitution of existence'. As a remedy the author recommends a 'fundamental anthropological interpretation', 'a science of man which we do not, as yet, possess'.

[3] Habermas, *Theory and Practice*, loc. cit., p. 267. In this connection he refers to a very interesting book by Max Horkheimer and Theodor W. Adorno, *Dialectic of Enlightenment*, loc. cit., where, within the framework of an analysis of the 'dialectics of myth and enlightenment', positivism is 'denounced' and Hegel's poor acquaintance with logic, mathematics and positive science is renewed.

Given his interpretation of positive science Habermas's thesis is at least plausible, even if it does not do justice to the fact that the relapse into mythology, where it has actually occurred, can in no way be laid at the door of the specific rationality of the scientific field.[1] Generally the positivism criticized by Habermas makes itself quite unpopular in totalitarian societies, in which such a remythologization is on the agenda, while dialectical attempts at the interpretation of reality are frequently able to gain recognition there.[2] Of course, it can always be said later that this was not true dialectics. But wherein can they be actually recognized? The treatment which Habermas bestows upon Polish revisionism is interesting in this connection.[3] This revisionism developed in reaction to Stalinist orthodoxy in an intellectual milieu which was greatly determined by the influence of the Warsaw school of philosophy. Among other things its critique was directed against the characteristics of a holistic philosophy of history with practical intent-characteristics which determine the ideological character of Marxism. Habermas wishes to take up positively those characteristics of Marxist thought which fell prey to revisionism's critique. This development is not accidental. It is

[1] It is interesting that in the Third Reich Carl Schmitt's decisionism which yielded to a 'concrete thought exclusively devoted to the upholding of order' (*Ordnungsdenken*) readily recalls Hegel, as the Hegelian Karl Larenz at that time attested to; see Karl Larenz's review of Carl Schmitt's book, *Über die drei Arten des rechtswissenschaftlichen Denkens*, Hamburg, 1934, in *Zeitschrift für Deutsche Kulturphilosophie*, Vol. 1, 1935, pp. 112 ff. This periodical also contains testimonies to a mode of thought which draws considerably upon Hegel and is right-wing in orientation. It is not difficult to incorporate it into the realm of fascist ideology.

[2] See Ernst Topitsch's article 'Max Weber and Sociology Today' in O. Starrmer (ed.), *Max Weber and Sociology Today* (Oxford, 1971). Also very interesting in this respect is the book by Z. A. Jordan, *Philosophy and Ideology. The Development of Philosophy and Marxism–Leninism in Poland since the Second World War*, Dordrecht, 1963, in which the confrontation of the Warsaw school of philosophy, which ought to fall under Habermas's broad concept of 'positivism', with the dialectically orientated Polish Marxism, is analysed in detail.

[3] See *Theory and Practice*, loc. cit., pp. 324 ff. This is the final section— 'Immanente Kritik am Marxismus'—a very interesting essay, 'Zur philosophischen Diskussion um Marx und den Marxismus' which also includes a discussion of Sartre and H. Marcuse. In this essay Habermas's intentions concerning a philosophy of history which is practically orientated and which reworks the insights of the empirical social sciences are well expressed.

connected with the fact that in Poland, after the opportunities for a certain amount of free discussion had been created, the arguments of the dialecticians collapsed—one could say, along the whole line— under the impact of the counter arguments from the Warsaw school.[1] It is a bit too simple to attribute an epistemological naïvety, as Habermas does, to the theoreticians who were compelled to relinquish untenable positions in the face of the critical arguments of philosophers who belonged to a dominant tradition in the theory of knowledge. Leszek Kolakowski's retreat to a methodological rationalism and a more positivistic revisionism, which Habermas so sharply criticizes, was motivated by a challenge to which our own inheritors of Hegelian thought must first prove equal, before they have cause to lightly dismiss the results of the Polish discussion.[2]

It seems to me that a close connection exists between the particular features of dialectical thought and the fact that dialectical attempts to interpret reality, in contrast to the 'positivism' which Habermas criticizes, are frequently popular in totalitarian societies. One can recognize a basic achievement of such forms of thought precisely in the fact that they are appropriate for disguising random decisions as knowledge, and thereby legitimating them in such a way as to remove them from the possibility of discussion.[3] A 'decision' veiled in this manner, however comprehensive it may be, will look no better even in the light of reason than that 'naked' decision which one imagines one can overcome in this way. Demasking through critical analysis can then, only with difficulty, be criticized in the name of reason.[4]

Habermas cannot, it is true, completely incorporate this critique of ideology into his scheme of a technically rooted and therefore

[1] See the above-mentioned book by Jordan, *Philosophy and Ideology*, parts 4-6. The relevant argument for Habermas's conception is to be found in part 6: 'Marxist–Leninist Historicism and the Concept of Ideology.'

[2] This is all the more the case since one can hardly claim that the Polish Marxists did not have access to the arguments which our representatives of dialectical thought believe they have at their disposal.

[3] See, for example, the critical examination of Ernst Topitsch in his book *Sozialphilosophie zwischen Ideologie und Wissenschaft*, loc. cit., and also his essay 'Entfremdung und Ideologie. Zur Entmythologisierung des Marxismus' in *Hamburger Jahrbuch für Wirtschafts- und Gesellschaftspolitik*, 9, 1964.

[4] The 'superficial' enlightenment which has to be overcome dialectically seems to me largely identical with the 'flat' and 'shallow' enlightenment

randomly utilizable knowledge. He is compelled to recognize a 'reified critique of ideology' which apparently has to a certain extent severed itself from this root,[1] and in which 'honest positivists whose laughter is dispelled by such perspectives', namely, those who shrink back from irrationalism and re-mythologization, 'seek support'. He regards the motivation of such a critique of ideology as unclarified, but this is only true because here he can hardly impute the only motive which he finds plausible, namely, that of the provision of new techniques. He sees that this critique 'itself [makes] an attempt to illuminate consciousness' but fails to see from whence it draws its strength 'if reason divorced from decision be wholly devoid of any interest in an emancipation of consciousness from dogmatic bias'.[2] Here he encounters the *dilemma* that scientific knowledge of this sort is, in his opinion, only possible as 'a kind of committed reason, the *justified* possibility of which is precisely what the critique of ideology denies' but with a renunciation of justification, however, 'the dispute of reason with dogmatism itself remains a matter of dogmatics'.[3] He sees behind this dilemma that 'the critique of ideology must tacitly presuppose as its own motivation just what it attacks as dogmatic, namely, the convergence of reason and decision—precisely a comprehensive concept of rationality'.[4] In other words, this form of critique of ideology is not in a position to see through itself. Habermas, however, sees through it, namely, as a veiled form of decided reason, a thwarted dialectics. One sees where his restrictive interpretation of non-dialectical social science has led him.

The critique of ideology analysed in this manner can, on the other hand, admit without further ado an underlying interest in an 'emancipation of consciousness from dogmatic bias'. It is even

which for a long time in Germany has been met with suspicion as a dubious metaphysics of the state or in the name of concrete life-references; on this subject see Karl Popper, *Selbstbefreiung durch das Wissen*, loc. cit., Ernst Topitsch, *Sozialphilosophie zwischen Ideologie und Wissenschaft*, loc. cit., and my contribution to the *Jahrbuch für kritische Aufklärung 'Club Voltaire'*, 1, München, 1963, 'Die Idee der kritischen Vernunft'.

[1] See Habermas, *Theory and Practice*, loc. cit., pp. 267 ff. He refers initially to the studies of Ernst Topitsch which are printed in *Sozialphilosophie zwischen Ideologie und Wissenschaft*, loc. cit. The book seems to provide him with certain difficulties of categorization.

[2, 3, 4] Habermas, loc. cit., p. 267.

capable of reflecting on its foundations without running into difficulties. But as far as Habermas's *alternative of dogmatism and rational justification* is concerned it has every cause to expect information as to how dialectics is capable of solving the problem of rational justification which arises here. Above all dialectics is dependent upon such a solution since it sets out from the standpoint of the legitimation of practical intentions. Whether positivism is in a position to offer a solution, indeed whether it is interested at all in a solution of such problems, is a question whose answer will depend, among other things, upon what one understands by 'positivism'. We shall return to this point.

According to Habermas one can distinguish between one type of critique of ideology and, correspondingly, a rationality which is only orientated to the value of scientific techniques, and another which, over and above this, also develops from 'the significance of a scientific emancipation for adult autonomy'.[1] He is prepared to admit that possibly 'even in its positivistic form can pursue an interest in adult autonomy'. The Popperian conception, 'the critique of ideology', to which he makes this concession, apparently in his opinion,[2] comes closest to the comprehensive rationality of the dialectical sort. For it cannot be denied that Popper's critical rationalism, which was developed precisely as a reaction to the logical positivism of the thirties, recognizes in principle no boundaries to rational discussion and consequently can take up problems which a more narrowly understood positivism is not wont to discuss.[3] But he has no cause however to attribute all such problems to positive science. Critical reason in

[1] *Theory and Practice*, loc. cit., pp. 268 ff., 276.

[2] Habermas, loc. cit., p. 251. Ernst Topitsch on the other hand, if I understand correctly, must it seems be classified under the first type. I am not in a position to recognize the basis for this classification. Nor do I see how one can carry out a cataloguing in accordance with this scheme at all. What criteria are applied here? Does not the first form of the critique of ideology perhaps owe its fictitious existence to his restrictive interpretation of scientific knowledge?

[3] Incidentally, it is thoroughly questionable to discuss such problems against the background of the positivism of the thirties which has long been abandoned by its early representatives. Even at that time, there was also, for example, the Warsaw school which never indulged in some of the restrictions. The statement of Wittgenstein which Habermas quotes in connection with the question of value-freedom ('The analytical theory of science and dialectics', loc. cit., p. 171) seems to me to be rather uncharacteristic of most

Popper's sense does not stop at the boundaries of science. Habermas concedes to him the motive of enlightenment but draws attention to the 'resigned reservation' which, it is claimed, lies in the fact that here rationalism 'only appears as his professed faith'.[1] It can be presumed that his critique at this point is linked with the above mentioned expectation of justification.

Undoubtedly this expectation remains unfulfilled. Popper develops his view in a confrontation with a 'comprehensive rationalism' which is uncritical in so far as it—in analogy to the Liar Paradox—implies its own transcendence.[2] Since, for logical reasons, a self-grounding of rationalism is impossible, Popper calls the assumption of a rationalist attitude a decision which, because it logically lies prior to the application of rational arguments, can be termed irrational.[3] However, he then makes a sharp distinction between a blind decision and one taken with open eyes, that is, with a clear knowledge of its consequences. What is Habermas's position on this problem? He passes over it, presumably on the assumption that a dialectician is not confronted with it.[4] He does not take up Popper's arguments against comprehensive rationalism. He admits that 'if scientific insight purged of

'positivists'. It has nothing to do with Popper's view which hardly makes intelligible its appearance in connection with a critique of Popper.

[1] Habermas, *Theory and Practice*, loc. cit., p. 276.

[2] Karl Popper, *The Open Society and its Enemies*, loc. cit., p. 230.

[3] One can argue here as to whether the expressions used are not problematical in so far as they can possibly evoke misleading associations. One could, for example, restrict the use of the dichotomy 'rational–irrational' to cases in which both possibilities exist. The word 'belief' which appears in this context in Popper is similarly loaded in many respects, above all on account of the widespread idea that there hardly exists a connection between belief and knowledge. But despite this it is not here primarily a matter of the mode of expression.

[4] It is not without interest in this connection that the founder of dialectics as it is played against 'positivism' by Habermas failed to get by without a 'resolution' 'which one can also regard as an arbitrary action'; see G. F. W. Hegel, *Wissenschaft der Logik*, edited by Georg Lasson, Erster Teil, Band 56 of the Meiner Library, p. 54. Jürgen von Kempski has specifically drawn attention to this point in the essay already mentioned, 'Voraussetzungslosigkeit' in *Brechungen*, loc. cit., pp. 142, 146 and *passim*. Besides this von Kempski points out that 'the so-called German idealists have made the Kantian position on the primacy of practical reason and the doctrine of postulates into a focal point for a reinterpretation of the critique of reason subservient, in the last analysis, to theological motives', loc. cit., p. 146.

the interest of reason is devoid of all immanent reference to praxis, and if conversely every normative content is detached nominalistically from insights into its real relation to life—as Popper presupposes undialectically—then indeed the dilemma must be conceded: that I cannot rationally compel anyone to support his assumptions with arguments and evidence from experiences'.[1] He does not show, however, how far the assumption of an 'immanent reference to praxis' in knowledge or a combination of normative content and insight into things can be relevant here. His remarks in the final analysis amount to the fact that the problems of a comprehensive 'decided' reason can be adequately resolved. One does not learn, however, what this solution looks like. His idea that 'in rational discussion as such a tendency is irrevocably inherent which is precisely a decisive commitment entailed by rationality itself and which therefore does not require arbitrary decision or pure faith',[2] presupposes rational discussion as a fact and for this reason overlooks the problem raised by Popper. The thesis that even 'in the simplest discussion of methodological questions . . . a prior understanding of a rationality is presupposed that is not yet divested of its normative elements',[3] is scarcely appropriate as an objection to Popper, who has not denied the normative background of such discussions but rather has analysed it. Once again Habermas's tendency to point to 'naked' facts instead of discussing problems and solutions is revealed.

In the meantime, Popper has further developed his views in a way that should be relevant to the problems which Habermas treats.[4] He aims at the transcendence of views which are directed towards the *idea of positive justification*,[5] and he opposes to this the

[1] Habermas, *Theory and Practice*, loc. cit., p. 276.

[2] Habermas, loc. cit., p. 279.

[3] Habermas refers here to David Pole's interesting book, *Conditions of Rational Inquiry*, London, 1961, a book which despite partial critique of Popper adopts a great number of his views. Pole discusses his work, *The Open Society and its Enemies*, but not, however, later publications in which Popper has further developed his critical rationalism.

[4] See in particular his essay 'On the Sources of Knowledge and Ignorance' in *Proceedings of the British Academy*, vol. XLVI, 1960, reprinted in *Conjectures and Refutations*; see also William Warren Bartley, *The Retreat to Commitment*, New York, 1962; Paul K. Feyerabend, *Knowledge without Foundations*, Oberlin/Ohio, 1961, and my above-mentioned contribution.

[5] Even in his *Logik der Forschung*, Wien, 1935, one can find the basis for this development; see his treatment of the Friesian trilemma of dogmatism,

idea of *critical validation*, that is detached from justificatory thought which only has the choice between an infinite regress which cannot be fulfilled, and a dogmatic solution. Habermas, too, is still in the grip of this justificatory thought when he has recourse to factual certainties of some kind in seeking to legitimate practical intentions from an objective context, and when he expects that meta-ethical criteria be derived and justified from underlying interests.[1] The alternative of dogmatism and rational justification which he considers, no matter how obvious it sounds, is affected by the argument that recourse to positive reasons itself is of a dogmatic procedure. The demand for legitimation which Habermas's practically orientated philosophy of history inspires, makes respectable the recourse to dogmas which can only be obscured by dialectics. The critique of ideology aims at making such obscurantism transparent, at laying bare the dogmatic core of such arguments and relating them to the social context of consequences in which they fulfil their legitimating function. In this respect it counteracts precisely such edifices of statements as Habermas demands for the normative orientation of practice—it must provide not legitimating but critical achievements. Anyone undertaking to solve the problem of the relationships between theory and practice, between social science and politics from the perspective of justification is left, if he wishes to avoid open recourse to a normative dogmatics, only with retreat to a form of obscurantism such as can be achieved by means of dialectical or

infinite regress and psychologism in the chapter on the problem of an empirical basis.

[1] See *Theory and Practice*, loc. cit., p. 280, where he discusses my essay 'Ethik und Meta-Ethik' which appears in *Archiv für Philosophie*, Vol. 11, 1961. In my treatment of the problem of verification for ethical systems he objects to the fact that here the positivistic limitations would involuntarily become evident, since material questions would be prejudiced in the form of methodological decisions and the practical consequences of the application of the relevant criteria would be excluded from reflection. Instead of this he suggests a hermeneutic clarification of historically appropriate concepts and, in addition, the justification from interests mentioned. Just before this, however, he quotes a passage of mine from which it becomes clear that a rational discussion of such criteria is quite possible. Here nothing is excluded from a reflection nor is anything prejudiced in the sense of decisions which cannot be revised. It would be difficult to determine whether something is 'in itself' a 'material question' and for this reason has to be discussed on a quite specific level.

hermeneutic thought. In this, language plays no small part, namely one which stands in the way of a clear and precise formulation of ideas. That such a language dominates even methodological reflections which precede the actual undertaking and also the confrontation with other conceptions on this level, can presumably only be understood from the angle of aesthetic motives if one disregards the obvious idea of a strategy of relative immunization.[1]

6. CRITICAL PHILOSOPHY VERSUS DIALECTICS

The problem of the relations between theory and practice which stands at the centre of Habermas's thought is interesting from many standpoints. The representatives of other views also have to come to grips with this.[2] It is a problem in whose treatment philosophical views inevitably play a role. This may lead to useful solutions, but may also in certain circumstances render a solution more difficult. Habermas's manner of tackling the problem suffers from the fact that he exaggerates the difficulties of the views he criticizes by means of restrictive interpretations and, at best, indicates his own solutions vaguely and in metaphorical turns of phrase.[3] He behaves hypocritically towards his opponents but more than generously towards dialecticians. He is unsparing with advice to his opponents that they should overcome their limitations by creating the unity of reason and decision, the transition to a comprehensive rationality, however this might be formulated.

[1] However, one has the impression that wherever this language makes an appearance in works by members of the Frankfurt School, even when their ideas seem quite interesting, they are themselves 'setting up a hedgehog defence' (*einigeln*) in advance against possible critics.

[2] Over a long period, for example, Gerhard Weisser, schooled in the Fries–Nelson version of Kantianism, has concerned himself with this problem. In economics we find the so-called welfare-economics which primarily has utilitarian roots. Particularly in this discipline it has become evident to what difficulties the undertaking of the justification of political measures through theoretical consideration is exposed. It frequently seems here that the greatest difficulties lie in the details.

[3] I do not in any way wish to dispute that his book *Theory and Practice* contains interesting, partly historical analyses and confrontations upon which I cannot enter within the framework of the problems at hand. I have only been able here to deal with systematic ideas which come into question for his critique of 'positivism'. The relevant sections may not necessarily be decisive for an appreciation of the book as a whole.

But what he positively opposes to their 'specific' rationality are more metaphors than methods. He makes thorough use of the advantage that lies in the fact that Popper, for instance, explicates his views in clear formulations, but he exposes his readers to the disadvantage that they must painstakingly find their way in his own exposition.

Substantively, the fundamental weakness of his presentation lies in the manner in which he outlines the problem situation. His instrumentalist interpretation of the theoretical-empirical sciences forces him towards an interpretation of the 'positivistic' critique of ideology for which there are surely no indications in social reality. Where he cannot help but concede the motive of clarification, the emancipation of consciousness from dogmatic bias, he indicates restrictions which are difficult to identify on the basis of his formulations. The thesis of the complimentarity of positivism and decisionism which he upholds does not lack a certain plausibility if one relates it to the unreflected 'positivism' of everyday life; it may even have something in its favour if one presupposes his instrumentalist interpretation of science, but it can hardly be applied in a meaningful manner to the philosophical views which he wishes to attack with his thesis. In his attempts to demonstrate the questionability of the distinction between facts and decisions, between natural laws and norms, distinctions which he regards as mistaken oppositions, but which he has to presuppose constantly, it is precisely because of the obliteration of the distinction that a clarification of the relations between these things is made more difficult. That there are relations between them is in no way denied in the views he criticizes. Instead, such relations are analysed.

The crude 'positivism' of common sense may tend not only to distinguish *pure* theories, *bare* facts and *mere* decisions but also to *isolate* them from the original *fusion* of these elements in the language and thought of everyday life. But this is in no way true of the philosophical views which Habermas criticizes. Instead they reveal manifold relations between these moments which can be relevant for knowledge and action. The facts then appear as theoretically interpreted aspects of reality,[1] the theories as selective

---

[1] See, for example, Karl R. Popper, 'Why are the Calculi of Logic and Arithmetic Applicable to Reality?' in *Conjectures and Refutations*, loc. cit., especially pp. 213 f.

interpretations in whose judgement facts once again play a part and whose acceptance involves decisions. These decisions are made according to standpoints which on a meta-theoretical level are accessible to objective discussion.[1] As far as the decisions of practical life are concerned, they can be made in the light of a situational analysis which makes use of theoretical results and takes into consideration consequences which are actually expected. The distinction between facts and decisions, nomological and normative statements, theories and states of affairs in no way involves a lack of connection. It would hardly be meaningful to 'dialectically transcend' all such distinctions in a unity of reason and decision postulated *ad hoc*, and thus to allow the various aspects of problems and the levels of argumentation to perish in a totality which may certainly encompass all simultaneously, but which then makes it necessary to solve all the problems simultaneously. Such a procedure can only lead to problems being hinted at but no longer analysed, to a pretence at solutions but not their implementation. The dialectical cult of total reason is too fastidious to content itself with 'specific' solutions. Since there are no solutions which meet its demands it is forced to rest content with insinuation, allusion and metaphor.

Habermas is not in agreement with the solutions to problems offered by his partners in discussion. That is his right. They themselves are not particularly content with them. They are prepared to discuss alternatives if these are offered and to respond to critical reflections in so far as arguments can be recognized in them. They do not suffer from that restriction of rationality to problems of positive science which he frequently believes he has to impute to them, nor do they suffer under the restrictive interpretation of scientific knowledge which he makes the foundation of his critique. In the positive sciences they do not see the mere aid of technical rationalization but instead in particular a paradigm of critical rationality, a social realm in which the solution of

[1] Habermas admits (*Theory and Practice*, loc. cit., pp. 280 f.) that 'as soon as argument with rational warrants is carried on at the methodological—the so called meta-theoretical and meta-ethical—level, the threshold to the dimension of comprehensive rationality has already been breached', as if the discussion of such problems had not always been characteristic precisely for the types of rationalistic view which he covers with the collective name of positivism. One only has to glance at certain periodicals to determine this.

problems using critical arguments was developed in a way which can be of great significance for other realms.[1] But they believe, however, that they must meet the dialectics which Habermas favours with scepticism, because among other reasons, with its assistance pure decisions can so easily be masked and dogmatized as knowledge. If he sets store by the elucidation of the connection between theory and practice, and not in its metaphorical paraphrase, then Habermas has sought out false opponents and false allies; for dialectics will offer him not solutions, but simply masks under which lurk unsolved problems.

[1] That even science is not immune from dogmatism is quite familiar to them since science too is a human undertaking; see, for example, Paul K. Feyerabend, 'Über konservative Züge in den Wissenschaften und insbesondere in der Quantentheorie und ihre Beseitigung' in *Club Voltaire, Jahrbuch für kritische Aufklärung*, 1, edited by Gerhard Szczesny, München, 1963.

9 JÜRGEN HABERMAS

Rationalism Divided in Two:
a Reply to Albert[1]

Hans Albert[2] has dealt critically with an essay on the analytical theory of science and dialectics in which I took up a controversy which developed between Karl R. Popper and Theodor W. Adorno at the Tübingen working session of the German Sociological Association.[3] The strategy of mutually shrugging one's shoulders which has been practised up until now is not exactly productive. For this reason, then, I welcome the existence of this polemic no matter how problematical its form. I shall restrict myself to its substance.

Before entering into the discussion I must make certain comments in order to establish agreement concerning the basis of our dispute. My criticism is not aimed at research practices in the exact empirical sciences, nor against those in behavioural-scientific sociology, in so far as the latter exists. It is another question whether this can exist beyond the confines of a social psychologically orientated small-group research. My critique is exclusively directed at the positivistic interpretation of such research processes. For the false consciousness of a correct practice reacts back upon the latter. I do not dispute that the analytical theory of science has promoted the practice of research and has helped to elucidate methodological judgements. At the same time, however, the positivistic self-understanding has restrictive effects; it limits the scope of essential reflection to within the boundaries of the

---

[1] First published in *Der Positivismusstreit in der deutschen Soziologie*. Translated by Glyn Adey and David Frisby.

[2] Cf. Hans Albert, 'The myth of total reason'. Page references in the text refer to this essay.

[3] *Der Positivismusstreit*, pp. 155 ff.; in addition Albert refers to several passages in my essay 'Dogmatism, Reason and Decision', in Jürgen Habermas, *Theory and Practice* (Boston/London 1974) pp. 253 ff. He does not take the book as a whole into account.

empirical–analytical (and formal) sciences. I reject this masked normative function of a false consciousness. According to limited positivistic norms, whole problem-areas would have to be excluded from discussion and relinquished to irrational attitudes, although, in my opinion, they are perfectly open to critical elucidation. Moreover, if those problems connected with the selection of standards and the influence of arguments on attributes were inaccessible to critical discussion, and had to be abandoned to mere arbitrary decisions [Dezisionen], then the methodology of the empirical sciences themselves would be no less irrational. Since our chances of reaching agreement on contentious problems in a rational manner are in fact quite limited, I consider reservations of principle which prevent us from exhausting these chances to be dangerous. In order to guarantee the dimension of comprehensive rationality and to penetrate the illusion of positivistic barriers, I shall adopt what is really an old-fashioned course. I shall trust in the power of self-reflection. When we reflect on what happens in the processes of inquiry we realize that we have been moving the whole time through the spectrum of reasonable discussion which is broader than positivism regards as permissible.

Albert isolates my arguments from the context of an immanent critique of Popper's view. Consequently they become confused— I myself scarcely recognize them. What is more, Albert creates the impression that, with their help, I intend to introduce something approaching a new 'method' alongside the already well-established methods of social science inquiry. I have nothing of the sort in mind. I selected Popper's theory for discussion because he himself had already confirmed, in some measure, my doubts about positivism. Influenced by Russell and the early Wittgenstein, it was above all the Vienna Circle around Moritz Schlick which had sketched out the now classic features of a theory of science. Within this tradition Popper occupies a peculiar position. He is, on the one hand, a leading representative of the analytical theory of science and as far back as the twenties he criticized, in a convincing manner, the empiricist presuppositions of this new positivism. Popper's critique concentrates on the first level of self-reflection of a positivism to which he remains bound in so far as he does not see through the objectivistic illusion which suggests that scientific theories represent facts. Popper does not reflect upon the technical cognitive interests of empirical sciences; what is more, he definitely repulses pragmatic interpretations. I am left with no alternative but to reconstruct the structure of my arguments utilizing Popper's problems—a structure which Albert distorts beyond recognition. In reformulating my previous critique in the light of Albert's strictures I hope that in its new form it will give rise to less misunderstanding.

The charge of misunderstanding, however, has already been levelled at me by Albert. In his opinion, I am mistaken on the following points:

on the methodological role of experience,
on the so-called 'basis problem',
on the relationship between methodological and empirical statements,
on the dualism of facts and standards.

Furthermore, Albert asserts that the pragmatic interpretation of the empirical analytical sciences is erroneous. In the last analysis, he considers that the opposition between dogmatically fixed and rationally substantiated positions is a falsely-posed alternative which has been made redundant by Popper's critical rationalism itself. I shall discuss these two objections with those four 'misunderstandings' which I wish to resolve in that order. The reader may then decide on whose side they lay.

I do not like encumbering a sociological journal with details of the theory of science but we cannot carry on a discussion as long as we stand above matters instead of in their midst.

1. CRITIQUE OF EMPIRICISM

The first misunderstanding relates to the methodological role of experience [*Erfahrung*] in the empirical–analytical sciences. Albert rightly points out that experiences of diverse origin can intervene in theories regardless of whether they spring from the potential of everyday experience, from historically transmitted myths or from spontaneous impressions. They merely have to fulfil the condition that they can be translated into refutable hypotheses. For the refutation itself, on the other hand, only one particular mode of experience is permitted, namely, sense experience, which is organized by experimental or analogous procedures. We also speak of systematic observation. I, for my part, have in no way questioned this influx of unordered experiences into the stream of imaginative leaps, out of which hypotheses are created, nor would I fail to recognize the merits of situations of refutation which organize sense experiences through replicable tests. But if one does not wish to enthrone philosophical innocence at any price the question must be permitted whether, through such a definition of the conditions of validation, the possible meaning of the empirical validity of statements has not been established in advance. And if this is the case, one might ask what interpretation of validity is thereby prejudiced. The basis of experience for the exact sciences is not independent of the standards which these sciences themselves attribute to experience. Obviously, the validating procedure which Albert suggests is the only legitimate one is merely one among several. Moral feelings, privations and frustrations, crises in the individual's life history, changes in attitude in the course of reflection—all these mediate different experiences. Through corresponding standards they can be raised to the level of a validating instance. The transference situation existing between doctor and patients which is utilized by the psychoanalyst provides an example of this. I do not wish to compare the advantages and disadvantages of the various procedures of validation; instead I simply wish to elucidate my questions. Albert is unable to discuss them because on the whole he calmly identifies tests with the possible validation of theories against experience. What I regard as a problem he continues to accept without discussion.

This question interests me in connection with Popper's objections to the empiricist presuppositions of neo-positivism. Popper challenges the thesis of the manifest self-givenness of the subject in sense experience. The idea of an immediately attested reality and of a manifest truth has not withstood critical epistemological reflection. Since Kant's proof of the categorical elements of our perception the claim of sense experience to be the final court of evidence has been dismissed. Hegel's critique of sense certainty, Peirce's analysis of the perception incorporated in sense of action, Husserl's explication of pre-predicated experience and Adorno's attack on First Philosophy have all, from their various points of departure, proved that there is no such thing as immediate knowledge. The search for the primary experience of a manifest immediacy is in vain. Even the simplest perception is not only preformed categorically by physiological apparatus—it is just as determined by previous experience through what has been handed down and through what has been learned as by what is anticipated, through the horizon of expectations and even of dreams and fears. Popper formulates this insight in the statement that observations always imply interpretations in the light of experiences made and knowledge acquired. More simply, empirical data are interpretations within the framework of previous theories: as a result, they themselves share the latter's hypothetical character.[1]

Popper draws radical conclusions from this state of affairs. He reduces all knowledge to the level of opinions, of conjectures, with whose help we complete an inadequate experience hypothetically and interpolate our uncertainties concerning a concealed reality. Such opinions and conjectures are differentiated purely in the degree to which they may be validated. Even conjectures which have withstood refutation, and which are constantly subjected to rigorous tests do not attain the status of proven statements; they remain suppositions, admittedly of a kind that hitherto have withstood all attempts to eliminate them—in short, they are well-tried hypotheses.

Empiricism, like the traditional critique of knowledge in general, attempts to justify the validity of exact knowledge by recourse to the sources of knowledge. Yet the sources of knowledge—pure thought, established tradition and sense experience—all lack authority. None of them can lay claim to immediate evidence and primary validity and consequently to the power of legitimation. The sources of knowledge are always contaminated; the way to their origins is barred to us. Hence the question of the derivation of knowledge must be replaced by the question of its validity. The demand for the verification of scientific statements is authoritarian because it makes the validity of statements dependent upon the false authority of the senses. Instead of inquiring after the legitimating origin of knowledge we have to inquire after the method by means of which definitively false opinions can be discovered and apprehended amidst the mass of opinions which are uncertain.[2]

[1] Karl R. Popper, *Conjectures and Refutations*, London, 1963, pp. 23. 387,
[2] *Conjectures*, pp. 3 ff., 24 ff.

Popper carries this critique so far that it unintentionally makes even his own suggested solution problematical. Popper strips the origins of knowledge of their false authority which are enlisted in empiricistic studies. He rightly discredits every form of primary knowledge, but even mistakes can only be falsified on the basis of criteria of validation. For their justification we must adduce arguments; but where then are we to look for these if not in precisely that dimension—not of the origin but, namely, of the formation of knowledge—which has been ruled out? Otherwise the standards of falsification remain arbitrary. Popper wants to mediate the origins of theories, namely, observations, thought and tradition alike as opposed to the *method* of verification which is to be the way of measuring solely empirical validity. Unfortunately, however, this method, in its turn, can only be substantiated by recourse to at least one of the sources of knowledge, to tradition, in fact to the tradition which Popper calls the critical tradition. It becomes clear that tradition is the independent variable upon which, in the final instance, thought and observations are just as dependent as the testing procedures, which are made up of them. Popper is too unhesitating in his trust in the autonomy of the experience which is organized in the testing procedure. He thinks that he can dismiss the question of standards in this procedure because, for all his criticism, he shares in the last analysis a deep-seated positivistic prejudice. He assumes the epistemological independence of facts from the theories which should descriptively grasp these facts and the relations between them. Accordingly, tests examine theories against 'independent' facts. This thesis is the pivot of the positivistic problematic which Popper still retains. Albert does not indicate that I might have succeeded in even making him aware of what is at issue here.

On the one hand, Popper rightly counters empiricism with the objection that we can only apprehend and determine facts in the light of theories.[1] Moreover, he occasionally describes even facts as the common product of language and reality.[2] On the other hand, he assumes for protocol statements, which are dependent on a methodically secured organization of our experiences, a simple relationship of correspondence to the 'facts'. Popper's

[1] *Conjectures*, p. 41, note 8.
[2] *Ibid* p. 241.

adherence to a correspondence theory of truth does not seem to me to be consistent. This theory presupposes that 'facts' exist in themselves without taking into account that the meaning of the empirical validity of factual statements (and indirectly the meaning of theories in the empirical sciences too) is determined in advance by the definition of the conditions of refutation. It would instead be more meaningful to attempt a basic analysis of the connection between the theories of the empirical sciences and the so-called facts. For in this way we should apprehend the framework of a preliminary interpretation of experience. At this level of analysis, it would seem obvious to apply the term 'facts' only to the class capable of being experienced, a class which has been organized in a preliminary manner to refute scientific theories. Then one would conceptualize the facts as that which they are: namely, produced. One would thus recognize the concept of 'facts' in positivism as a fetish which merely grants to the mediated the illusion of immediacy. Popper does not complete the retreat into the transcendental dimension but the consistency of his own critique leads in this direction. Popper's presentation of the basis problem shows as much.

2. THE PRAGMATIC INTERPRETATION OF EMPIRICAL–ANALYTICAL RESEARCH

The second misunderstanding, of which Albert accuses me, refers to the so-called 'basis problem'. Popper gives the name 'basic statements' to those individual existential statements which lend themselves to the refutation of a causal hypothesis expressed in the form of negative existential statements. Normally, these formulate the result of systematic observations. They mark the point of contact at which theories strike the basis of experience. Basic statements cannot of course rest upon experience without contact with it, for none of the universal expressions which occur in them could be verified, not even with the aid of a large number of observations. The acceptance or rejection of basic statements rests in the last instance on a decision but the decisions, however, are not made in an arbitrary fashion. Rather, they are made in accordance with rules. Such rules are only laid down institutionally, not logically. They motivate us to orientate decisions of this sort towards an implicitly pre-understood goal but they do not define it. We behave in this way in the course of everyday communication and also in the interpretation of texts. We have no choice when we move in a circle and yet do not wish to forego explication. The basis problem reminds us that even applying formal theories to reality entangles us in a circle. I have learned of this circle from Popper: I did not invent it myself as Albert seems to suppose. Even in Albert's own formulations it is not difficult to discover it.

Popper explains it in a comparison of the research process with a juridical process.[1] A system of laws, regardless of whether we are dealing with a system of juridical norms or empirical scientific hypotheses, cannot be applied unless agreement has previously been attained concerning the facts of the case to which the system should be applied. Through some kind of decision the judges agree which representation of the factual course of events they intend to approve. This corresponds to accepting a basic statement. The decision is made complicated, however, since the system of laws and the facts of the case are not given independent of one another. On the contrary, the facts of the case are even sought under categories of the system of laws. The comparison of the research process with the juridical process is intended to make us aware of this circle which is inevitable when general rules are applied. 'The analogy between this procedure and that by which we decide basic statements is clear. It throws light, for example, upon their relativity, and the way in which they depend upon questions raised by the theory. In the case of the trial by jury, it would be clearly impossible to apply the "theory" unless there is first a verdict arrived at by decision; yet the verdict has to be found in a procedure that conforms to, and thus applies, part of the legal code. The case is analogous to that of basic statements. Their acceptance is part of the application of a theoretical system; and it is only this application which makes any further application of the theoretical system possible.'[2]

What does this circle, resulting when theories are applied to reality, signify? I think that the area of the empirical is established in advance by means of theoretical assumptions concerning a certain structure, in combination with a certain type of conditions

[1] Karl R. Popper, *The Logic of Scientific Discovery*, London, 1960, pp. 109 ff. (hereafter cited as *Logic*).

[2] *Logic*, pp. 110 ff.

of validation. Such things as experimentally established facts upon which empirical scientific theories could founder are only constituted in a preliminary context of the interpretation of possible experience. This context is produced in an interplay of argumentative discourse and experimental action. The combination is organized with a view to controlling prediction. An implicit pre-understanding of the rules of the game guides the discussion of the investigator when he is deciding whether to accept basic statements. For the circle within which they inevitably move when they apply theories to what has been observed refers them to a dimension in which rational discussion is only possible with the assistance of hermeneutics.

The demand for controlled observation as the basis for decisions concerning the empirical plausibility of causal hypotheses entails a pre-understanding of definite rules. It is certainly not sufficient to know the specific aim of an investigation and the relevance of an observation for certain assumptions. Instead, the meaning of the research process as a whole must be understood in order that I may know to what the empirical validity of basic statements refers at all, just as the judge must always have understood the meaning of judicature as such. The *quaestio facti* must be determined with reference to a *quaestio juris* understood in its immanent claim. In legal procedures this question is prominent in everyone's mind. The whole affair revolves around the question of an offence against general prohibitive norms positively set down and sanctioned by the state. However, what does the *quaestio juris* look like in the research process and how is the empirical validity of basic statements measured in this case? The form of the propositional system and the type of conditions of validation which are used to measure their validity suggest the pragmatic interpretation: namely, that empirical–scientific theories disclose reality under the guiding interest in the possible informative security and extension of feedback-controlled activity.

Clues to this interpretation can be found in Popper himself. Empirical scientific theories possess the significance of permitting the derivation of universal propositions concerning the covariance of empirical quantities. We develop such causal hypotheses above all in anticipation of law-like regularity, without being able to justify empirically this anticipation itself. This methodical anticipation of possible empirical uniformity, however, corresponds to the elementary requirements of behavioural stability. Feedback-monitored activities can only be established for a long period of time to the extent to which they are directed by information as to empirical uniformities. In addition, this information must be capable of translation into expectations of behavioural regularity under given conditions. The pragmatic interpretation refers the logical generalization to general behavioural expectations. Viewed pragmatically, the disjunction between universal propositions, on the one hand, can be explained by the structure of feedback-monitored action which always allows itself to be guided by anticipations of behavioural regularity.[1]

---

[1] In this context Popper's comment that all universal terms can be regarded as dispositional terms is of interest (*Logic*, pp. 94 f., note X, pp. 423 ff. and *Conjectures*, pp. 118 f.). On the level of individual universal terms the problematic of universal statements is repeated. For the dispositional concepts implied in such terms are in their turn only to be explained by means of assumptions about a causally regular behaviour of objects. This is proved in doubtful cases when we contemplate possible tests which would be sufficient to elucidate the significance of the universal terms used. In all this, the recourse to the conditions of validation is not perhaps fortuitous. For it is only the relation of the theoretical elements to the experiment which closes the functional circle of feedback-monitored action within which such things as empirical regularities first 'exist'. The hypothetical surplus, beyond each particular content of an immediately perceived entity which, in the logical form of law-like statements and in the universal terms of observational statements comes into its own, does not relate to the regular behaviour of things 'in themselves' but instead to the behaviour of things in so far as this forms a part of the horizon of expectations of actions requiring orientation. In this way, the degree of generality of the descriptive content of judgements of perception is hypothetically projected beyond the particularity of that perceived in each case, because under the selective pressure towards the stabilization of successful actions we have always gathered experiences and articulated meanings—'for what a thing means is simply what habits it involves' (Peirce).

A further clue for a pragmatic interpretation is given by Popper in connection with a sociology of tradition ('Towards a Rational Theory of Tradition', in *Conjectures*, pp. 120 ff.). He compares the analogous roles which traditions and theories acquire in social systems. Both inform us about reactions which we can expect regularly and in accordance with which we can confidently orientate our action. Likewise they bring order into a chaotic environment in which, lacking the capacity for prognosticating answers or events, we would not be able to form suitable behavioural habits.

This interpretation, according to which the empirical–analytical sciences allow themselves to be guided by a technical cognitive interest, enjoys the advantage of taking account of Popper's critique of empiricism without sharing a weakness of his falsification theory. For how is our uncertainty in principle about the truth of scientific information to fit in with its highly varied and very permanent technical utilization? By that moment at the latest, in which knowledge of empirical uniformities is consumed in technical productive forces and becomes the basis of a scientific civilization, the manifestations of everyday experience and of a permanent experimentation is overwhelming; logical misgivings are unable to assert themselves against the plebiscite of functioning technical systems, a plebiscite which is renewed daily. However great the weight of Popper's objections to verificationism, his own alternative seems for that reason less plausible, since it is only an alternative under the positivistic presupposition of a correspondence between statements and the actual state of affairs. The moment we abandon this supposition and take technique in its widest sense seriously as a socially institutionalized regulatory system which, in accordance with its methodical meaning, is designed to be technically utilizable, one can conceive of another form of verification. The latter is exempt from Popper's objections and concurs, in fact, with our pre-scientific experiences. All the assumptions, then, are empirically true which can guide experimental activity without having been previously rendered problematic through experimentally striven for mistakes.[1]

Albert imagines that by referring to Popper's criticism of instrumentalism he is released from any argument of his own against my interpretation, which he does not even reproduce. But

[1] According to this view, Popper's reservation regarding definitely valid knowledge can be thoroughly compatible with the pragmatic verification of knowledge. Popper admits experimental tests exclusively as an instance of falsification while in the pragmatic view they are controlled experiments which refute assumptions but can also confirm them. However, verification through results can only be globally allocated and not in a strictly correlative manner since, with a given theory, neither in their scope nor in respect of their area of application can we definitively ascertain the factually working elements of knowledge. Definitively we only know those parts of a theory which are controlled through its results and that means that a prognostically validated theory is proved correct in the sphere of application of the validation situation.

I do not really need to answer his criticism since it is directed against theses which I do not expound. In the first instance Popper concentrates on the thesis that theories are instruments.[1] Here he can easily counter that rules of technical application must be tried out, while scientific information must be tested. The logical relationships in the case of suitability tests for instruments and the validation of theories are not symmetrical—instruments cannot be disproved. The pragmatic interpretation, which I wish to give to empirical-analytical sciences, does not include this form of instrumentalism. It is not the theories themselves which are instruments but rather that their information is technically utilizable. Even from a pragmatic viewpoint the failures, whereby causal hypotheses founder under experimental conditions, possess the character of refutations. The hypotheses refer to empirical regularities; they determine the horizon of expectation of feedback-monitored activity and consequently can be falsified by disappointed expectations of success. Yet the causal hypotheses in this methodical sense refer to experiences which are constituted exclusively in the functional sphere of such action. Technical recommendations for a rationalized choice of means under given purposes are not derivable from scientific theories merely at a later stage and as if by chance. But these theories themselves are not therefore technical implements. This is true possibly in a figurative sense. Technical utilization of knowledge is, of course, in no way intended in the process of inquiry: actually, in many cases it is even excluded. Nevertheless, with the structure of propositions (restricted prognoses concerning observable behaviour) and with the type of conditions of validation (imitation of the control of the results of action which is built naturally into systems of societal work) a methodical decision has been taken in advance on the technical utility of information from the behavioural sciences. Similarly the range of possible experience is prejudiced, precisely the range to which hypotheses refer and upon which they can founder.

The descriptive value of scientific information cannot be disputed, but it is not to be understood in such a way that theories represent facts and relations between facts. The descriptive content is only valid with reference to prognoses for feedback-monitored actions in predictable situations. All the answers which

---

[1] 'Three views concerning knowledge', in *Conjectures*, pp. 111 ff.

the empirical sciences can supply are relative to the methodical significance of their presentation of problems and nothing more. No matter how trivial this restriction may be, it contradicts the illusion of pure theory which has been preserved in positivistic self-understanding.[1]

3. CRITICAL JUSTIFICATION AND DEDUCTIVE PROOF

The third misunderstanding to which, according to Albert, I have succumbed, refers to the relationship between methodological and empirical statements. He finds me guilty of an especially trivial positivism since I do not forego empirical arguments in methodological contexts and thereby mix the logic of inquiry with the sociology of knowledge in an unacceptable manner. After Moore and Husserl, commencing from different sides, had effected the strict division between logical and psychological studies, and in so doing had reinstated the old Kantian insight, the positivists broke with their naturalism. Influenced, in the meantime, by the advances which had been made in formal logic, Wittgenstein and the Vienna Circle made the dualism of statements and the facts of the case the basis of their linguistic analyses. Since then it has not been possible to lump together naïvely questions of genesis with those of validity. Presumably, Albert wished to

---

[1] Another of Popper's objections is directed against operationalism according to which basic concepts can be defined through modes of behaviour (*Conjectures*, p. 62; *Logic*, pp. 440 f.). Rightly, Popper on the other hand asserts that the attempt to trace concepts of disposition back to measurement operations in its turn presupposes a theory of measurement for no operation could be described without universal terms. This circle, in which universal terms point to empirically regular behaviour, while the regularity of behaviour can only be established through measuring operations, which in turn presuppose general categories, seems to me, however, to require interpretation. The operationalist point of departure rightly insists that the semantic content of empirical scientific information is only valid within a frame of reference which has been transcendentally posited by the structure of experimental activity, and furthermore the semantic content cannot be projected on to reality 'in itself'. It is incorrect to assume that every content could be simply reduced to criteria of observable behaviour. The circle in which this attempt is ensnared shows instead that the systems of actions, of which the research process forms a part, are mediated through language, but at the same time language is not subsumed in categories of behaviour.

draw attention to this triviality. Once again, in so doing, he does not touch upon my presentation of the problem. For I am interested in the peculiar state of affairs that, despite that clear distinction, non-deductive relationships between formal and empirical propositions are produced precisely in the methodology of the empirical sciences and in the dimension of scientific criticism. The logic of science possesses an element of the empirical precisely in that sector in which the truth of empirical scientific theories should prove itself. For criticism, in Popper's sense, cannot be fitted in an axiomatized form into the formal sciences. Criticism is the unreserved discussion of propositions. It employs all available techniques of refutation. Such a technique is the juxtaposition of hypotheses with results of systematic observation. Though test results find a place in critical discussion, they do not constitute criticism. Criticism is not a method of refutation, it is this refutation itself as discussion. On the other hand, the dimension in which critical discussion of the validity of theories is made is not that of the theories themselves. For not only statements and their logical relations find a place in criticism but so do empirical attitudes which are influenced with the aid of arguments. Albert can of course rule out, by means of a postulate, that we consider in any way a connection which is neither completely logical nor completely empirical. In so doing, he would at most evade a discussion which I should like to develop in order to elucidate the question whether such a postulate can be justified for the realm of meta-theoretical discussion. Rather it seems to me that there is reason to repeat Hegel's critique of Kant's division between the transcendental and empirical realm in the form of a contemporary critique of the division between the logical–methodological and the empirical realms. In both cases, the critique is far removed from ignoring the distinctions mentioned; rather it uses them as a starting point.

A reflection on what Popper himself does makes us aware of the peculiar form of meta-theoretical discussions in so far as they advance beyond linguistic analysis. On the one hand, Popper pursues the immanent critique of given theories and in so doing employs the systematic comparison of logically compelling deductions. On the other hand, he develops alternative solutions; he makes suggestions of his own and attempts to support them with arguments. In this case he cannot confine himself to the verification of deductive connections. Rather, his interpretation pursues the aim of critically altering old attitudes, of making new standards of judgement plausible and new normative points of view acceptable. That takes place in the hermeneutical form of a line of argument which evades the rigid monologues of deductive systems of propositions. It sets standards for critical discussion as such. This is revealed in every choice between possible techniques of inquiry, between several theoretical starting points, between various definitions of basic predicates; it is revealed in decisions as to the linguistic framework within which I express a given problem and form its hypothetical solution. A choice of standards is constantly repeated and in the attempt to support this choice through suitable arguments Morton White has shown that, even at the highest level, meta-theoretical discussions remain bound to this form of argumentation. Even the distinction between categorial and non-categorial being, between analytic and synthetic statements, between descriptive and emotive contents, between logical rules and empirical causal regularities, between controlled observations and moral experience—even these fundamental distinctions, upon which exact empirical science rests, are in no way exempt from discussion. They presuppose criteria which do not result from the things themselves, that is, that are open to criticism, which in their turn cannot be strictly substantiated by arguments but can be supported or weakened by them.[1]

White makes the attempt which Popper neglects, the attempt to examine the logical relations of this non-deductive form of argumentation. He demonstrates that methodological decisions are quasi-moral decisions and, as a result, can only be justified in discussion of the kind familiar from the old topics and rhetorics. For neither the conventionalistic nor the naturalistic interpretation does justice to the choice of methodological rules.

Critical argumentation differentiates itself from deductive argumentation in progressing beyond the dimension of the logical connection of statements and includes a moment which transcends language-outlooks. A relationship of implication between outlooks and statements is impossible: outlooks cannot be deduced from statements nor, vice-versa, statements from outlooks.

---

[1] Morton White, *Toward Reunion in Philosophy*, Cambridge, 1956.

Nevertheless agreement upon a mode of procedure and the acceptance of a rule can be supported or weakened with arguments; at any rate, it can be rationally considered and judged. This is the task of critique with reference to both practical and meta-theoretical decisions. Since the supporting or weakening arguments do not stand in a strictly logical relation to the statements which express the application of standards, but instead only in a relation of rational motivation, then meta-theoretical discussions can also include empirical propositions. However, the relation between arguments and attitudes does not itself thereby become an empirical one. It can be taken as such as for instance in a Festinger experiment on change ·of outlook, but then the mode of argument at the level of observable language behaviour would be reduced and the moment of rational validation, which forms part of every motivation, would be suppressed.

Popper does not consider that a rationalization of attitudes is out of the question. This form of argument is the one possible in order to tentatively justify decisions. Yet since it is never conclusive, he considers it to be unscientific in comparison with deductive modes of argument. He prefers the certainty of descriptive knowledge, a certainty guaranteed by the deductive combination of theories and the empirical constraint of facts. Yet even the interplay of statements and experiences of this particular type presupposes standards which require justification. Popper evades this objection by insisting on the irrationality of the decision which precedes the application of his critical method. According to him, the rationalistic approach comprises the willingness to decide upon the acceptance of theories on the basis of experiences and arguments. It cannot, however, be substantiated either through arguments or through experiences. Certainly it cannot be justified in the sense of a deductive proof, but it can in the form of a supporting mode of argument. Popper himself, in fact, makes use of it at some length. He explains every critical attitude in terms of certain philosophical traditions. He analyses the empirical presuppositions and consequences of scientific criticism. He examines its functions within the given structure of public political life. In fact, his methodology as a whole is a critical justification of criticism itself. It may be that this non-deductive justification is unsatisfactory for a logical absolutism. However, no other form of justification is known to scientific criticism which goes beyond an immanent critique and validates methodological decisions.

Popper terms the critical attitude a belief in reason. Therefore, he claims, the problem of rationalism does not consist of the choice between knowledge and belief, but rather in a choice between two sorts of belief. But, he adds paradoxically, the new problem is which belief is the correct one and which the false.[1] He does not totally reject non-deductive justification but he believes that he can avoid its problematical combination of logical and empirical relations if he foregoes a justification of criticism—as if the Black Peter were not already there in the criticism.

Albert saddles me with the onus of proof for the substantiation problem. He seems to assume that all problems are resolved for him with the abstention of rationalism from the problem of self-substantiation. Apparently, he falls back on William W. Bartley who attempted to prove in a consistent manner the possibility of such an abstention.[2] However, it seems to me that this attempt was not successful.

Bartley commences from the assumption that for logical reasons a deductive self-substantiation of rationalism is out of the question. Instead, he discusses the possibility of a critical philosophy (*Kritizismus*) which does in fact accept every proposition which can be rationally established, but not exclusively such propositions. He does not hold any views which might not be accountable to criticism, but neither does he demand that all views, including the critical attitude itself, be rationally established. Is this view still tenable, however, when logically the conditions of critical validation are themselves exposed to criticism? Bartley neither questions the standards according to which experience is organized in testing situations nor does he pose sufficiently radically the question of the sphere of validity of deductive justification. For by means of a premise he exempts from criticism all those standards which we must presuppose in order to criticize. He introduces a so-called revisability criterion: 'namely, whatever is presupposed by the argument revisability situation is not itself revisable within that situation'.[3] We cannot accept this criterion. It is introduced in

[1] Karl R. Popper, *The Open Society and Its Enemies*, London, 1957, II, p. 30.
[2] *The Retreat to Commitment*, N.Y., 1962, especially chs. 3 and 4; also, 'Rationality versus the theory of rationality', in M. Bunge, ed., *The Critical Approach to Science and Philosophy*, London, 1964, pp. 3 ff. [3] Ibid., p. 173.

order to secure the form of the argument, but it would stifle the line of argument in precisely that dimension in which its peculiar achievement displays itself: the subsequent revision of previously applied standards. Something approaching critical justification consists precisely in the fact that it produces a non-deductive connection between selected standards and empirical propositions, and consequently also supports or weakens attitudes by means of arguments which, for their part, are first found in the perspective of these attitudes. As soon as it progresses beyond the verification of deductive systems, the argument takes a reflexive course. It employs standards which it can only reflect upon in their application. The argument differentiates itself from mere deduction by always subjecting the principles, according to which it proceeds, to discussion. To this extent criticism cannot be restricted in advance to conditions which form the framework of possible criticism. What can pass as criticism always has to be determined on the basis of criteria which are only found, elucidated and possibly revised again in the process of criticism. This is the dimension of comprehensive rationality which, although incapable of ultimate substantiation, develops in a circle of reflexive self-justification.

Bartley's unconditional rationalism makes too many reservations. He does not put criticism into effect as the sole and most extreme horizon within which the validity of theories is determined in relation to reality. As a makeshift, we can conceive of criticism, which cannot be defined because the standards of rationality can only be explained within criticism itself, as a process which in an open [*Herrschaftsfrei*] discussion leads towards a progressive resolution of disagreement. Such a discussion is guided by the idea of a general and unconstrained consensus among those who participate in it. In so doing, 'agreement' should not reduce the idea of truth to observable behaviour. Rather, the categories with whose help agreement can be achieved in such cases are themselves dependent upon the process which we interpret as a process for achieving consensus. The idea of overall agreement does not therefore exclude a distinction between true and false consensus; but this truth cannot be absolved from the possibility of future revision.[1] Albert replies that I presuppose something resembling a free discussion in methodological contexts as a

[1] See D. Pole, *Conditions of Rational Inquiry*, London, 1961, p. 92.

fact. I presuppose it as a fact since we still find ourselves in a communication which is intended to lead to agreement. At the same time, however, this empirical fact possesses a distinctive feature: namely, a transcendental condition. Only in discussion can agreement on the standards be reached on the basis of which we differentiate facts from mere spectres. The rejected link between formal and empirical propositions attempts to do justice to a context in which methodological questions can no longer be meaningfully separated from questions of communication.

4. THE SEPARATION OF STANDARDS AND FACTS

The fourth misunderstanding with which Albert charges me relates to the dualism of facts and evaluations [*Entscheidungen*]. This can be explained on the basis of the difference between natural laws and cultural norms. Assumptions about empirical regularities can definitely founder on the facts, while the choice of standards can at most be upheld critically through additional arguments. One easily differentiates, then, a realm of scientifically reliable information from that realm of practical knowledge which we only acquire through a hermeneutic form of argument. I am anxious to call into question this optimistic distinction which is traditionally termed the division between science and ethics. For, on the one hand, theoretical knowledge which has been proved against facts is derived within a normative framework which is capable of a critical but not of a deductive-empirical justification. On the other hand, the critical discussion of standards precisely includes empirical considerations—that is, recourse to so-called facts. A critique which establishes a rational connection between outlooks and arguments is the comprehensive dimension of science itself. Even theoretical knowledge can be no more certain than critical knowledge. Once more the 'misunderstanding' appears to result from Albert in no way having apprehended my intention. I do not deny the distinction between facts and standards. I merely ask whether the positivistic differentiation which permits a dualism of facts and decisions, and correspondingly a dualism of propositions and proposals—that is, a dualism of descriptive and normative knowledge—is an appropriate one.

In the appendix to a new edition of *The Open Society*[1] Popper develops the asymmetrical relation between standards and facts: '. . . through the decision to accept a proposal we create the corresponding standard (at least tentatively); yet through the decision to accept a proposition we do not create the corresponding fact.'[2] I should like to grasp this relation more precisely. We can discuss proposals and statements. Yet the discussion entailed produces the standards just as little as it does the facts. Rather, in the first case, it draws upon arguments in order to justify or contest the act of accepting standards. Such arguments can include empirical considerations. But these, for their part, are not under discussion. In the second case, the reverse occurs. Here it is not the choice of standards which is under discussion, but their application to a state of affairs. The discussion draws in arguments in order to justify or contest the act of incorporating a basic statement with reference to a given hypothesis. These arguments include methodological considerations. Their principles, however, are not under discussion in this case. The critique of an empirical scientific hypothesis and the critical discussion of the choice of a standard are not symmetrical. Yet this is not, in this instance, because the logical structure of the discussion is different in the two cases—it is the same.

Popper terminates this reflection by reference to the correspondence theory of truth. Ultimately the dualism of facts and standards goes back to the assumption that, independent of our discussions, there exists something resembling facts and relations between facts to which propositions can correspond. Popper denies that the facts themselves are only constituted in combination with the standards of systematic observation or controlled experiment. In so far as we intend true propositions we always know that their truth is measured against a correspondence of propositions and facts. He meets, in the following manner, the obvious objection that with just this concept of truth a criterion or standard or definition has been introduced which itself must be exposed to critical discussion. 'It is decisive to realize that knowing what truth means, or under what conditions a statement is called true, is not the same as, and must be clearly distinguished

---

[1] 4th Edition, London, 1962, vol. 2, pp. 369 ff.: 'Facts, Standards and Truth.'

[2] Ibid., p. 384.

from, possessing a means of deciding—a criterion for deciding
—whether a given statement is true or false.'[1] We must forego a
criterion, we must forego a definable standard of truth: we cannot
define truth—but nevertheless we 'understand' in each individual
case what we intend when we test the truth of a proposition: 'I
believe that it is the demand for a criterion of truth which has
made so many people feel that the question "what is truth" is
unanswerable. But the absence of a criterion of truth does not
render the notion of truth non-significant any more than the
absence of a criterion of health renders the notion of health non-
significant. A sick man may seek health even though he has no
criterion for it.'[2]

In this passage, Popper makes use of the hermeneutic insight
that we understand the meaning of statements from the context
even before we can define individual terms and apply a general
standard. Anyone familiar with the business of hermeneutics
would certainly conclude that we intend the meaning of such
terms and statements without any standard at all. Rather the
preunderstanding which guides interpretation before any definition—even Popper's interpretation of truth—always includes
standards implicitly. The justification of these preliminary standards is not really excluded; instead it is just the abstention
from a definition which permits a continuous self-correction of
the diffuse preunderstanding in the progress of the explication
of the texts in hand. The interpretation throws the light of a
growing understanding of the text back on to the standards
with which it was initially opened up. The hermeneutic course of
interpretation itself produces its own justifications too with the
adaptation of the originally employed standards. The standards
and the descriptions which they permit in application to the text
still stand in a dialectical relationship. It is just the same with
the standard of a correspondence truth. It is only the definition
of standards and the establishment of criteria which tears apart the
standards and the descriptions which make them possible. First,
they create a deductive connection which excludes a retrospective
correction of the standards through the thing measured. Only
now does the critical discussion of standards free itself from their
usage. Yet standards are also used implicitly before a critical

[1] *Open Society*, vol. 2, op. cit., p. 371.
[2] Ibid., p. 373.

justification on the meta-theoretical level stands out from the object level of applied standards.

Therefore Popper does not manage to evade the dialectical connection between descriptive, postulatory and critical statements by reference to a correspondence concept of truth. Even this concept of truth, which allows such strict differentiation between standards and facts is, no matter how implicitly we orientate ourselves by it, still in its turn a standard which requires critical justification. A critical discussion, regardless of whether it concerns the acceptance of proposals or propositions, includes a threefold usage of language: the descriptive, in order to describe a state of affairs; the postulatory, in order to establish rules of procedure; and the critical, in order to justify such decisions. Logically these forms of speech mutually presuppose each other. The descriptive usage is in no way limited to a certain class of 'facts'. The postulatory usage covers the establishment of norms, standards, criteria and definitions of all types, no matter whether practical, logical or methodological rules are involved. The critical usage employs arguments for considering, evaluating, judging and justifying the choice of standards; it includes therefore language transcendent approaches and attitudes in its discussion. No proposition concerning reality is capable of rational examination without the explication of a connection between arguments and attitudes. Descriptions are not independent of standards which are used, and standards rest upon attitudes which are in need of justification through supporting arguments but which are, at the same time, incapable of deduction from propositions. If attitudes are altered under the influence of arguments, then such a motivation apparently combined a logically incomplete constraint with an empirical one. The only constraint of this sort originates in the power of reflection which breaks the power of the unpenetrated by rendering it conscious. The emancipatory insight translates logical constraint into empirical constraint. Precisely this is achieved by criticism; it overcomes the dualism of facts and standards and in this way first produces the continuum of a rational discussion which otherwise would degenerate immediately into mere decisions and deductions.

As soon as we discuss a problem at all with the aim of reaching a consensus rationally and without constraint we move into a dimension of comprehensive rationality which embraces as its moments language and action, statements and attitudes. Critique is always the transition from one moment to another. It is, if I may put it like this, an empirical fact in a transcendental role of which we become aware in the execution of criticism. It can also, of course, be repressed and disguised from that moment on in which, with the definition of the initially implicitly applied standards, a language-immanent realm of logical relations is freed from living reflection. This repression is expressed in Popper's critique of Hegel: 'To transcend the dualism of facts and standards is the decisive aim of Hegel's philosophy of identity—the identity of the ideal and the real, of the right and the might. All standards are historical: they are historical facts, stages in the development of reason, which is the same as the development of the ideal and the real. There is nothing but facts; and some of the social or historical facts are, at the same time, standards.'[1] Nothing was further removed from Hegel's mind than this metaphysical positivism which Popper counters with the logical insight that statements and states of affairs belong to different spheres. Hegel in no way reduced the logical and empirical, the criteria of validation and factual relations, the normative and the descriptive to the level of historical facts. However, he did not exclude from his mind the experience of critical consciousness which showed that reflection also holds together the separated moments very well. The critique moves from the argument to the outlook and from the outlook to the argument, and acquires in this moment the comprehensive rationality which, in the natural hermeneutics of colloquial speech, is still as it were at work by habit, but which in the sciences must be produced between the now-separated moments of formalized language and objectivized experience by means of critical discussion. Only because this criticism relates chosen standards non-deductively to empirical states of affairs and can measure one moment by another is the statement, which according to Popper's own presuppositions would be untenable, correct: '. . . that we can learn by our mistakes and by criticism; and that we can learn in the realm of standards just *as well* as in the realm of facts.'[2]

[1] *Open Society*, vol. 2, op. cit., p. 395.
[2] Ibid., p. 386.

5. TWO STRATEGIES AND A DISCUSSION

Albert seizes upon a series of questions, polemicizes and lets them drop again. I cannot discover any principle behind this sequence. I have attempted to clear up four fundamental misunderstandings in order to create a basis of agreement upon which further problems—for instance, the role of historical reflection, the postulate of value-freedom or the position of the critique of ideology—could be discussed without linguistic confusion. Now, I believe, my intention will no longer be open to misunderstanding. In opposition to positivism, I should like to justify the view that the process of research which is carried out by human subjects belongs to the objective context which itself has to be recognized by virtue of the cognitive act.

The dimension in which this combination of the process of research with the social process of life is formed belongs neither to the sphere of facts nor that of theories; it is separated from such a dualism, which only has meaning for theories in empirical science. Rather in the comprehensive communicative context of scientific criticism one moment links itself to another. I would say, in old-fashioned language, that the transcendental conditions of possible knowledge are here created under empirical conditions. As a result neither the sociology of knowledge nor pure methodology are apposite at this level of reflection. Their combination, which used to be called the critique of ideology, is more appropriate. I do not like to use this expression for I do not wish the present discussion to cover all forms of personal interests. I am concerned with knowledge-guiding interests which in each case form the basis for a whole system of inquiries. In contrast to positivistic self-understanding, I should like to point out the connection of empirical–analytical science with technical interests in acquiring knowledge. But this has nothing to do with 'denunciation' as Albert insinuates. It has quite escaped Albert's notice that a critique of empirical–analytical inquiry itself is far from being my intention. He imagines that I desired to play off the methods of understanding against those of explanation. On the contrary, I regard as abortive, even reactionary the attempts which characterized the old methodological dispute, namely, attempts to set up barriers from the outset in order to remove certain sectors altogether from the clutches of a certain type of research. It would be a bad dialectician who immunized himself in this way.

Naturally the analysis of cognitive interests is not without consequences. It makes us aware of attitudes upon which fundamental decisions concerning the methodological framework of whole research systems are dependent. Only in this way do we learn to know what we are doing; only in this way do we know what, when we do something, we can learn. We make ourselves aware, for instance, of the fact that empirical–analytical inquiries produce technically utilizable knowledge, but not knowledge which makes possible a hermeneutical elucidation of the self-understanding of acting subjects. So far, sociology has primarily, and by no means in an unproblematic manner, assisted the self-reflection of social groups in given historical situations. It cannot escape this today, not even where it has professed its intention to provide merely information on empirical regularities of social behaviour. I agree with Albert that in our discipline we ought to devote all efforts to acquiring more and better information of this kind. I do not agree with him that we could, should or even must restrict ourselves to this. I shall not examine here the reason why in this country sociology has taken over the role of a historically oriented theory of society, while other social sciences were free from this burden and have therefore made faster progress within the limits of an exact empirical science. But what would it be like if a successful, positivistic, scientific strategy were able to completely reject this task and banish it to the vestibules of scientific discussion? For the critique of ideology in the hands of the positivists has this purpose. It concerns itself with cleansing the practical consciousness of social groups of those theories which cannot be reduced to technically utilizable knowledge and none the less insist upon a theoretical claim. How would it be then if this purge was feasible and was successfully carried out?

Under the conditions of reproduction of an industrial society individuals who only possessed technically utilizable knowledge, and who were no longer in a position to expect a rational enlightenment either of themselves or of the aims behind their action, would lose their identity. Since the power of myth cannot be broken positivistically, their demythologized world would be full of demons. I fully accept the risk of this language. It belongs to a sphere of experience which is in no way reserved for a clairvoyant elite. However, I do have to admit that the power of imagination only forms in contact with traditions which one has initially acquired and not immediately immersed oneself in. The possibility of rational agreement even in this dimension can be verified by reading a recently published book by Klaus Heinrich.[1]

A sociology, which restricted itself in its critical intention to empirical–analytical inquiries, would only be in a position to examine the self-preservation and self-destruction of social systems in the sphere of pragmatically successful adjustment processes and would have to deny other dimensions. Within sociology as a strict behavioural science questions relating to the self-understanding of social groups cannot be formulated. Yet they are not meaningless on that count nor are they beyond binding discussion. They arise objectively from the fact that the reproduction of social life does not merely pose technically soluble questions and includes more than the processes of adaptation along the lines of the purposive–rational use of means. Socialized individuals only acquire their life through group identity, which contrasts with animal societies which must be constantly built up, destroyed and formed anew. They can only make their existence secure to the extent to which it is secured by the process of adaptation to their natural environment, and by readaptation to the system of social work in which they mediate their metabolism with nature by means of an extremely precarious equilibrium of individuals among themselves. The material conditions for survival are most closely bound up with the most sublime organic equilibrium, with the broken balance between separation and unification in which the identity of each ego is able, through communication with others, to first adapt. A failed identity for the person attempting to assert himself, and an unsuccessful communication between those talking to one another are both self-destructive—which ultimately has physical effects. In the individual sphere these are familiar as psychosomatic disturbances, but dismembered life histories also reflect the dismembered reality of institutions. We are acquainted with the painful process of constantly identifying oneself anew through Hegel's 'Phenomenology of Mind' as well as Freud's psycho-

[1] *Versuch über die Schwierigkeit, Nein zu sagen*, Frankfurt, 1964; cf. my review in *Merkur*, November 1964.

analysis. The problem of an identity which can only be produced through identifications, and that means solely through externalizing the identity, is at the same time the problem of communication which makes possible the happy balance between silent, isolated existence and silent estrangement, between the sacrificing of individuality and the isolation of abstract individual persons. Everyone repeats such experiences of impending loss of identity and the silting up of verbal communication in the crises of his life-history. Yet they are no more real than the collective experiences in the history of the species which the total societal subjects have made for themselves in their confrontation with nature. Questions from this realm of experience, because they cannot be answered by technically utilizable information, are not capable of explanation by empirical–analytical inquiries. Nevertheless, since its beginnings in the eighteenth century, sociology has raised and above all tried to discuss these questions. In so doing it cannot forgo historically-orientated interpretations and nor, apparently, can it evade a form of communication under the spell of which alone these problems pose themselves. I refer to the dialectical network of a communicative context in which individuals develop their fragile identity between the dangers of reification and formlessness. This is the empirical core of the logical form of identity. In the evolution of consciousness the problem of identity presents itself as a problem of survival and, at the same time, of reflection. From here dialectical philosophy first took up its starting point.

In the shirt-sleeved world picture of many a positivist, dialectics plays the part of hobgoblin. For others who occasionally become aware of the fact that they lapse into dialectical trains of thought, dialectics only expresses that we think and are in a position to think when according to the traditional rules of resolution we really should not be able to do so. In dialectics, thought does not become entangled because it scorns the rules of formal logic: because it clings to them in a particularly stubborn manner— even on the level of self reflection, rather than of breaking off reflection at this point. The self-reflection of the strict empirical sciences, in my opinion, strikes a cautionary note as far as positivistic expectations are concerned. It contains the realization that our theories do not simply describe reality. On the other hand, it does not permit itself to be discouraged by definitions from explaining such connections which, according to the demarcation upon which for good reason empirical science analysis is based, should not exist.

Given these points of departure, a discussion between positivists and others who are not ashamed of dialectical trains of thought has its moment of treachery. Nevertheless, since both parties are convinced of the unity of human reason, as well as of the possibility of a consensus achieved in a rational manner and, in addition, do not intentionally deny the comprehensive rationality of an unreserved criticism, it is possible for them to carry on a discussion. In so doing, however, both parties pursue a different strategy.

Albert accuses me of an utterly unscientific strategy. He calls it immunization and masking. If one considers that I subject to debate—the very conditions of validation themselves, upon whose exclusiveness Albert insists—neither description seems particularly meaningful to me. I should prefer to talk of a flanking strategy. You have to make it clear to the positivist that you have already taken up a position behind his back. I have no idea whether this is a sympathetic manner in which to proceed but, at any rate, it was dictated to me by the course of the discussion. Albert's objections rest on presuppositions which in their turn I have called into question. Albert's strategy,[1] on the other hand, I could characterize, with a certain symmetry to his accusation of obscurantism, as one of pretending to be stupid. One will not understand what the other person is saying. This strategy, intended to force the opponent to accept one's own language, is several centuries old and has been successful since the days of Bacon. The advances of the exact sciences rest, to a large extent, upon translating traditional ways of putting questions into a new language. They find no answer to questions which they themselves have not formulated. Yet, on the other hand, this very same strategy becomes a brake-like drag if one wishes to discuss the status of such inquiries as a whole. The systematic pretence of failure to understand drains a discussion dry, since any discussion must always move within the compass of a pre-understanding which is mutually taken-for-granted. In this way, one promotes

[1] Here I do not wish to include Albert's slip which creeps in on pp. 184 f. I do not accept that Albert makes the nationally widespread anti-communism a part of his strategy.

an ethnocentricity of scientific subcultures which destroys the candour of scientific analysis.

The accusation of unintelligibility belongs to this context. In so far as this touches me as an empirical subject I take it repentantly to heart. But in so far as it is aimed at a structure of thought it requires explanation. Understanding is a two-sided relationship. While carrying out my required reading of ingenious positivistic studies, I have had the painful experience of not, or not immediately, understanding a great deal. I attributed the difficulty to my defective learning processes and not to the unintelligibility of the texts. I would not venture to exclude altogether the feeling that the same thing could happen the other way round with someone who quoted Hegel at second hand.

I speak here of tradition with respect to learning processes which it makes possible and not in anticipation of authorities to which a descent could be traced back. Perhaps it is precisely for this reason that Popper's work belongs to the series of great philosophical theories because he still maintained learned acquaintance with traditions which many a member of his retinue hardly knows even by name.

10 HERBERT MARCUSE

On Science and Phenomenology[1]

The Crisis of European Science and Transcendental Phenomenology is Husserl's last work. Written in the thirties, the first part was published in 1936, the second part only after Husserl's death.

I would like to indicate first where I see the general historical locus of this work. It seems to me that we have to place it into the context of the radical re-examination of the Western concept of Reason, of Western rationality that begins in the last decades of the nineteenth century and to which so essentially different thinkers as Bergson, Dilthey, Max Weber, Spengler, Piaget and Bachelard belong. All of them have in common this questioning of the very idea which has guided Western thought since its Greek origins, i.e., the rationality typical of the occident. It seems to me that Husserl is the last in this group, and in a certain sense, (which may strike you as strange) the most radical of these re-examiners. In Husserl, it is modern science itself, this most sacrosanct child of Western rationality, that is questioned. In this re-examination, modern science appears as the end of a fateful development which begins with Greek thought, that is, with the origins of Western thought itself—as the 'end' of this development in the twofold sense of termination and of fulfilling the *telos*, the purpose, the objective of this thought.

According to Husserl, science—modern science, Galilean as well as post-Galilean—originates in the Greek idea of knowledge and truth and comes to rest in a scientific rationality in which truth and validity contain in themselves illusion and repression. Before I try to present Husserl's radical thesis, I have to stress that it is not the result of a sociological analysis or of a sociology of knowledge. It is precisely the fascinating aspect of Husserl's work that it is a *philosophical* analysis within the academic framework of intellectual history, even within the academic division of

[1] First published in *Boston Studies in the Philosophy of Science*.

labour. Husserl emphasizes philosophy as *Beruf*, as calling, and that philosophy is done in the *Berufszeit*, that is to say, in the time reserved, in the academic division, for such investigations. Husserl adds (and this is important: I come back to it at the end) that the calling of the philosopher is a unique calling because (and I quote him)

> this calling is linked with the 'possibility of a radical transformation of humanity', and not only a radical transformation of humanity but also a 'liberation', and this possibility makes the calling of the philosopher unique within the division of labor.[1]

In the course of such a philosophical undertaking (philosophical also in the sense of a discipline!), in the course of its own inner development Husserl's analysis transcends itself, or rather it descends from the pure theoretical to the impure pre-theoretical, practical dimension. Better—the pure theoretical analysis discovers its own internal impurity, but only to return from this impure sphere to the still pure theoretical dimension of transcendental phenomenology as constituent of the practical, pre-theoretical dimension, the *Lebenswelt*. (I use the German term *Lebenswelt*. The literal translation 'life-world' is too large and too vague in this context; what Husserl means is our own empirical day-to-day world as it is given in immediate experience, practical and other—the world of life and death, in our empirical reality. So I will use either '*Lebenswelt*' or 'empirical reality'.)

I will now devote some time to presenting Husserl's own thesis (the work is not fully translated; we only have Gurwitsch's excellent abstract of it)[2] but I shall focus it in such a way that the critical problems stand out. Husserl begins with a very brief description of what he considers the Greek concept of Reason, namely, the idea of human being as self-determination and determination of its world by virtue of man's intellectual faculties, the concept of Reason, according to which man's intellectual faculties are at the same time capable of determining his own life and of determining, defining and changing the universe. This conception

---

[1] Husserl, *Gesammelte Werke*, vol. VI (Den Haag, 1954), ed. W. Biemel, p. 154.
[2] Ed. note: this is no longer so. See the translation by David Carr.

presupposes that the universe itself which is thus rationally comprehended is in its very structure a rational system and therefore
accessible to knowledge and change on the grounds of man's own
rational knowledge. In other words, Reason for the Greeks, is
objective and subjective at one and the same time, and on this
basis, Reason is the subjective as well as objective instrument for
changing the world in accord with man's rational faculties and
ends. But in this process, Reason itself as *theoria*, is and remains the
basis of the transformation of the world. Philosophy is thus
established as *science*, and as first, most excellent and general
science, which must give direction and the end to all other
sciences.

What are the implications of this original concept of Reason?
First, it implies a supra-factual, supra-temporal validity of Reason,
so that the really real as discovered and defined by Reason is
rational as *against* the immediately given fact. Reason establishes
an authority and reality which is in this way antagonistic to the
immediately given facts. Secondly, true being is ideational being
(a conclusion from the first implication), not being as we experience it immediately in the flux of our empirical, practical
world. Thus 'Platonism' is the basis of all scientific knowledge.
Thirdly, objectivity is necessarily correlated with subjectivity,
again the subjective as well as objective structure of Reason.
Husserl here gives a formulation which, in an entirely different
context, recaptures the very question and thesis with which
Western philosophy began, namely, the final identity of Being
and Reason. He says:

Can Being and Reason be separated if cognitive Reason determines (the essence of being?)[1]

So we find at the very beginning and at the late stage of western
philosophy this almost literal identity in the formulation of the
basic problem, the mysterious union and even identity of Reason
and Being, Knowing and Being. Now this concept of Reason,
which is theoretical and practical Reason in one, is understood by
Husserl as a *project*. I use the term here as it was elaborated in the
philosophy of Sartre: 'project' in the sense that this idea of

[1] Husserl, *Gesammelte Werke*, loc. cit., pp. 9, 12.

rationality and its application is a specific way of experiencing, interpreting, organizing and changing the world, a specific historical project among other possible ones, not the only, necessary project. This project, according to Husserl, came to fulfilment with the foundation of modern science, namely, in Galilei's mathematization of nature. Galilei's mathematization of nature established that purely rational, ideational system which was the dream of all Platonism; Galilei established the ideational world mathematically as the true reality, substituting this scientific universe for the only given reality, namely, our empirical *Lebenswelt*. But the very fulfilment of this project was also its collapse, according to Husserl. For this scientific rationality, this idea of Reason and its application proved successful only in the positive sciences and in the technological conquest of Nature, while the original foundation of this entire science, that which originally was supposed to constitute the very structure, content and end of science, namely, philosophy, remained an impotent, abstract meaningless metaphysical sphere of knowledge and continued in this impotent form a hopeless academic existence which, in addition, was more and more dissolved into psychology. Thus separated from the basic philosophy which, according to the original ideas of Reason, was supposed to give the ends, the objectives, the meaning of science, separated from this basic philosophy which was supposed to provide the truly universal concepts, Reason was at the same time divorced—and this is decisive for Husserl—from that rational *humanitas* envisaged in the original philosophical project. Scientific, technological rationality became reason *kath' exochen*. Divorced from the validating 'ends' set by philosophy, the rationale set by science and the rationale of its development and progress became that of the *Lebenswelt* itself, in which and for which this science developed.[1] Instead of rationally transcending the *Lebenswelt*, science comprehended, expressed and extended the specific rationale of the *Lebenswelt*, namely, the ever more effective mastery of the environment (*Herrschaft über die praktische Umwelt*), including the ever more effective mastery of man.[2] But that was not the inherent *telos* of science, which was first and foremost, and not only in a chronological sense, the *telos* defined by the empirical reality in which science developed. Thus theoretical Reason, pure Reason,

[1] Ibid., pp. 49 f.   [2] Ibid., p. 67.

without losing its scientific character as theory, becomes practical Reason. Theory, by virtue of its internal dynamic rather than on external grounds, becomes a specific, historical practice. But (and this is decisive for Husserl and the justification of his own subsequent phenomenological reduction) this entire development, this entire transformation of Reason, this essential, structural, internal commitment of pure Reason, pure theory and pure science to the empirical reality in which they originated, this entire transformation *remains hidden to science itself*, hidden and unquestioned. The new science does not elucidate the conditions and the limits of its evidence, validity and method; it does not elucidate its inherent historical denominator. It remains unaware of its own foundation, and it is therefore unable to recognize its servitude; unable to free itself from the ends set and given to science by the pre-given empirical reality. I should like to stress again, because these formulations can be easily misunderstood, that it is not a sociological relation which is here established between an empirical reality and the pure science which develops in this empirical reality. Husserl's concept goes much farther. He maintains that the empirical reality is the framework, and dimension in which the pure scientific concepts develop. In other words, the empirical reality constitutes, in a specific sense, the very concepts which science believes are pure theoretical concepts.

Before I go on with Husserl's interpretation of this development, I would like to reformulate and to extend his thesis in a way which may bring out its provocative implications. What happens in the developing relation between science and the empirical reality is the abrogation of the transcendence of Reason. Reason loses its philosophical power and its scientific right to define and project ideas and modes of Being beyond and against those established by the prevailing reality. I say 'beyond' the empirical reality, not in any metaphysical but in a historical sense, namely, in the sense of projecting essentially different, historical alternatives.

Now back to Husserl's interpretation.

The new science (by which he understands mainly Galilean science) establishes a rational 'infinite' universe of Being (I follow his words here literally), systematically organized and defined by science itself. Within this universe, every object becomes accessible to knowledge, not incidentally, in its contingent, particular occurrence, but necessarily and in its very essence.[1] Thus, it becomes object of scientific knowledge, not as this individual object but as exemplification of general objectivity (the falling feather as *res extensa* in motion).[2] That is to say, the concrete and particular object, the Aristotelian totality is no longer the *Wesen*, the essence; Platonism supersedes Aristotelianism, not only in physics, but in the very concept of scientific rationality. And concomitant with this de-individualization, which is the prerequisite for the quantification of the scientific universe, is the familiar reduction of secondary to primary qualities; devaluation of the inexorably individual sense experience as nonrational.[3]

As a result of this twofold process, reality is now idealized into a 'mathematical manifold': everything which is mathematically demonstrated with the evidence of universal validity as a pure form (*reine Gestalt*) now belongs to the true reality of nature.[4] But (and here is the great gap which separates the new science from its classical original) in contrast to the ideational forms of Plato, the ideational forms of mathematical physics are freed from any substantive connection with other than mathematical ends. The ideational realm of Galilean science no longer includes the moral, esthetic, political Forms, the *Ideas* of Plato. And separated from this realm, science develops now as an 'absolute' in the literal sense no matter how relative within its own realm it may be, absolved from its own, pre-scientific and nonscientific conditions and foundations. According to Husserl, the absolute evidence of mathematics (which as we shall see we question), was for Galilei so self-evident that he never asked for the actual foundation of its validity, for the validating ground of this evidence, and of its extension to the whole of nature. Thus, the validation of the new science remained in the dark; its own basis never became the theme of scientific inquiry; science contained an unmastered, unscientific foundation. This is of the utmost importance for *the validity of science* itself, because the relation between science and the pre-scientific empirical reality is for Husserl not an external one but one which affects the very structure and meaning of the scientific concepts themselves.

Now according to Husserl, where is this pre-scientific validating ground of mathematical science? It is originally in geo-

[1] Ibid., p. 19. [2] Ibid., p. 40.
[3] Ibid., p. 54. [4] Ibid., pp. 20–21.

metry as the art of measuring (*Messkunst*) with its specific means and possibilities.[1] This art of measuring in the empirical reality promised and indeed achieved the progressive calculability of nature, subjecting nature to the ever more exact 'foresight' in mastering and using nature. (Foresight—*Voraussicht*, perhaps better translated as projection and valid, rational anticipation.) Foresight and anticipation, rational anticipation can then guide the practical orientation in and the transformation of the empirical *Lebenswelt*, without however (and this is decisive) setting or defining or changing the goals and ends of this transformation. Geometry can and does furnish (and the same holds true for the extension of geometry, mathematics) the methods and ever more exact, ever more calculable approaches for the transformation and extension of the established *Lebenswelt*, but remains forever incapable of defining, anticipating or changing, by its own concepts, the ends and objectives of this transformation. In its method and concepts, the new science is essentially non-transcendent. This is what I consider as Husserl's key sentence: Science 'leaves the *Lebenswelt* in its essential structure in its own concrete causality unchanged'.[2]

As to the interpretation of this paradoxical and provocative thesis (so obviously paradoxical since we are used to seeing in science one of the most dynamic forces in the world): In my view, what is at stake is not the more or less external relation between science and society, but the internal conceptual structure of science itself, its pure theory and method which Husserl now reveals in their essential historicity (*Geschichtlichkeit*), in their commitment to the specific historical project in which they originated.[3] Pure science retains, *aufgehoben* (to use Hegel's term now) the practice out of which it arose, and it contains the ends and values established by this practice. The empirical reality thus performs the *sinngebende Leistung* (constituent act): It is constitutive of scientific truth and validity. Science is *Aufhebung der Lebenswelt*

(1) inasmuch as science cancels the data and truth of immediate experience,

(2) inasmuch as science preserves the data and truth of experience, but

---

[1] Ibid., pp. 27, 30.   [2] Ibid., p. 51.   [3] Ibid., p. 152.

(3) preserves them in a higher form, namely, in the ideational, idealized form of universal validity.

And this threefold process takes place in the scientific abstraction. The quantified ideational forms are abstracted from the concrete qualities of the empirical reality, but the latter remains operative in the very concepts and in the direction in which the scientific abstraction moves.

In this way, the pre-scientific, pregiven empirical reality enters the scientific enterprise itself and makes it a specific project within the pre-established general project of the empirical reality. However, the abstract, ideational, mathematical form into which science transforms the empirical conceals this historical relation:

> The *Ideenkleid* (the ideational veil) of mathematics and mathematical physics represents and [at the same time] disguises the empirical reality and leads us to take for True Being that which is only a method.[1]

This is perhaps the most effective and lasting mystification in the history of Western thought! What is actually only one method appears as the true reality, but a reality with a *telos* of its own. The mathematical ideation, with all its exactness, calculability, foresight, leaves a void (*Leerstelle*) because the objectives and ends of this calculability and anticipation are not scientifically determined. This void can thus be filled by whatever specific end the empirical reality provides, the only condition being that it is within the range of scientific method. This is the famous neutrality of pure science which here reveals itself as an illusion, because the neutrality disguises, in the mathematical–ideational form, the essential relation to the pregiven empirical reality.

In Husserl's terms: The objective *a priori* of science itself stands under a hidden empirical *a priori*, the so-called *lebensweltliche a priori*.[2] Moreover, as long as this empirical *a priori* remains hidden and unexamined, scientific rationality itself contains its inner and own irrational core which it cannot master. According to Husserl, modern science thus operates like a machine which everyone can learn to handle without necessarily understanding the inner necessity and possibility of its operation.[3] In other words, pure science has an inherently instrumental character prior to all speci-

---

[1] Ibid., p. 52.   [2] Ibid., pp. 49, 143 f.   [3] Ibid., p. 52.

fic application; the Logos of pure science is technology and is thus essentially dependent on external ends. This introduces the irrational into science, and science cannot overcome its irrationality as long as it remains hidden from science. In Husserl's words: Reason is Reason only as manifest Reason (*offenbare Vernunft*), and Reason 'knows itself as Reason only if it has become manifest'.[1] In as much as Reason remains non-manifest in science, scientific rationality is not yet the full rationality of science. How can Reason become conscious of itself?

Husserl proposes to break the mystification inherent in modern science by a phenomenological analysis which is in a literal sense a *therapeutic* method. Therapeutic in the sense that it is to get behind the mystifying concepts and methods of science and to uncover the constitutive *lebensweltliche a priori* under which all scientific *a priori* stands. This is to Husserl first a methodological problem. The pregiven empirical reality as a whole must become the object of the philosophical analysis, otherwise the *a priori* prior to the scientific *a priori* could never come to light. But obviously philosophy itself is part of this empirical reality and philosophy itself stands under the *a priori* of the empirical reality. The circle is to be broken by a dual phenomenological reduction (suspension, *epoché*): first the suspension of the objective *a priori*; the suspension of scientific truth and validity; secondly the suspension of the *lebensweltliche a priori*, of the *doxa* and its validity.

Now what do we retain, what remains as the residuum of this twofold suspension? In the first *epoché*, 'we put in brackets' (that is to say, we do not deny but simply suspend judgement on) scientific truth and scientific validity. What remains as the residuum is (*a*) the entire general structure of the empirical reality,[2] the infinite manifold of things in time and space, the orta, and (*b*) the world itself in which all these things necessarily appear—the world as the universal, unsurpassable horizon of all particular objects. But this first *epoché* is not sufficient: it cannot do what it is supposed to do, namely, break through the mystification and uncover the ultimate foundation of scientific truth. It cannot do this because with this first 'bracketing' we are still on the basis (*auf dem Boden*) of the empirical reality, within the 'natural position' of our day-to-day experience. A second *epoché* is necessary which 'at one stroke' leads to a total alteration of the

[1] Ibid., p. 53. [2] Ibid., pp. 143 f.

'natural position' of experience, to the suspension of the natura
validation of everything that we naturally accept as valid in our
immediate experience.[1] Once we have suspended these judgements
too, we reflect no longer on the pregiven world and the particular
objects appearing in it, but on *how* these objects appear, on the
modes in which this entire world is given to us. The residuum of
this *epoché* is thus the world as correlate of a totality of *modes of
consciousness*, as a 'synthetic totality'. What we have now as residuum is the *transcendental* subjectivity,[2] and to this transcendental
subjectivity the world is now given as phenomenon of and for an
absolute subjectivity.[3] This transcendental subjectivity is no longer
any particular or individual or group subjectivity. It is 'absolute'
because whatever object or object-relation may appear, now
appears as necessarily constituted in specific acts of synthesis
which inseparably link objectivity and subjectivity. In other
words, we have now what we might call the absolute original
experience: the experience which is at the origin of and is constitutive of any possible objectivity that can ever become the object
of scientific and of any other thought. The phenomenological
reduction has now opened the dimension in which the original
and most general structure of all objectivity is constituted.

I shall add only a few critical remarks. The breakthrough to
the transcendental subjectivity is supposed to be the road to uncover the foundation on which all scientific validity rests. I ask
the question: can the reductive phenomenological analysis ever
attain its goal, namely, to go behind scientific, and pre-scientific,
validity and mystification? I shall offer three suggestions.

First: The phenomenological analysis is confronted with the
fact of reification (Husserl does not use this term). Reification is a
form which is usually not examined. Scientific as well as pre-
scientific experience are false, incomplete inasmuch as they experience as *objective* (material or ideational) what in reality is subject—object, objectivation of subjectivity. In founding the
analysis on the constitutive subject—object correlation, Husserl's
dual *epoché* does go behind the reification—but so does all transcendental idealism. Thus far we are, in my view, in no way beyond
Kant. I know Husserl's own interpretation of the difference
between phenomenology and Kant; I think that in the context of
my criticism this difference is not very relevant. My point is that

[1] *Ibid.*, pp. 151 f.   [2] *Ibid.*, pp. 147 f.   [3] *Ibid.*, p. 155.

the phenomenological breakthrough stops short of the *actual* constituent subjectivity. Husserl transcends the objective *a priori* of science in the first *epoché* and the empirical *a priori* in the second *epoché*. He thus creates a conceptual metalanguage for the critical analysis of the empirical reality. But my question is: does this conceptual metalanguage really come to grips with the constituent subjectivity? I think not.

Second: The phenomenological reduction arrives at a subjectivity which constitutes only the most general forms of objectivity, for example, the general form of appearing as object, changing as object, being related to other objects. But does this subjectivity give us 'manifest Reason' behind the disguising Reason, the validation of scientific truth? Can this transcendental subjectivity ever explain—and solve—the crisis of European science? Husserl's transcendental subjectivity is again a pure cognitive subjectivity. One does not have to be a Marxist in order to insist that the empirical reality is constituted by the subject of thought *and* of *action*, theory and practice. Husserl recognizes the historical subject in its *sinngebende Leistung*; but then, by suspending, bracketing it, the phenomenological analysis creates its own *a priori*, its own ideation and its own ideological veil. Pure philosophy now replaces pure science, as the ultimate cognitive lawgiver, establishing objectivity. This is the *hubris* inherent in all critical transcendentalism which in turn must be cancelled. Husserl himself seems to have been aware of this *hubris*. He speaks of the philosopher as *'urquellend fungierende Subjektivität'*: the philosopher functions as the primordial source of what can rationally be claimed as objective reality.

I come to the conclusion and leave it as a question. Husserl recognizes the fetishism of scientific universality and rationality by uncovering the specific historical–practical foundations of pure science. He sees that pure science is in its very structure technological—at least potentially applied science. The scientific method itself remains dependent on a specific *Lebenswelt*. This is the hidden irrational element in scientific rationality. Husserl finds the reason for this dependence in the loss of the philosophical dimension, which was originally the basic dimension of science. Classical philosophy defined the method and function of science in terms of an idea of Reason which claimed higher truth and validity than those embodied in, and established by, the given empirical reality. This validating idea of Reason was that of the *telos* of man as man, the realization of *humanitas*. According to Husserl, the humanistic structure of Reason collapses with the release of science from this philosophical foundation. This would imply that humanism becomes an ideology at the very time when modern humanism is born. In other words, the birth hour of humanism itself would be the degradation of humanism to a mere ideology. Apparently there must be something wrong with this formulation. The fact remains that humanism is still today an ideology, a higher value which little affects the inhuman character of reality. The question with which I would like to conclude is this: Is philosophy entirely innocent of this development, or does it perhaps share the *hubris* of science? Does it share the reluctance to examine its own real foundation and function and is it therefore equally guilty of failing in the task of *Theoria*, of Reason—to promote the realization of *humanitas*?

INDEX

INDEX